Drawing Conclusions

Drawing Conclusions

An Artist Discovers His America

Tracy Sugarman

 Syracuse University Press

Syracuse University Press, Syracuse, New York 13244-5160

First Edition 2007

07 08 09 10 11 12   6 5 4 3 2 1

All illustrations are courtesy of the artist.

The paper used in this publication meets the minimum requirements
of American National Standard for Information Sciences—Permanence
of Paper for Printed Library Materials, ANSI Z39.48–1984.∞™

For a listing of books published and distributed by Syracuse University Press,
visit our Web site at SyracuseUniversityPress.syr.edu.

ISBN-13: 978-0-8156-0871-4

ISBN-10: 0-8156-0871-3

Library of Congress Cataloging-in-Publication Data

Sugarman, Tracy, 1921–

    Drawing conclusions : an artist discovers his America / Tracy Sugarman. — 1st ed.

        p. cm.

    ISBN 978-0-8156-0871-4 (hardcover : alk. paper)   1. Sugarman, Tracy, 1921–   2. Illustrators—United
States—Biography. I. Title.

NC975.5.S84A2 2007

741.6092—dc22

[B]

2007031392

Printed in China by Everbest through Four Colour Imports, Ltd., Louisville, Kentucky

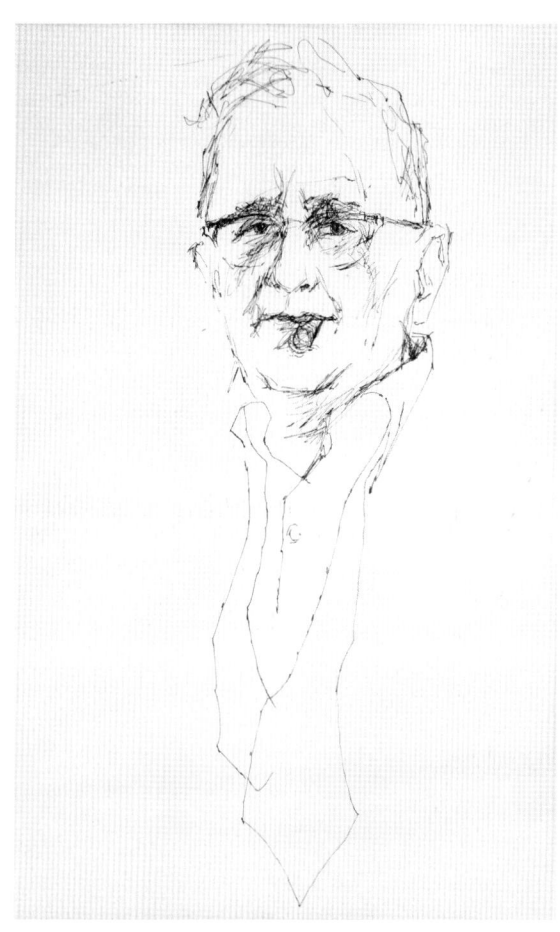

David Sugarman

For my father, David Sugarman,
Syracuse University, Class of 1907
With love and deep appreciation

Tracy Sugarman's art was first seen by a national audience in the pages of *Fortune,* the *Saturday Evening Post,* and *Colliers.* Publishers who commissioned him to illustrate their books include Simon and Schuster, Doubleday, Random House, and Time-Life Books. In an age of photography, Sugarman has continued to capture the disparate images of America with his pen and his watercolors. His reportage in words and drawings on the Seventh Avenue garment-center world of New York, his searing reportage for the *New York Times* on the Rikers Island prison, his documenting of the fascinating diversity of American corporate life, and his capturing of the lyrical world of the Tanglewood music culture and of the excitement of the Alvin Ailey Dance Group have all been preserved in his documentation. His paintings of the first rollout of the space shuttle *Columbia* are now a permanent part of the National Aeronatics and Space Administraton (NASA) Smithsonian Collection at the Kennedy Space Center, and his entire collection of art from World War II has been acquired by the U.S. Library of Congress.

Most significant for Sugarman has been his exploration of many of the areas in America where the struggles for change and growth are still being waged. His drawings of Appalachian life for VISTA, his dramatic drawings of the Malcolm X murder trial for the *Saturday Evening Post,* and his poignant coverage of marginal Hispanic American life in Texas for the Housing Investment Trust of American Federation of Labor and Congress of Industrial Organizations (AFL-CIO) have all contributed to ongoing dialogues in our society. But his recording of the civil rights movement in Mississippi in his book *Stranger at the Gates: A Summer in Mississippi,* published by Hill and Wang in 1966, marked the beginning of a searching fascination with a state that continues to challenge and intrigue him. The entire portfolio of his drawings of the "long, hot summer" in Mississippi is now a permanent archive at Tougaloo College. His most recent book, *We Had Sneakers—They Had Guns,* is a sympathetic journey into the past of the civil rights struggle in Mississippi with blacks and whites with whom he worked in 1964 and 1965.

In 1970, Mr. Sugarman partnered with filmmaker Bill Buckley to create Rediscovery Productions, Inc. In the intervening years their documentary film company has produced nearly forty educational films about social, political, and cultural challenges to American society. He continues to serve as artist, scriptwriter, and coproducer for Rediscovery.

Contents

Illustrations

Preface

For sixty years as a reportorial artist I have been struggling against the thievery of time. Always there have been paintings to finish, deadlines to meet, publishers to placate, pockets of stolen time to be ferreted out so I could enjoy the beauty or wonder of the journey. But always, half a step from my elbow, has been my voracious fellow traveler, time. He has whistled the tune and I have danced. So my joy as an artist and writer has come in time-encapsulated chunks, disparate in their challenges but total in their demands.

Often I have been like a sprinter, clutching sketchpads and notebooks, racing to a finish line at a Rikers Island holding pen, or the launchpad for the doomed space shuttle *Columbia*, or the jury box at the Malcolm X murder trial, or a Boston Symphony rehearsal at Tanglewood, or the picket headquarters for an International Ladies' Garment Workers' Union (ILGWU) labor strike on Seventh Avenue, or scrambling to capture Alvin Ailey dancers in midflight. And sometimes I have been like a middle-distance runner, pacing myself through the minefields of the D-day invasion in Normandy, or sweating out the perilous days and nights in the Mississippi Delta as an archivist for the civil rights movement. But I have never, until now, regarded myself as a long-distance runner. Over sixty years there have been so many finishing lines, and the race is hardly over. If there's a finite finishing line, I've not yet discerned it.

What has intervened in my hopscotched career has been the arrival of a benign and smiling advocate, the U.S. Library of Congress. Distanced from my quirky, crazy-quilt stops and starts as I have scratched my impressions of the twentieth century in America, the library has chosen to acquire my collection of images on paper as a significant body of work, a reflection of my time and place.

I am deeply grateful for this honor and its breathtaking nod to posterity. But at such a moment I feel compelled to look inward rather than forward. As my life's most significant work is being trundled into the library's august archives, I have to make a reckoning. What indeed do all those drawings, paintings, and words add up to? What conclusions have I drawn?

Drawing Conclusions

Introduction

June 6, 1943, D+7 Utah Beach, Normandy

Through the rain and sheets of spray, we could barely see the ship as it was making its way toward our Normandy beachhead. In the hollows between the cresting waves, the great bow doors of the large amphibious craft would be almost lost to view, then rise again like a great leviathan, water cascading across its decks. As the landing ship tank (LST) approached our seawall of sunken ships, it swung wide to port, hoping to make a run for the beach. It was then that my boatswain spotted the hundreds of army troops on its deck. They were in a long, ragged line stretching the length of the ship, waiting for chow. Now they were stumbling and falling on the heaving deck as torrents of water threatened to pitch them into the sea. The boatswain was handing me his binoculars when we felt, and then heard, an enormous explosion. As I wiped the water from my glass, I could suddenly see the nightmare that was happening two hundred yards away.

The LST had hit a magnetic mine and simply been eviscerated. The center of the ship had been blown away, and the crashing seas were racing between the remains of the bow and the stern of the sinking ship. Its small boats had been blown from their davits and dangled from the wreckage on their useless lift lines. Some dazed men still clung to the wreck, but most had been hurled into the furious English Channel. Their screams and shouts were almost lost in the rising wind as we all raced to our boats to attempt a rescue.

As we cleared our seawall of sunken ships, the full power of the storm caught our open boats. Our bows would be hurled up on a wave and then come crashing down, filling our small deck and making our footing treacherous. Trying to reach over the gunnels to grab the desperate hands was nearly impossible in the churning water. On every side frightened and bloody faces would simply slide from sight. Fewer and fewer voices could be heard over the keening wind, and we searched desperately for bodies still afloat. It was a bad dream, and it was happening in maddeningly slow motion.

The bad dream of the tragic sinking continued to trouble my heart and mind for weeks. It was only after I had put those images into my sketchpads that I was able to put the horror

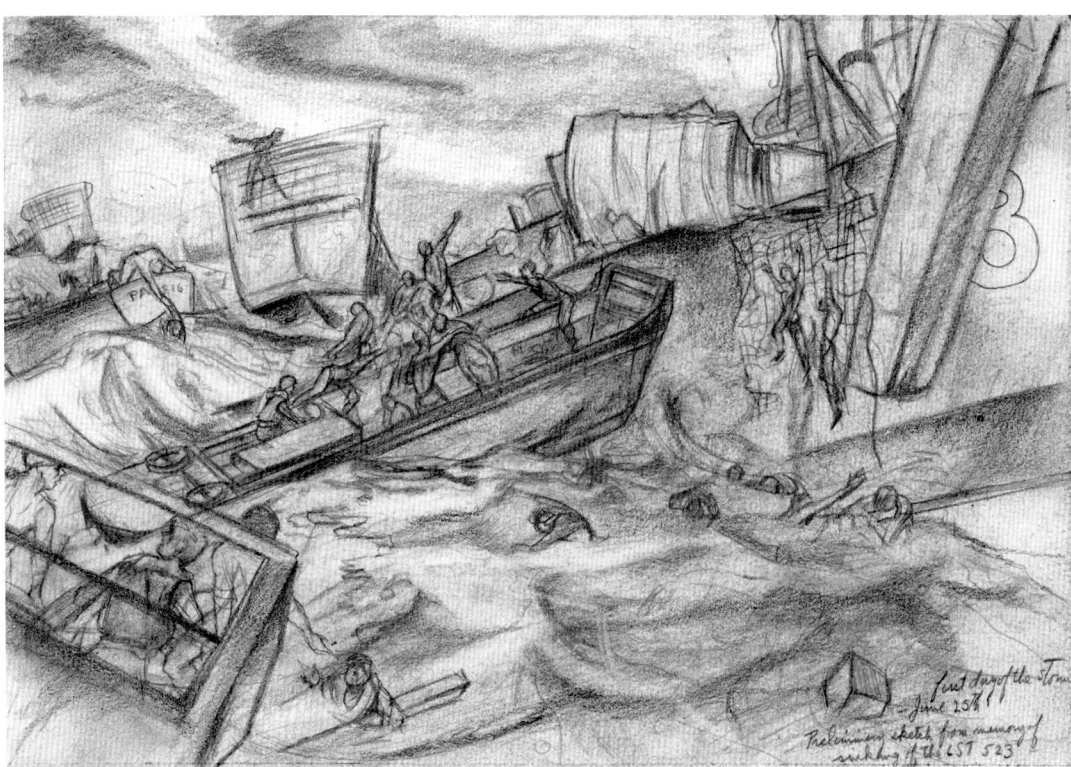

1. *The Sinking of
the Last LST 523,
Utah Beach*

into perspective, and move on. It was revelatory to me. For the first time I realized that the work of my eyes and my hands could bring comfort to my heart. It was a lesson learned at war that would help me through many heartbreaking moments when I was recording the unfinished business of peacetime America.

1

New York City

In the fall of 1945, my "ruptured duck" discharge pin securely attached to my prewar sports jacket, I started to seek work in New York City as an illustrator. All of New York seemed intoxicated with a buoyant air of promise and purpose, a joyous recapturing of the peacetime pleasures so long denied by the endless war. I watched enviously the scurrying crowd of New Yorkers who all seemed to have a wonderful destination waiting. I didn't, and I felt very much the stranger.

In our tiny Greenwich Village apartment my now pregnant wife and I would leaf through the countless magazines I aspired to work for. The confidence, experience, and skill of a coterie of remarkable illustrators, many just returned from their own tours of duty, were daunting reminders that the magazines were comfortably their domain. The slick, beautiful, and arresting images of Al Parker, Austin Briggs, Earl Blossom, Dean Cornwall, all artists I had admired before the war, seemed to tumble from every glossy page, leaving me wide-eyed and desolate. What in the world could I show to any art director that would commend me to be included in such a pantheon? The very personal war drawings that I had sent home to June from England and Normandy seemed oddly remote from the images America wanted to see.

Our first child was now on his way, so, timid or not, I would leave our apartment every day, fiercely clutching the want-ad section of the *New York Times*. I was determined to find a job, any job, in the art world I longed for.

Persistence, not talent, finally brought me into the frantic warrens of a commercial art studio. It was only much later that I learned that the diminutive lady boss who hired me was moved to do so because I was a former navy officer and was over six feet tall. Had I known, it wouldn't have given me any pause. Her two qualifications for hiring me were then and now a source of bewilderment. All I knew was I was finally off the intimidating streets and was now a working New Yorker. When June heard that I was to receive the princely sum of fifty dollars a week, we celebrated with a bottle of wine. We felt that we now had the world by the tail.

For a whole year, I explored the sobering new world of a working New Yorker, making realistic and totally forgettable drawings. But I found delight in the companionship of

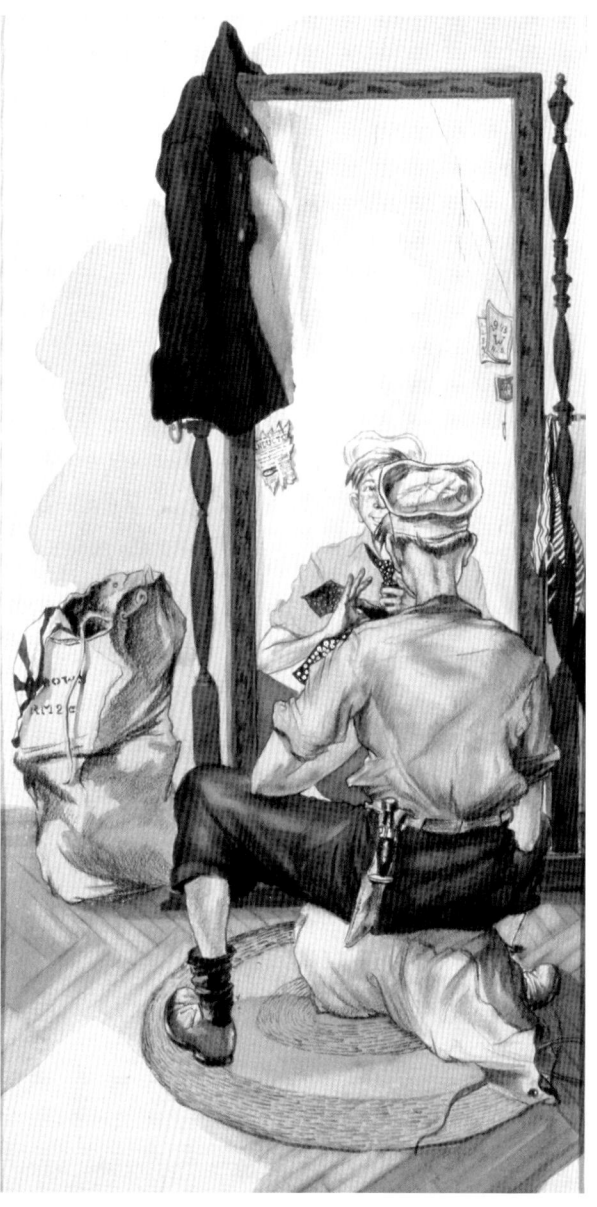

2. Coming Home

young art professionals who had the skills I was struggling to acquire. My essential mentor, however, was an Italian gentleman named Salvatore Garone. Not only could he render a Seagrams rooster in a rich flourish of sparkling watercolor, but he could and did recite Dante's *Inferno* by the hour. When not in thrall to the great poet, I busily sought to escape the critical scrutiny of my boss. When the inevitable inspection of my studio output did take place, my renderings of liquor bottles, lingerie, furniture, and shoes were declared quite satisfactory, but my drawings of Popsicles were found sadly lacking. This was a failure of great proportion because Popsicle was a most important client. My lady boss bade me a fond farewell, and the six-foot former naval officer was relieved of his duties. Once again I found myself back on the sidewalks of New York. It had been an extraordinary twelve months and the last year I would ever know when there was a predictable paycheck at the end of every month.

A week later we had a surprise visit from June's father. It was his first since our baby was born. A stocky man of fifty-five with prematurely white hair, ice-blue eyes that impassively scrutinized the world from behind wire-rimmed glasses, and a ruddy complexion, Max Feldman was a formidable presence. With a wife and two daughters, he had been a martinet who was rarely challenged at home and never at his successful business.

Max kissed June at the door, stopped for an instant at the crib in the living room where his first grandchild was sleeping, and turned to me. "Where can you and I talk privately?" I glanced briefly at June and then led him into our bedroom. I closed the door behind us, pulled out the chair for him, and sat on the edge of our bed. "Max," I said, "June and I have no secrets from each other. Why . . . "

His eyes held mine. "Because this is between you and me. I want you to come work for me in Peekskill." Without further preamble, his voice rising, he continued. "You've got responsibilities now . . . family responsibilities . . . and you are going to need money. You can have money at the Feldman News Company. And you can start tomorrow."

I looked at him with astonishment, incapable of responding. This was the man who so objected to our wartime marriage, let alone my liberal politics, that he refused to come to our wedding until the very last moment when it was clear we were going ahead without him.

Max stared at me. "My daughter deserves a man who can provide for her." There was a long silence. His voice softened. "We haven't been close, Tracy. We're very different. But we can get along, and we can build the company together." Richard awoke from his nap hungry, and his cries from the living room made Max pause. He stared at the closed door. "I have no sons." He rose from his chair and faced me. "One day the Feldman News Company can be yours."

I finally found my voice. "Thank you for that offer, Max. It's very generous. June and I will talk it over seriously, and I'll call you."

After he left the apartment, I told June everything that had been said in the bedroom. Her eyes blazed, and she exploded with anger. "Damn him! Damn him! Does he really think an artist like you would come work for him to distribute newspapers? Oh, yes! Money is all he respects and all he understands. Well, baby, if you ever say yes to an offer like that, you'll have to find another wife!" She scooped up our hungry baby and disappeared into the bedroom.

The call to Max that night turning down his offer was received in an angry silence. Then he said, "I hope you can draw good-enough pictures to provide for June and Dickie," and hung up. I hoped so, too.

It was now past time for a serious discussion of my professional future. Where to turn? In an act of blind loyalty and incredible bravery, June voted that I give up the commercial art world that obviously did not appreciate me. "You always wanted to be a magazine illustrator, and that's what you should be doing," she said firmly. I stared at my wife, feeling like a trapeze artist who was condemned to perform without a safety net at the very top of the tent. Only the thought that I would never ever again have to struggle with drawing Popsicles made me seriously consider June's quixotic proposal. Richard woke from his nap and regarded me with an unblinking gaze. I swallowed hard and voted with June. *"Ally ally in free, ready or not here I come!"*

Until the advent of television that reshaped American advertising, magazines were among the most vital conduits for selling everything to postwar Americans. To bring the buyer into the heart of the publications where the ads were in the back of the magazine, publishers employed a stellar galaxy of illustrators from every genre to bring alive the stories of MacKinlay Kantor, Scott Fitzgerald, Willa Cather, and hosts of other leading lights in the literary world. Many of the artists who created the pictures for the most popular magazines themselves became celebrities. The next cover of the *Saturday Evening Post* by Norman Rockwell or the next episode of *Tugboat Annie* illustrated by Harold Von Schmidt was anticipated eagerly by millions of Americans at newsstands across the nation.

For my new generation of illustrators who came on the scene after World War II, fighting our way into the slick pages was a hard task, requiring equal parts of talent, ambition, and patience. New York was the mecca to which we all had flocked from every point on the compass. The competition was fierce, and it soon became clear to me that if I was to crack the magazines, I would first have to financially survive while I honed my skills and prayed for a break.

In the pecking order of the illustration world, the commercial art studio was perhaps the lowest rung of the ladder, and I was determined never to return to that barren place. I soon discovered that there was another way one could go: the art sales representative. Scattered across midtown Manhattan were a number of large studios, owned by enterprising men and women who represented illustrators. Most of them had been selling in the art field from before the war. They had cultivated relationships with the art directors at the advertising agencies and with the art buyers at the magazines. With the postwar frenzy of starting over, the sales reps were bringing fresh newcomers, young artists with promise, to all parts of Madison Avenue. To be represented by a sales rep, many of the artists who needed work space would agree to sharing 50 percent of their commission fees with their rep. For those of us who had our own space (mine was a windowless foyer in our crowded Bronx apartment), the commission to be paid the rep was 25 percent. I leaped at the chance to have my work shown, and was grateful for the small jobs that my agent could find me.

Many of the striving young artists who populated those studios became my friends. When we could afford it, we would meet at the sanctum sanctorum of illustration, the Society of Illustrators. Partly, it was to savor the elegant ambience of the Sixty-third Street town house whose walls were adorned with paintings by all our heroes; partly, it was to enjoy each other's company; and partly, it was to watch our professional role models in the flesh. At our end of the bar were we new members of the Society. Frank, the bartender, his mahogany face shining and smiling, would skillfully keep the drinks flowing, Pabst and Budweiser to us and bourbon and water and scotch and soda to the old-timers who gathered together at the far end. With Frank's diplomacy and tact, he made us feel just as welcome as Norman Rockwell, just in from Vermont, Bob Fawcett from Ridgefield, or a coterie of famous artists just arrived from Westport. At the end of our buffet lunch, we would take our subways back to work. Some people, we said, were more equal than others. But one day . . .

In those busy, skittish years of finding my footing as a wage earner and assisting when I could in the rearing of our kids, there developed a tight mutual dependency between June and me. She was a knowledgeable partner in evaluating the options that might be open that I could pursue in my career. From our earliest days at Syracuse University when she was doing honors work in the college of liberal arts, she began to explore with me the world of illustration, which was what she knew I passionately wanted to enter. Even during the war, my letters would often be thick with illustrations clipped by June, keeping me in touch with that beckoning world even on a Normandy beachhead. For my part, I relished working at home, a sanctuary that I cherished, which allowed me over the years to savor with June the wonder of watching our kids grow.

Late one evening after Richard had been read to sleep, we settled on the living room couch, finally scanning the *New York Times*. A Glenn Miller record crooned softly around us. Minutes later I heard June murmur, "David Stone Martin. How come I know that name?"

"Because you've seen his work, Snoon. He's the guy who illustrated the Lead Belly record we got last month. A wonderful artist. His work doesn't resemble anyone else's. Personal as hell. He was perfect for a Lead Belly album." I put down my paper. "Why did you ask?"

"Because the Brooklyn Museum has hired him to teach a course in drawing." She examined my face, and then said, "You've been working very hard, chasing every dumb job that you can find to keep us happy. I think it would be great if you could have some fun. Maybe you'd get something out of a class with this guy you admire so much." She handed me the page she'd been reading, and smiled. "The class is going to be in the evening, Trac. If you go, you can skip doing the dishes."

"In Brooklyn? Oh, my aching back. It's a thousand miles away, Snoon."

She patted my knee and took the paper back. "You take the D Train at the Fordham Road station over at the corner of the Concourse, go to Grand Central, and change to the Brooklyn train. Bet you a Schrafft's chocolate soda it doesn't take longer than forty minutes."

"Forty minutes going, and forty minutes coming back. That's eighty minutes," I said. "Plus two hours at the museum." But June was lost in the crossword puzzle.

Doing the dishes would have been a lot quicker and a lot easier. But my decision "to go have some fun" with David Stone Martin proved to be one of the most provocative learning experiences of my professional life. Canny and enigmatic, Martin spoke a graphics language that it took me sessions to translate. But with time I came to understand that drawing could be much more than the skilled reproduction of what I was viewing. In all the long hours drawing and painting from the model at Syracuse I had gained the academic skills to do that. But now I was beginning to examine the object to be captured through the prism of my personal vision. It wasn't just an old woman before me. It was my feelings and my perceptions about "old" that were also important. It wasn't just a Negro horn player David Stone Martin was drawing. It was Martin's feelings about blacks, about that piece of jazz, that specific milieu. By the time I would leave class and start the long journey home, my head would be racing. And invariably, by the time my train reached Fordham Road, I would be deep asleep. Usually, I would wake as the train sped away from Fordham Road and home. I would stumble, exhilarated and exhausted, from the D Train at the last station, Gun Hill Road. Then I would walk the long half-mile through St. James Park to our apartment.

For our young family, New York City seemed stunningly alive with promise. Did everything really shine as I remember? For this upstate boy, I confess that Manhattan appeared dazzling, even from our apartment way up in the top of the Bronx. Everything was in arm's reach, and everything seemed newly hatched. We clutched New York like ardent lovers, an affair of the heart that was to last a lifetime. For this young artist's family, life in the postwar forties was exhilarating. In a two-minute walk I could enter the subway, and in twenty minutes, for a nickel, I could reach a client on Madison Avenue. For loose change we could visit the Metropolitan Museum of Art, the Whitney, and the Museum of Modern Art. For a very few dollars we could listen to Billy or Ella or Gillespie on Fifty-second Street, go to see a new Balanchine ballet at City Center, delight in a new musical by Leonard Bernstein or a new play by Tennessee Williams or Arthur Miller on Broadway. We could plumb the tiny, exciting world of "off-Broadway" theaters that were surfacing in profusion in Greenwich Village. And, at no charge at all, we could explore the rich, small treasures on Fifty-seventh Street where abstract expressionists like De Kooning, Miro, and Pollack were moving the margins of what we had long accepted as "art" and Alexander Calder, Henry Moore, and a legion of young sculptors were redefining form and space. New York was an adult feast that constantly whetted the appetite, and it was affordable even to a struggling illustrator and his family. But even Eden had its perils.

Young adults become different young adults when they procreate. We did. Fun and games remained fun and games, but time created a different dynamic when fun might be possible and games might be schedulable. When kids join your troupe, life often gets in the way. And the kids are so beautiful and exciting and demanding that old lifestyles are eagerly exchanged for new responsibilities while you're enjoying them. Most often, it was not a deal we made with the devil but an arrangement we willingly made. With the birth of our son and the anticipation of our daughter's arrival, "New York, New York" lost some of its carefree luster, and the early sparkle often took on a wan aspect as you watched your newborn and your new self coping with the big city that was no longer the familiar turf you had trod, hand in hand.

"You can take the boy out of the country, but you can't take the country out of the boy." How banal is that? I had been away from Syracuse for years, seen some of the world during the war, and had been leading all the hedonistic life I could afford in the Manhattan of my dreams. Yet "upstate" lingered, an itch in memory that was unscratchable. I longed to get my kid onto some grass and into a swing hanging from a tree limb, "no matter what." And "what" was the unleashed genie that started to shred the gossamer net that had held me to New York. "What" was the half-parched grass in St. James Park.

There are probably perfectly sane and balanced grown-ups, now well into their middle years, who can attest to the series of lunatic confrontations that took place in the summers of 1949 and 1950 when Dickie Sugarman was three and four years old. The Irish and the Jews who then lived around the park have been replaced in the New York tradition of musical-chair neighborhoods by the newer arrivals, the African American and Hispanic citizens who now live there. So those who bore witness to my travails when they were children probably now reside in East Orange or White Plains or Darien. But I can attest that my suffering bought them joy and a richer life than they had hitherto known in the Bronx.

June had grown up in the glades and glens of Peekskill, New York, a leafy town at a great bend in the Hudson River. Attuned to the verdant beauty she had known as a child, she, too, longed for our son to share those fragrant pleasures. So for the first two years of our son's life in the Bronx, as I wrestled with my art deadlines in our tiny apartment foyer, she would bundle him into his carriage and push him more than a mile away to the oasis of the Bronx Botanical Garden and the wonderful Bronx Zoo. June was game, Dickie was delighted, and I was living in a fool's paradise where babies forever remain babies. Babies don't stay babies. After a while they dismount from their carriages and want to go play in the park. "Like all the other kids, Daddy."

Now ambulatory and curious, Dickie became my fascinating companion on our short hikes from 190th Street to the beckoning green of St. James Park. Hand in hand we paused at its edge, scanning the little oasis. A cement sidewalk was alive with boys playing tag and girls scratching out hopscotch boxes with fragments of chalk. Through the thicket of kids some older boys were threading their way on roller skates, pushing the smaller children out of the way. Dickie's hand tightened in mine, and we were both reluctant to enter the jostling group. The cement sidewalk meandered toward some ancient, empty asphalt tennis court. The rusted wire enclosure of the scrabbly courts abutted a hard-packed dirt playground with a clutch of filled seesaws and a few busy sets of swings. Just beyond, in the shade of a dusty maple tree, was a little shack marked "Park Attendant." Unsullied by children, adults, dogs, or roller skaters, a virgin greensward stretched invitingly across the park, and I led my wide-eyed son onto the empty lawn. The grass had been recently mowed, and the nostalgic smell made me smile. "Go, Dick! I'll race you. And I'll give you a head start up to ten." He skittered away across the grass, laughing as I started my count, "One! Two! Three!"

A furious bellow interrupted my cadence. "You! Hey, you!" I stopped, glancing back over my shoulder in time to see a large, heavyset man lumbering through the sea of children on the sidewalk. Suddenly hushed, they parted at his approach as the Red Sea had opened for Moses. I stopped dead in my tracks, waiting for the park attendant to reach me.

"It's okay, Dick," I called to my startled son. "Stay right there. The man wants to talk to me."

The flushed red face was now closing fast, and he pointed a stubby finger at me. "What the hell do you think you're doing?" The voice was as astonished as it was angry.

"I'm taking my kid to the park, and you're scaring the hell out of him." I glanced at the swarm of silent children who puddled around the two of us. I lowered my voice. "And you're scaring the hell out of these kids."

"Who the hell do you think you are? The pope? You get that kid off the lawn right now. Kids aren't allowed on the lawn here. They play on the sidewalk or over at the swings." He waved his fist. "And that applies to you, too! Off the lawn!"

Two years in the navy had exposed me to a lot of orders that I had had to follow. I wasn't in the navy now. I said, "No. This is a public park, and I say my kid is allowed to play on the grass. And he's staying with me." I called to Dick. "We'll start the race again. One! Two! Three!"

"I'm reporting you to my superintendent," the attendant yelled.

"You do that," I replied. "Four! Five! Six! Seven! Eight! Nine! Ten! Ready or not, I'm coming!" Dickie and I raced away, and the kids on the sidewalk started to laugh, and then they bolted onto the welcoming lawn of St. James Park.

I don't know whether it was more of a nightmare for the park attendant or me. The confrontations continued on a regular basis of shouting and gesticulation every time Dickie and I would set foot in St. James Park. At our arrival the crowds of kids on the sidewalk would, as if on cue, race onto the lawn, kicking balls and shouting the rules of pickup games. As the attendant and I would once again stand rooted and furious on the cement, the liberated kids would spread across the lawn like sparrows.

The feeling of being a kind of Bronx St. Francis was fleeting, however, and by the time I would return a sleepy son to the apartment, I was frustrated and angry. The apartment foyer that had been my studio now seemed cramped and dark. The image of a tree branch and a swing in an Edenic suburb grew ever more alluring. June noted my growing dyspepsia and, with a new baby waiting to light on the forever-embroiled St. James lawn, started planning for new vistas away from our beloved New York. It seemed time to move on.

The summer before we left New York for Westport, Connecticut, a chance meeting with Jerrold Beim brought me into the world of book publishing. He was the author of several successful children's books published by William Morrow. I was to discover that this tall, awkward, and quiet man had a wonderfully wry sense of humor, and an abiding respect for the intelligence of the children he served. Sensitively dealing with real-life issues, Jerry's books won critical acclaim as well as a loyal following.

When he invited me to come meet Edith Hamilton, the splendid woman who was his chief editor at Morrow, I found out that Jerry had requested me to work with him on his next book. I was flattered by his confidence in me, delighted at the chance to work with a renowned editor like Edith Hamilton, and terrified at having the responsibility to create the visual story. Happily, it was successful enough to have Edith Hamilton declare us a team, and to provide us the opportunity to fashion five more books. That commitment made our transition to the new world of suburbia financially easier to manage.

Jerry and his family grew to be dear friends, and we were all devastated when he and his son, Seth, were killed in an automobile accident. We lost very special friends, and I lost a wonderfully generous and talented collaborator.

2

Fifty Miles from America

Growing up in prewar America, I knew about "the suburbs." They were just down the road, small, leafy bedroom towns a little beyond the country clubs and the drive-in barbecue stands, nestling just beyond the city-limits sign. For the upwardly mobile, they were nesting places for expanding families, promising more trees, bigger lawns, and room for the additional bedrooms that would certainly be needed sooner or later. Nothing much changed for those who settled there other than the tax base. Their social, professional, and political life remained rooted in the city right next door, the community home they had always had, only minutes away.

But the "suburbia" of the postwar years was very different from the suburbs I had known as a child. New networks of superhighways and commuter railroads were transforming the landscape, shrinking distance, and making the real country available to those who longed to get away from the incessant demands of their urban workplace. The business that sustained you might still be back in the city, but the city was now often an hour or more away. The new commuters who, like us, had fled the city quickly discovered that our new community had discrete needs of its own. "Our town" was the schools our kids would go to, the PTAs we'd join, the church our family might pray at, the Scout troops, Brownies, and Little Leagues our kids would be part of. And the enhanced "quality of life" we had invested our hopes and bankroll in was now in the hands of men and women at the Westport, Connecticut, Town Hall who would be seeking our vote in a local election. Everything was all right here, in suburbia, where we slept. Westport would be our home for the next fifty years. It has been a wonderful place to live and work in. But in some ways we found that it is also fifty miles from America.

My Westport studio was a quiet haven for the day's labors, and the crowded life we lived as young suburban parents putting down new roots made our nights and weekends rich and full. New friends were being made constantly as the migration from the city gained acceleration, and our focus became increasingly on the community and our turf within it. The gentle innocence of those early-fifties years in our new Eden seems risible material for the laugh-track sitcoms of later, more cynical years. Was I really the father in *Father Knows*

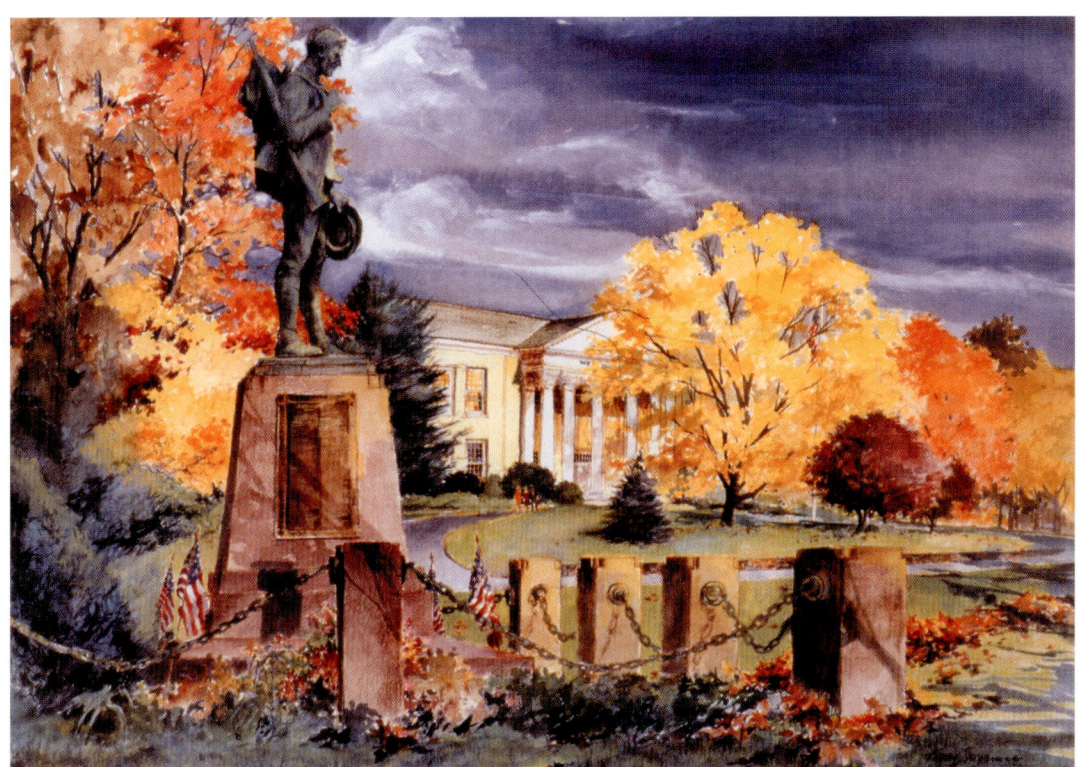

3. *Westport War Memorial and Town Hall*

Best when I marched with Dick's Boy Scout troop in the Memorial Day parade? Was June Sugarman really June Cleaver when she organized the new arrivals into a PTA at Laurie's school? Were we really that smug, that self-absorbed, that divorced from the world we had left in our journey to the Connecticut shore?

Our life in Westport was tranquil and quietly satisfying. There was the constant surprise and pleasure as each of our children stretched at a breathtaking pace into their teens. As a parent who worked mostly at home, I had a window on their world, and our house became a comfortable center for their friends. June's sea anchor was her involvement with the schools, a creative place for enriching the possibilities that are offered to the town kids. At points along the way both she and I invested time with the Brownies, the Cubs, the Girl Scouts, and the Boy Scouts. Our friends were artists, businesspeople, doctors, lawyers, and a rich mix of writers. Only one hour away from the soundstages of the burgeoning world of television, our town became a haven for a community of television writers, actors, and directors. The "golden age of television" was being explored in New York, and friends like Max Shulman, Rod Serling, Mason Adams, and Dick Berg were enthusiastic participants in the exciting new medium. If it wasn't the real world, it seemed very real to us.

Certainly, the challenge of global politics that had so absorbed us as a war generation and the racism that we had dissected in our endless bull sessions on campus as we played

"Strange Fruit" for the thousandth time, or in our navy years when I was seeing racial apartheid aboard every ship, had not vanished from our psyches. But they were a hidden subtext in our suburban lives. Politics was local, and there was no racial problem here because there were almost no minorities living here. But in the tranquil warp and woof of our family life there was an obstinate strand that kept coming loose, an irritating reminder that the world that had once so totally engaged our passions had not vanished simply because we had moved fifty miles up the road.

The new miracle of television was dramatically shrinking the space between the observer and the observed. The battles being waged in the new United Nations, the "cold war" with Russia, the McCarthy-Army hearings in Washington, and the extraordinary developments at the U.S. Supreme Court that destroyed the age-old excuse of "separate but equal," launching a thrilling civil rights movement, moved inexorably into our suburban living room. Wide-eyed, we could see that the world was changing, but we didn't have a clue as to how those changes might affect our comfortable lives. Ironically, it was a commission for a fifth-grade health book that loosened the strand for the first time. The fabric would be subtly altered, and never made quite so smooth again.

3

Scott, Foresman, and Company

The illustrated books I had completed for William Morrow had opened an exciting new door. A commission from Scott, Foresman, and Company, the textbook giant, to illustrate its first full-color health book appeared to be a remarkable opportunity. My meeting with the publisher was promising and cordial, and I flew back from Chicago with high hopes for the ambitious project. For the next months I was totally engaged in creating the first extended series of illustrations for the book. It promised to be an eventful and challenging time in the year ahead. Daughter Laurie's sweet arrival, the exciting new neighborhood vistas of playmates for Dick, the ready new companionship of a young, expanding community of artists and writers for June and me, and the easy access to beaches and countryside totally captivated us.

The drawings had gone well, and I was eager to show my new client this first batch of completed pages. The committee appeared pleased with the work as it circled the table in the boardroom, but the editor seemed unusually quiet as the enthusiastic comments were being made. As the pile of drawings completed their journey in front of him, the room became quiet. He smiled and said, "They're very good, Tracy. Very real kids. And a very warm environment in the work. Good job!" He paused, and a small frown creased his forehead. "But there's a small problem that you will have to adjust." He sifted through the stack and extracted several of the drawings. He framed one in his hands and turned it in my direction. "This is a Negro child brushing his teeth. And in this, there is a Negro girl jumping rope with white children. And in this, there is a Negro boy . . . " He stopped, aware that I had pushed my chair back from the table. The room was silent.

I cleared my throat and extended my hand across the table for the troublesome drawings. "Well, you are certainly correct," I said. "Those Negro children are indeed brushing their teeth and jumping rope. But what is the problem I have to adjust?"

He reddened, and when he spoke again he said in an aggrieved voice, "We can't have that in our textbook." His eyes held mine. "That is the problem. That is your problem to fix. This is a textbook, Tracy, and it must be accepted by textbook review boards in every southern state. And states like Texas will never accept a textbook that suggests there are racially integrated classrooms."

"Sir," I said, "it has been more than two years since the U.S. Supreme Court in *Brown vs. The Board of Education* declared that in education, separate but equal is separate but unequal. It is the law of the land. And it is certainly my belief that any textbook should reflect the law of the land."

The editor nodded and reexamined one of the drawings. "Well, couldn't you make this Negro child less Negro? Perhaps very light-skinned, so she might be Negro but perhaps not?" He smiled encouragingly. "A good artist could do that."

"I'm sure a good artist could," I said quietly. "But not this good artist." I got up from the table. "I think perhaps you should discuss this without me. I'll be flying back to Connecticut in the morning."

I called June on the phone from the hotel and warned her that our big breakthrough project might well be dead. "Honey," she said, "we've never been rich up to now, and we're still okay. You did right, baby. I'll meet you at the plane with the kids."

The trip home was desolate. The months of work I had already invested in the project plagued my thoughts, and I wondered if I would ever find another commission that offered such scope. The whole family had been witness to the creation of the portfolio, and I was running through scenarios that could comfortably explain the sudden end to what had been such a bright and exciting challenge.

But the reception by my kids in the terminal was sweet and welcoming, a sign that June had not shared my dolorous call with them. "Welcome home, sailor," she said brightly. "We missed you!" As we climbed into the car she murmured, "There was a call from Chicago. The editor wants you to call him as soon as you get home." Her eyes were questioning. "What do you think it means?"

"I haven't a clue," I said.

The editor's voice was upbeat and enthusiastic. "Get cracking on the rest of the illustrations, Tracy." There was a brief hesitation. "Everyone has signed on, and we think Texas will be doable. So we're betting on that. And I want you to know we're glad we had a chance to discuss it with you."

As I hung up the phone, I grinned at my wife. "It's a go!"

"It's a go?"

"It's a go. And I will never begin to understand the corporate mind."

"Maybe that's just as well," June replied with a big smile.

The minds of clients have long remained a mystery to me. What has really mattered has been the kind of working alliances that have been fashioned with a long series of editorial, institutional, and corporate sponsors that have kept me afloat as an illustrator for nearly sixty years. I feel most grateful for the level of mutual trust that has nearly always animated those business relationships. The candor and honesty that have been their hallmark have most often led to lasting friendships.

At an awkward moment in time when America was seeking to find its racial footing in public education, Scott, Foresman chose to do the brave thing. Together, we integrated a textbook even before the civil rights movement and the U.S. Congress changed the apartheid face of the South. In subsequent years, we created other textbooks that honestly reflected the interracial communities that distinguish our nation. I am proud of the accomplishments we achieved together.

I will always treasure the compliment paid to me by Mrs. Fannie Lou Hamer, the extraordinary heroine of the freedom struggle in Mississippi in the sixties. At the end of my work as an artist with the civil rights movement in 1965, she said, "You did important work down here with your drawings of confrontations and voter registration and Freedom Schools, Tracy. But I think the most important contribution you made was when you put black kids in an American textbook."

4

Casper Pinsker Jr.

On a long, lazy Sunday afternoon in August 1954, I was building a sand castle with my son on a sandbar at Compo Beach in Westport. Deep in concentration and working to finish our creation before the tide turned, we did not notice the little boy who stood hesitantly at our backs until he inched his way closer to get a better look at what we were doing. When I saw the fascinated look in his eyes, I asked him to join us.

He hesitated a moment and looked back at the crowd on the beach.

"It's okay, son. This is my boy, Dick, and I'm Tracy. What's your name?"

"Robbie. Robbie Pinsker."

"Well, Robbie, grab that shovel and help Dick build a moat. The tide is starting to creep in."

The boy grinned, knelt beside Dick, shovel in hand, and started digging.

Splashing his way through the low-tide puddles, a stocky young man looking quite concerned joined us. "Is Robbie bothering you?" he asked. "I told him not to!"

I stood up, brushed the sand from my knees, and reassured him. "I invited him to help. Looks like a good digger!"

The man smiled and stepped closer, extending his hand. "I'm Cap Pinsker, Robbie's dad. And my wife over there on the red blanket under the *New York Times* told me you are an artist. Of course, Helene thinks everybody in Westport but me is an artist! Is she right?"

"Well," I said, "just take a look at our castle. It should be obvious!"

In the days that followed, it turned out that his question was not just an idle inquiry. Pinsker was in the process of starting a record company called Grand Award, and he was seriously seeking artists for his covers. He asked to see my work and then gave me an assignment to design the cover of a New York album. "Let's see how it goes," he said.

Apparently, it went well. Grand Award was a great success, and in the next five years I drew or painted more than a hundred album covers. What was so gratifying for me was the total confidence shown by Grand Award in my choice of media and subject matter.

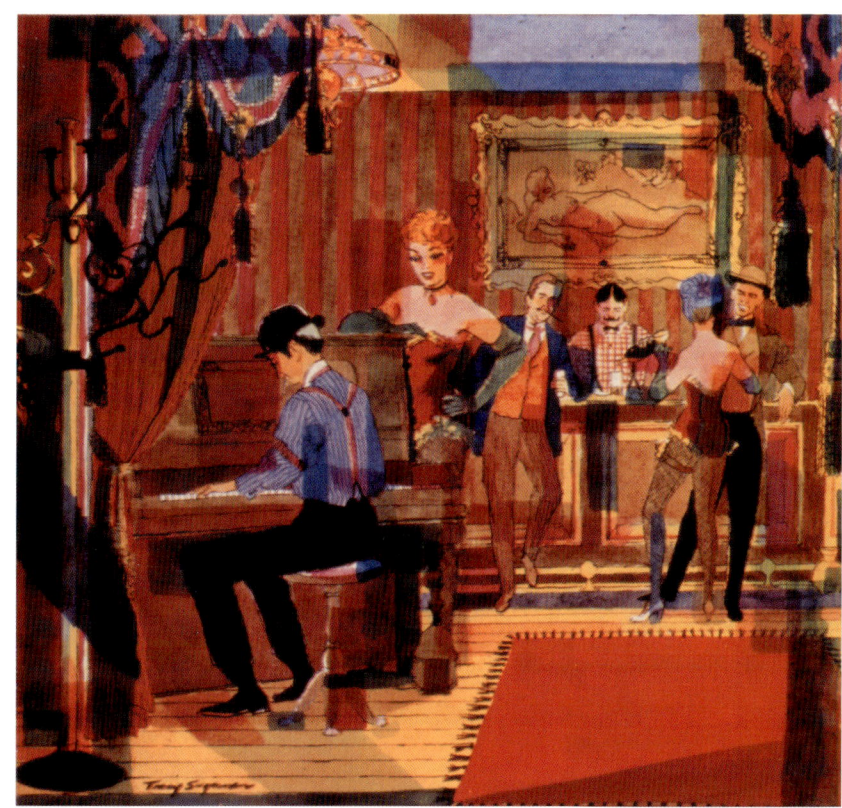

4. *Knuckles O'Toole*

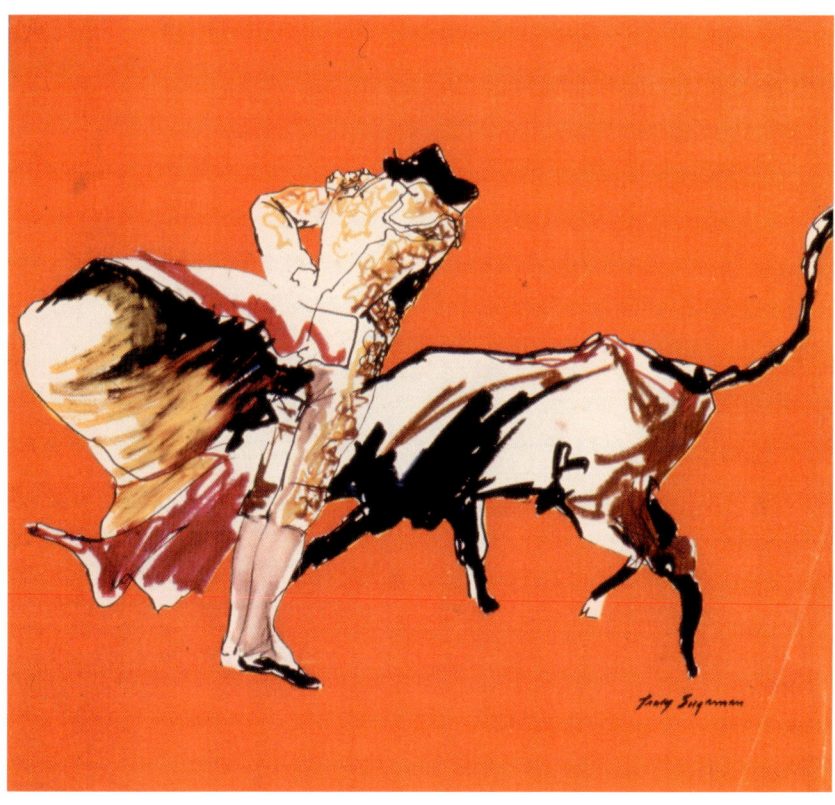

5. *Matador*

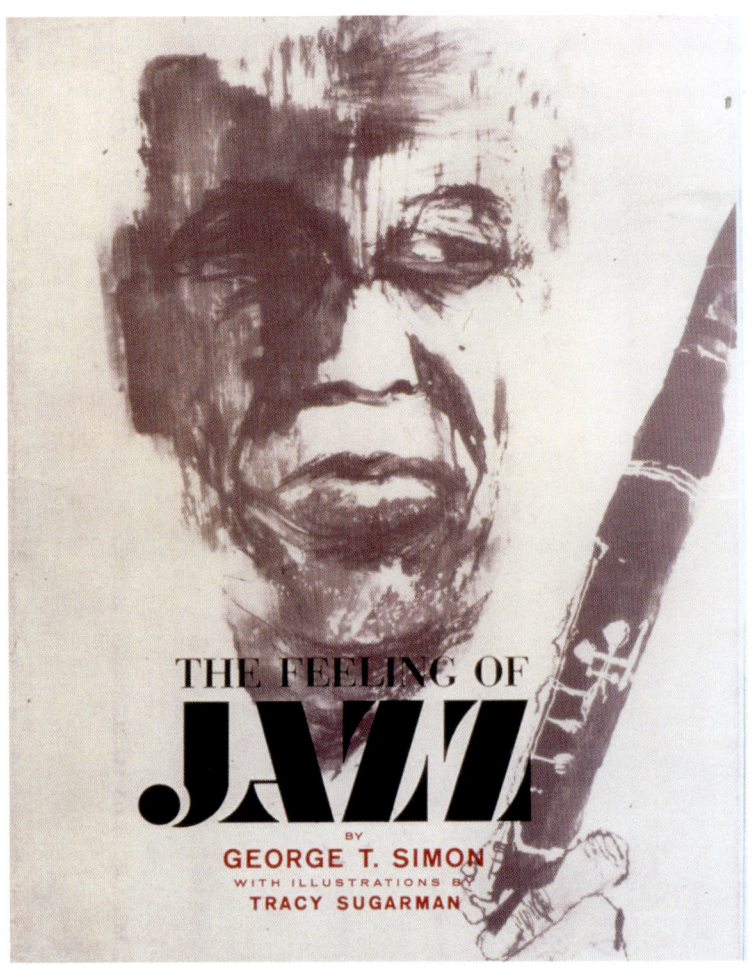

6. *The Feeling of Jazz*

From the very first album until the business was sold, I was never asked to make a correction or change.

While waiting for the break that would finally get me into magazines, thanks to Grand Award, I had been able to explore every medium from scratchboard to oils, from pastels to watercolors, and seen them reproduced. I had captured Mahalia Jackson singing gospel and Knuckles O'Toole playing ragtime piano. I'd painted bullfights and ballet dancers, lovers in Spain and children in France, cowboy balladeers and marching bands. I now knew I had the tools necessary to work anywhere.

On the back of all the jazz records produced by Grand Award were liner notes by George Simon. Simon was the jazz critic for the *New York Herald Tribune* and for twenty years had been the editor of *Metronome*, the jazz bible. He called me after the demise of Grand Award Records and invited me to illustrate *The Feeling of Jazz,* his roman à clef novel about the world he knew so intimately. "I like the way you show affection for the musicians you've drawn for the albums," he grinned. "After all, I am a drummer!"

Simon and Schuster produced a beautiful melding of George's words and my pictures. It was great fun working with Simon and getting to see and draw the inside of the music scene in the clubs of New York. It was the beginning of a love affair with jazz that has warmed me for more than forty years.

5

Bill Cooley

For a sales rep, Bill Cooley seemed remarkably unassuming and modest. We had met at the Society of Illustrators, and I liked his manner and his modesty. When he had examined my very full portfolio, he was enthused about representing me. "I think you should be a natural for *Colliers, Woman's Home Companion, American, Boy's Life,* maybe even the *Saturday Evening Post.*" No one could have tried harder to make those things happen, calling repeatedly on art directors who didn't share his enthusiasm. For months he was unable to get me a manuscript.

One late afternoon after searching Madison Avenue once again, we sat disconsolately, frustrated and impatient. "I just don't get it," Cooley said. "Unless . . . " He paused uncomfortably. "Look, Tracy, don't get me wrong." He was silent for a moment and then blurted out, "Maybe it's your name. Maybe you should think about changing your name."

I stared at him in disbelief, and then got angry. "My name? Why the hell should I change my name? No, Bill. I like my name, and so did my father. It stays Sugarman. Tracy Sugarman."

Cooley was silent and flushed.

"Maybe, Bill, I just have to get better. We both have to get better."

Two weeks after I stormed out of Cooley's living room, he called me on the phone. "Are you sitting down? Well, sit down. I've got a manuscript from *Colliers* magazine. And on the cover it says, 'This is for Tracy. Tracy Sugarman.'" He laughed. "Maybe we both got better!"

Recalling the unintentionally awkward discussion with Bill Cooley about names, more particularly a name that was probably recognized as a Jewish name, is like hearing a distant, discordant echo from another time. Certainly, Bill was in no stretch of the imagination an anti-Semite, nor did I even imagine he might be. Instead, he was realistically acknowledging that there were those in every field of endeavor who held tight to evil stereotypes of others in order to make themselves feel fulfilled. Being a Jew has always been a matter of quiet pride for me, and unlike many who have suffered unfairly from religious prejudice, my religion has never knowingly created obstacles for me in my professional or social life. In an era when the most unspeakable blood crime in all of history had destroyed six million Jews, I am disdainful and contemptuous of the pathetic men and women who still persist in gorging on that wicked fruit. If I have achieved some success in my career, it is not because of my religion. And if I have failed in meeting the challenges in my life, it is not because of my religion. As my aunt Rose would say, "Who has time for such nonsense in America?"

Though hardly celebrities, many of us young illustrators were able to support ourselves on the peripheries of the field, doing less important stories for the big books or filling the pages of a score of smaller magazines. During that decade I fulfilled assignments for *Colliers*, the *Ladies' Home Journal*, *Blue Book*, *Red Book*, *Parents Magazine*, *Coronet*, *Everywoman*, and *Esquire*. It was a busy life of sketches, meetings with art directors, constant deadlines, and delivering the finished work with a fair amount of trepidation and panic.

But I was troubled. I knew I was making a living being an illustrator of other people's visions. I began to long for the intimacy of drawing my world in peacetime as I had drawn it at war.

When, in 1956, I gave myself the assignment to put the garment center of Seventh Avenue in my sketchbooks, I joyously found my way back to where I truly lived as an artist. From that time on, I have explored my country and my time on my terms. For more than half a century I have been capturing images in words and pictures of this marvelous and contradictory place.

6

Seventh Avenue

The journey from my tranquil and homogeneous Connecticut town to the frenetic warrens of Seventh Avenue was a jolt into reality every morning. Every noisy, trundling rack of garments in every color that filled the thronging streets, every shout in Spanish, Italian, Yiddish, Caribbean, Brooklynese, was a strident reminder that the American pot was still furiously boiling. I was enthralled with the whole vibrant spectacle, and I'd move through the garment center itching to stop and capture the garden of faces, complexions, and gestures that were so exotic and alive.

For weeks I made my odyssey from suburbia to prowl the world of garment workshops, salesrooms, and the helter-skelter of delis, trucks, and cops that seemed to fill every side street. I became a familiar if odd addition to the life, hanging around, drawing pictures, and asking questions of the men and women who always clustered around my sketchpads. I liked their easy banter and friendliness as we would share a pastrami sandwich or argue about the Dodgers, who were making a run for the pennant. I laughed at their jokes, admired their kids' pictures, and listened avidly as they told me about their jobs, their pride in their craft, and their dissatisfaction with their wages and their bosses. When they'd see me actually drawing, they would become quiet, closely observing what I was seeking to put down. "You do this? You make a living from it? Jesus!" They'd pat me on the shoulder and return to their presses and workrooms after their lunch break. "Wait till I tell my old lady that a real artist drew my picture while I was pressing!" The hours would rush by before I had to run to catch my train at Grand Central, suddenly remembering I had to get home for a PTA meeting or Boy Scout cookout, but in Westport. Fifty miles from America.

I remember the day dawned brilliant and crisp. White steam from the grates along Thirty-sixth Street rose straight in the chill air. But it was one of those rare March mornings in New York when the wind from Jersey carried a fragrant hint of spring as it swept across the Hudson and into the garment district. Outside the sweating window of Max's Bagel and Hot Knishes, two salesmen lingered with their "coffees to go," reluctant to leave the pale disk of sun that flooded the street. Beneath their freshly shined shoes, the pavement

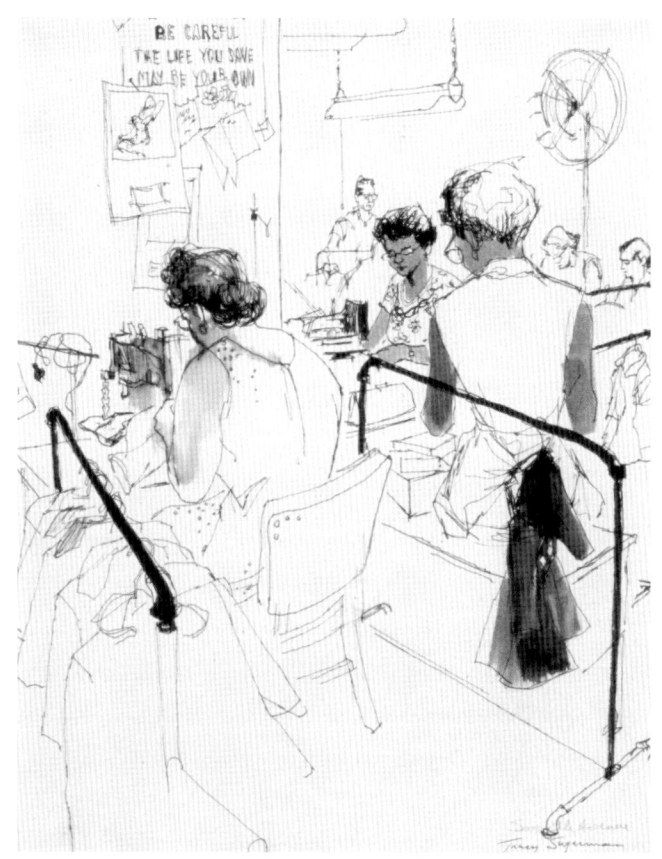

7. *Three Women*

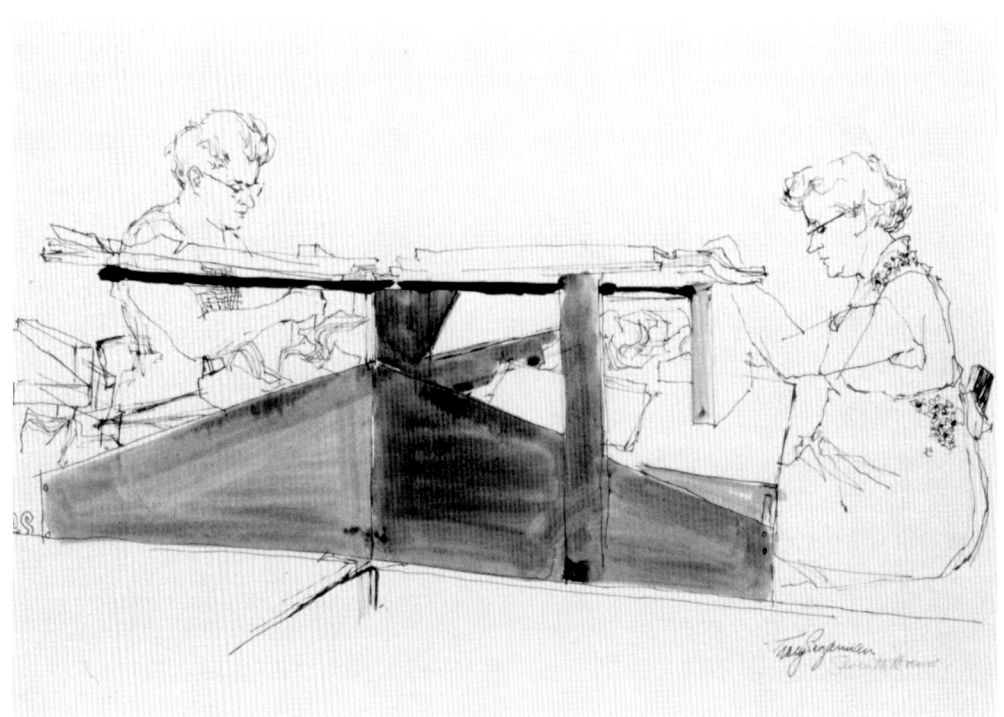

8. *Mrs. Flores and Mrs. Zeoli*

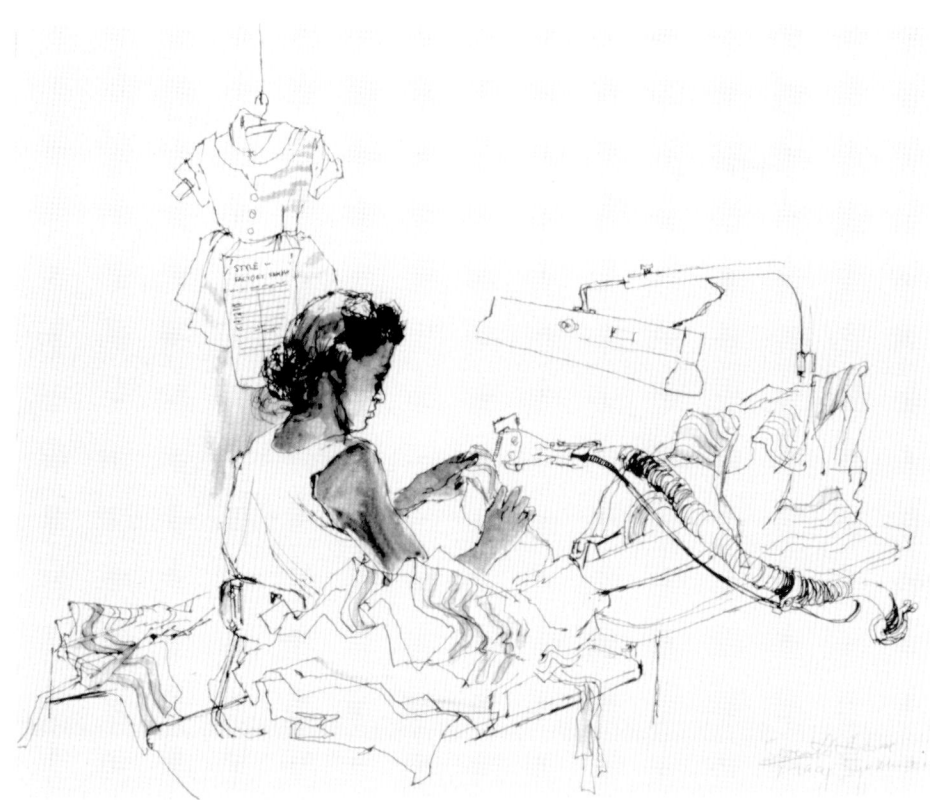

9. *Threads*

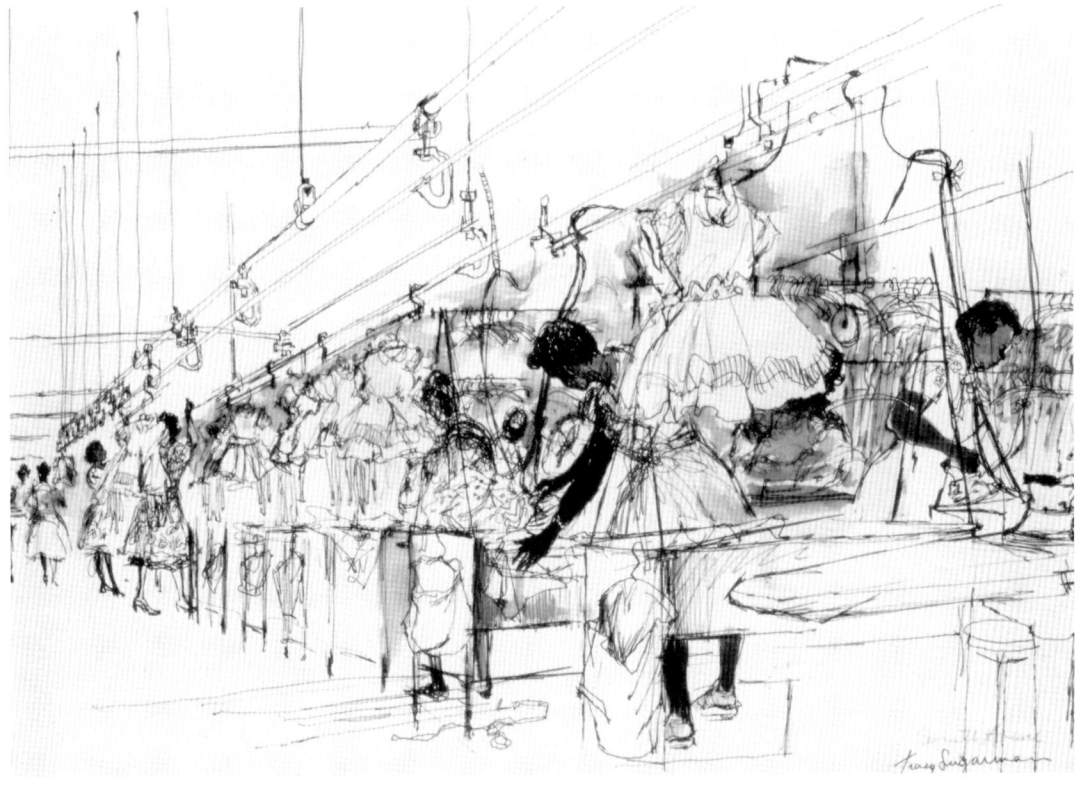

10. *Children's Dresses*

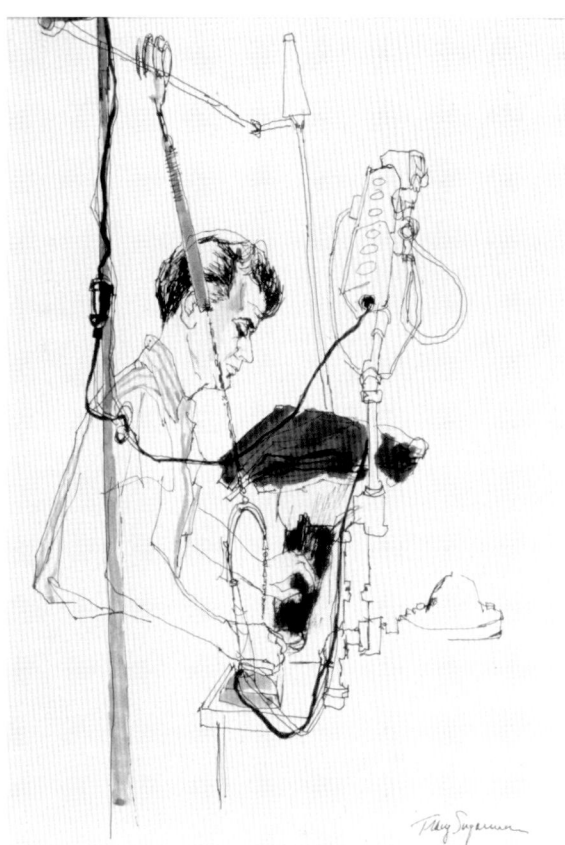

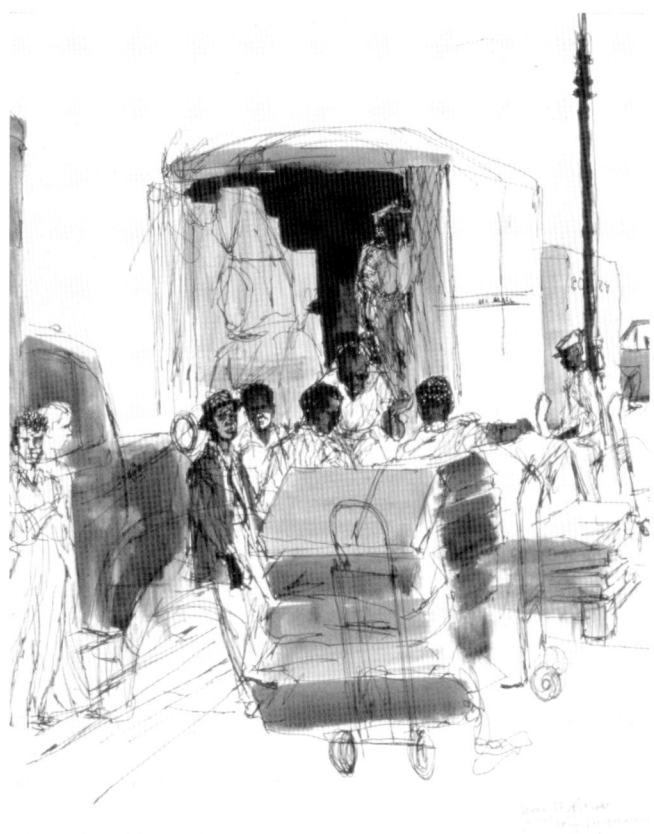

11. *Sidney*   12. *Loading Trucks*

trembled as the Seventh Avenue subway racketed below. Up and down the side streets, the jumble of trucks and passenger cars honked their raucous battle for space. "Ged oudda de way! Yeah, you!"

A young Hispanic fought to keep his hand truck moving across the frantic intersection of Thirty-sixth Street and Seventh Avenue, grateful for the flushed policeman who momentarily held the impatient traffic at bay. The miniature bouquet of children's dresses on his racks whipped in the wind, a stray flash of color in the gray clutter.

Heading east, a station wagon equipped with a public address system slithered through the herd of trucks. "CALLING ALL DRESSMAKERS! THIS IS A GENERAL STRIKE! LEAVE YOUR MACHINES! LEAVE YOUR SHOPS! PROCEED TO MADISON SQUARE GARDEN!"

The two salesmen seemed rooted to the sidewalk, their eyes staring at the station wagon in disbelief. Then they bolted down the suddenly hushed avenue. For a long moment nothing seemed to move. Then every door burst open. Men and women, some still in work smocks and aprons, clutching their jackets and hats, poured onto the sidewalks. More and more streamed from the buildings, blinking in the sudden brightness.

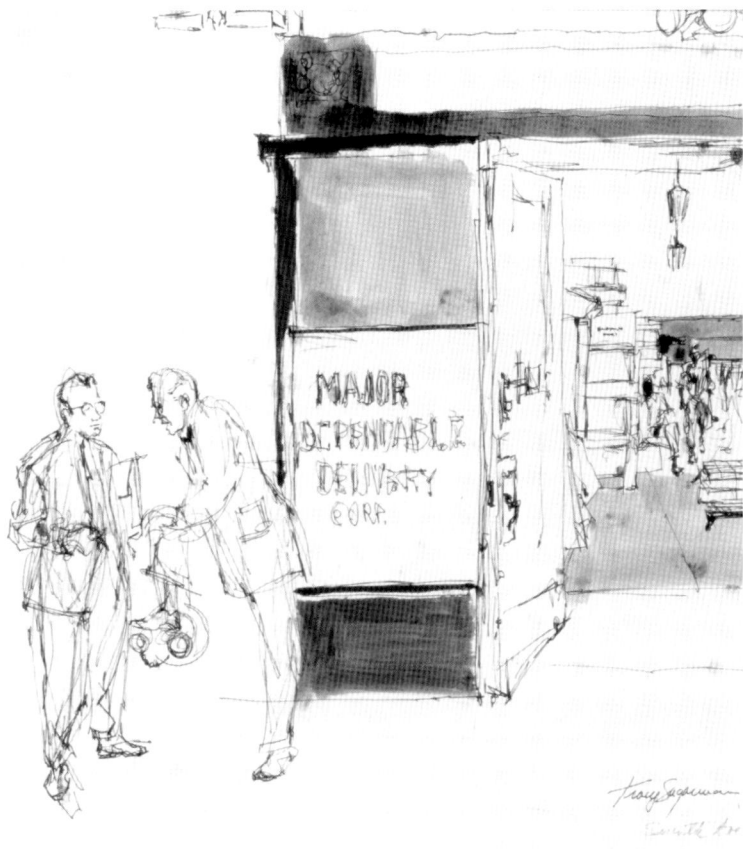

Calling out to friends, they spilled into the street, moving inexorably west. When they reached Eighth Avenue, they joined the flood of pressers, shipping clerks, cutters, finishers, and floor women as they swept north toward Madison Square Garden.

13. *Two Salesmen*

Nathan, a cutter I had drawn, fell in step with me. His eyes raked the crowd, and he was grinning broadly. "Look at that, artist! Just look at that!" I knew he was a union shop steward, and there was pride on his face as he looked about him.

As we moved slowly up the avenue, Nathan turned to me. "Let me tell you what happened to me. One day I'm on the way to the job, and as I'm crossing Union Square Park a big pigeon flies over me and shits on my head. I got so mad that I chased him across the park, where he settled on a branch and just looked at me. I wagged my finger at him and screamed, 'You bastard! For the bosses, you sing!'" As we both laughed, he nodded at the large parade. "You know, artist," he said quietly, "there have been a lot of birds flying over this bunch for years."

The crowd seemed released and festive. Shouts of "Strike! Strike!" and chants of "Join us!" mingled with laughter. A clutch of women started to sing "Solidarity Forever" in Spanish, and applause rippled through the crowd. Now it was taken up by others, more than ten thousand strong, and the marchers left the sunshine and entered the cavernous space of Madison Square Garden.

From the podium, smiling union officers waved excitedly to the thousands who had answered their call. Overhead, a great banner had been hung from the lights. "ON WITH THE STRIKE! ON TO VICTORY!" It was March 5, 1958. And it was the first

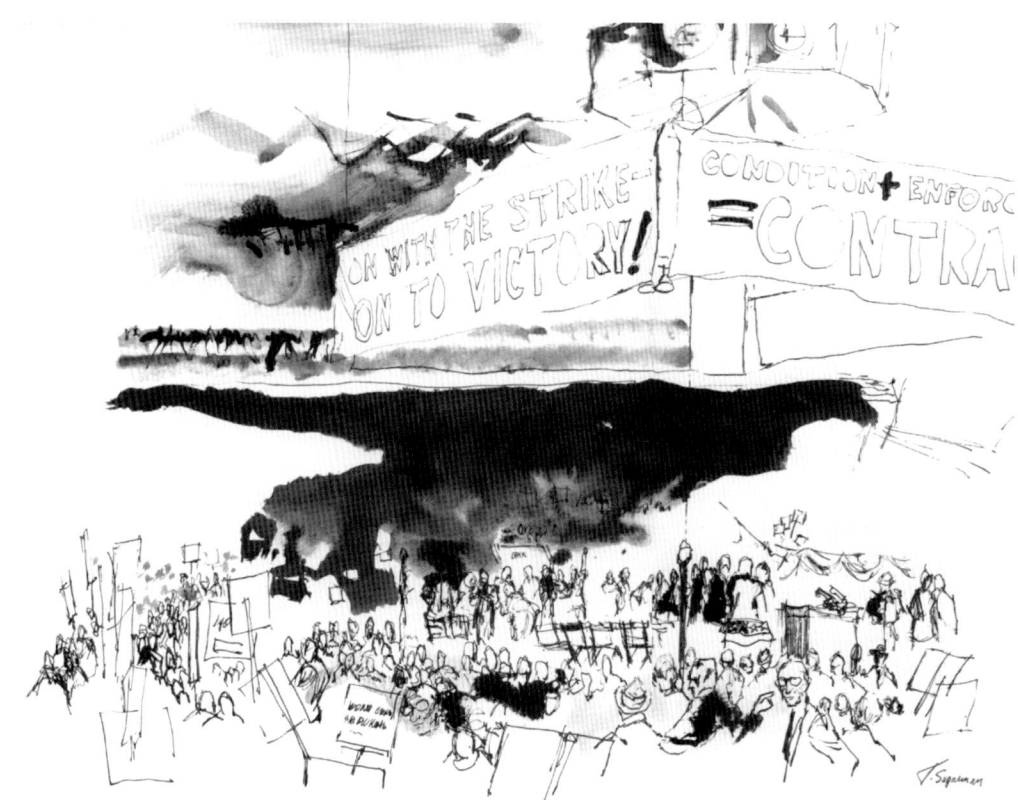

14. *Madison Square*
Garden Rally

day of the first strike by the International Ladies' Garment Workers' Union in twenty-five years.

By the time the strike took place, I had filled my sketchbooks with images of intent Hispanic women organizing endless racks of dresses; of sweating black men, skillfully pressing garments in a welter of lint and steam; of fastidious fitters whose hands moved effortlessly over the draped fabrics on the forms, cursing in Yiddish at a dropped pleat. The whole unbuttoned world of New York labor was unfolding on my pages, and now it was going out on the picket lines. I simply moved with my friends into the uncertain world of labor confrontation, and I took my sketchpads with me.

For the days and nights of the strike, I prowled their picket lines, sketched their strike headquarters at the old Diplomat Hotel and the Armory, and put down my impressions of them and their leaders when they packed Manhattan Center and the Garden for the great rallies. When International Ladies' Garment Workers' Union president David Dubinsky, the great orator Luigi Antonini, and the AFL-CIO's George Meany thundered their challenges to the billion-dollar-a-year garment industry, I was there with my friends. And I was recording it all for posterity.

My folio of the garment center would not be seen by the public until 1998, when the ILGWU and the Fashion Institute of Technology mounted a handsome monthlong

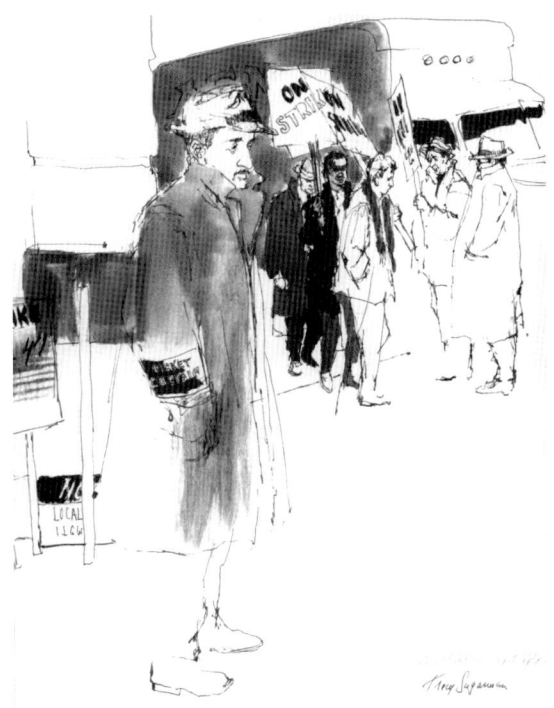

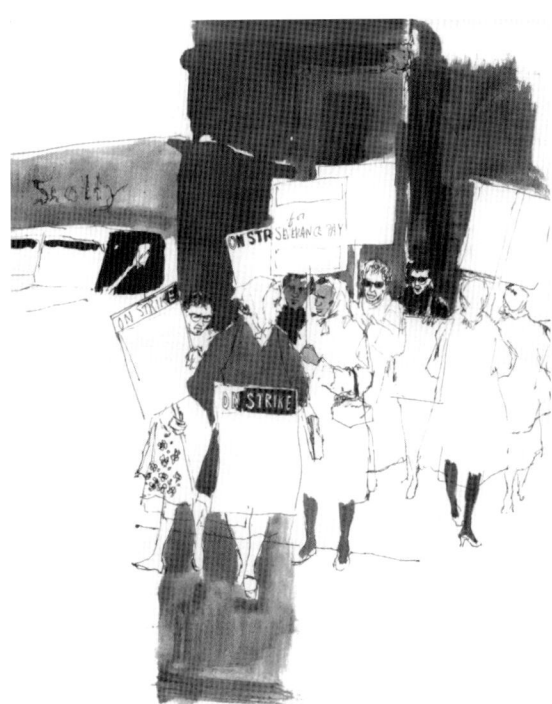

(*Left*) 15. *Pickets*

(*Right*) 16. *Solidarity*

exhibition of all the work. After forty years, my personal sketchbooks were now considered archival. It was gratifying to see what pride the workers felt as they pointed out aspects of the various drawings to their children and grandchildren. "That's how it was," they said. "That's exactly how we looked then! Jesus, there's Solomon in his old fedora! And will you look at that ancient punch-card machine in shipping!"

When the union won its strike, I returned to Madison Avenue where I made my living as a magazine illustrator. I took with me the drawings I had made during the turbulent weeks on Seventh Avenue. With them, I hoped I could convince magazine art directors to give me the meaty reportorial assignments rather than the fictional manuscripts that felt increasingly ephemeral. My gritty images of strikers and picket lines were respectfully received, but often in silence. "But we don't do things like that at this magazine, Sugarman."

One art director, however, after viewing the portfolio with obvious pleasure, said, "My dad was a cutter on Thirty-seventh Street. He could be in any of these wonderful drawings." He looked thoughtful as he handed me my portfolio. "Do you know a man named Tony Schwartz?" he asked.

When I said I did not, he scribbled a number on his memo pad and handed it to me. "Here's Tony's number. You should call him." I was puzzled. "Who is Tony Schwartz? And what does he do?" The man smiled as he showed me to the door. "He's an artist, like you. But he's doing what you do with a tape recorder. You guys should know each other."

7

Tony Schwartz

Meeting Tony was memorable for me. He, too, was striving to capture a reality that was unvarnished, authentic, and unrehearsed. I listened to his recorded interviews with children, cab drivers, gospel singers, and politicians and to his extraordinary tone poems composed from the sounds of the city he knew and loved so well. I was enchanted by the originality and honesty of it all. Schwartz had first worked as a graphic artist, but soon found that his real passion was the medium of sound.

He slowly leafed through my story of Seventh Avenue. When he finished, he grinned at me. "So when do we start working together?"

I gazed at this tall, gentle, rumpled man who would now play an important role in my life. "Well," I said in a wondering voice, "I don't know. Now?"

Our first team assignment was a request to prepare four half-hour documentary programs for CBS-TV's religious program *Lamp unto My Feet*. The theme was modest enough—simply an examination of God! We were to interview and draw four sets of people: children, teenagers, adults, and the elderly and record their perceptions of the Lord.

Those hours with Tony, drawing as he conversed with our participants, were pure delight. I found myself in the company of one of the greatest listeners I had ever met. Tony's obvious pleasure in the dialogues was so apparent and flattering that no one seemed even aware of his recorder or my sketchbooks. His openness and respectful, sensitive questions were disarming, and the atmosphere of the conversations was totally relaxed. As a result, the contemplative and surprising responses were often candid, funny, and moving.

It was the first time I had ever shared a creative project with another artist, and it was a reassuring and valuable learning experience for me. Each of us valued the other's unique contribution, and we both were careful to respect the other's needs and space.

When we presented the tapes and the drawings to CBS, we were both excited that we had created something of unique value. Our producer was delighted with the work, and we were wide-eyed as we watched her transform our collaborations into four cohesive and moving half hours of programming. The exploratory journeys of the camera about

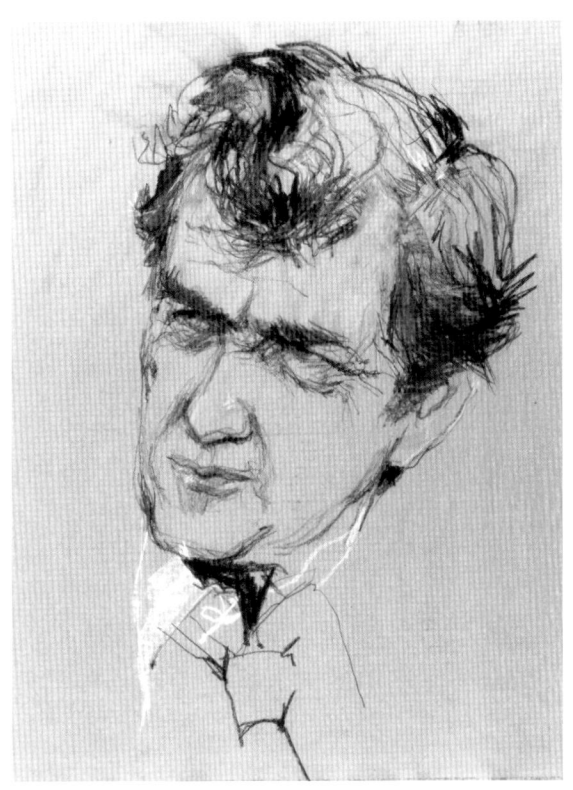

17. *Senator Edmund Muskie*

my drawings seemed seamlessly wed to the voices of those being interviewed, and another dimension was created for the observer. It was my initiation into the art of filmmaking, an intriguing medium that in ten years would become central to my life as an artist and a writer.

Schwartz's innovative use of reality sound and authentic, unscripted people unlocked a massive door into the commercial warrens of Madison Avenue and the political offices of congressmen, senators, and men and women seeking office from across the country. On my infrequent visits to Tony's studio, I became aware that Madison Avenue movers and shakers as well as familiar faces from Washington were often in attendance, seeking his uniquely persuasive analysis. Tony was flying high, tickled that the simple unadorned truth he had sought out as his medium was now being appreciated. From his studio he now often broadcast lectures to schools of communication on prestigious campuses. I realized that my once socially reticent friend was now an icon to many young people who analyzed his work and found it provocative. For a generation that was exploring his friend Marshall McCluhan's "global village," Tony Schwartz was providing new evidence that slick, packaged information could be well improved by simplicity and honesty.

Though our collaborations were mostly confined to the more introspective venues of Sunday-morning television, with themes of ethnic celebrations, religious ruminations, or civil rights, we did take an adventurous shot at making a political television commercial for Senator Edmund Muskie's bid for the presidency in 1968. We put together a series of drawings of Muskie that I prepared with Tony's audiotapes of statements by the senator. It broke exciting new ground in how to present a candidate, and we and the Muskie camp were enthusiastically awaiting its first run on the air. Alas, it was never to be. When in a television interview on the campaign trail he was challenged on some statement regarding his wife, the usually affable senator was infuriated, breaking into tears in the heat of his defense. Like the shot heard 'round the world, Muskie's tears were reported by his opponents as a sign of unmanly behavior to the furthest corners of the political landscape.

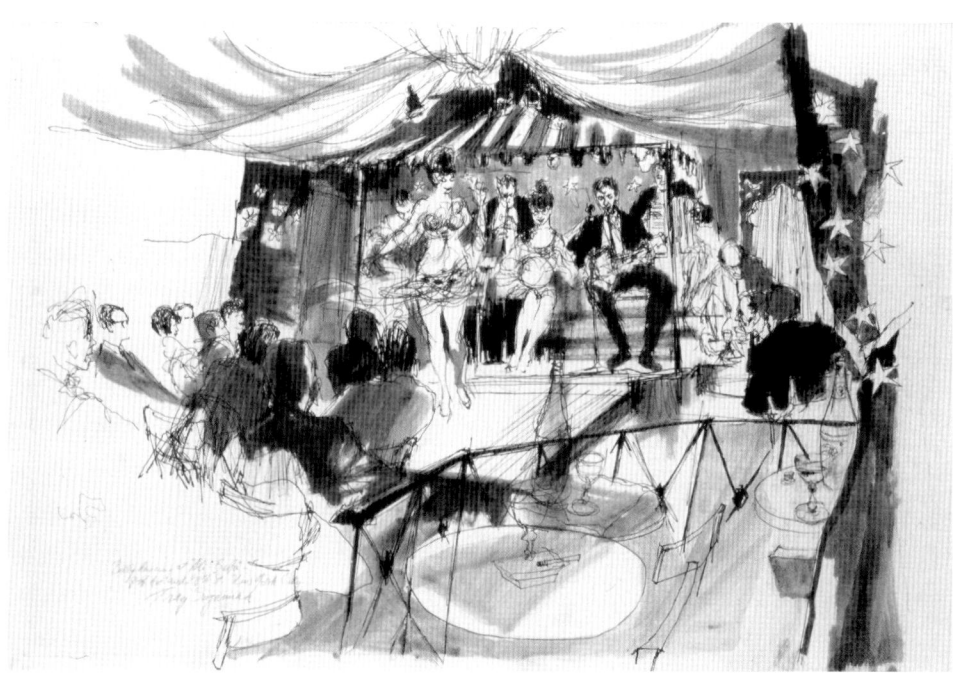

18. *Ninth Avenue Belly Dancer*

The incident was so exploited that the Muskie campaign never recovered. The Washington-bound *Muskie Special* left the rails, never to return. And our wonderful commercial died in the womb.

My collaboration with Tony seemed to open exciting new doors for me. I was no longer merely an illustrator who helped adorn the fictional pages of magazines. Now more of my assignments were to create my own images of on-site life in America. When art directors called me in, it was because specific stories could better profit from the point of view of an artist than a photographer. Photographs in a manufacturing site, on an assembly line, or in an oil-cracking plant were hard to make in a focused way that was visually arresting. The camera lens was simply too democratic and inclusive. Too often, the art director had to struggle with all the photograph's intrusive and irrelevant background that was distracting. In contrast, as an artist I could select the subject I wanted to paint, and include only that which could best tell the story. My contribution seemed very welcome, and for the next six years I found receptive clients in both the corporate and the publishing worlds.

I was off and running, and having an exhilarating time with my reportage. I drew and painted textile mills across the South, research labs for Western Electric in New Jersey, satellite tracking stations in the wilds of Maine for AT&T and recorded on paper the magic of glass making in Corning, New York. Only in the elegant offices of Standard Oil on Wall Street where I was drawing their executive hierarchy did I feel any constraint or pressure. In all honesty, it was my own psychological problem, perhaps a holdover from

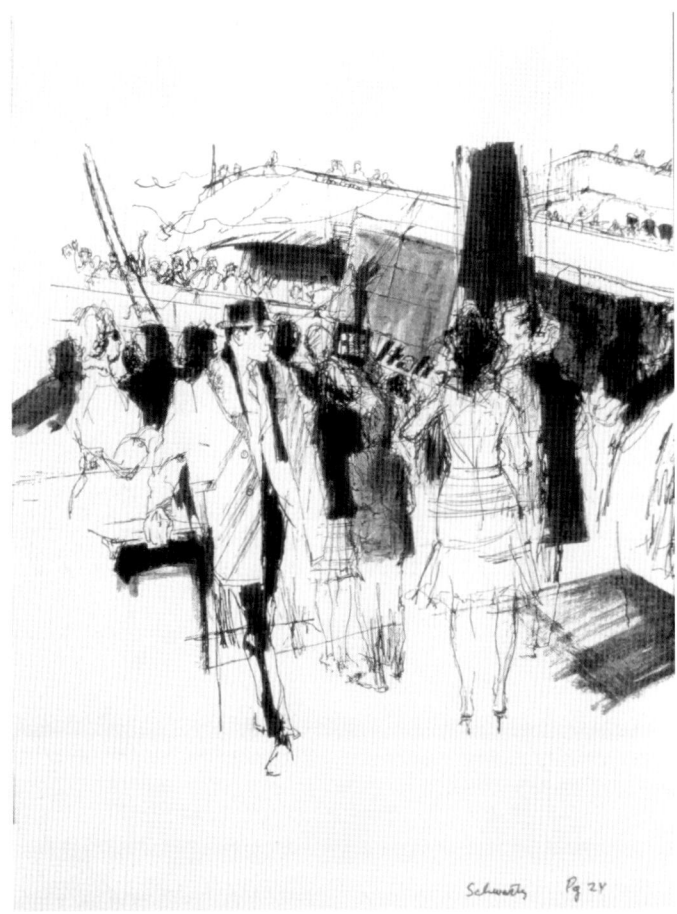

19. *Sailing of the* Leonardo da Vinci

my nights on the picket lines during the garment workers' strike. For that intensive period I had identified with people who felt powerless and were struggling against men of power like the ones I was drawing. *"For the bosses, you sing!"* But the people at Standard Oil could not have been more accommodating or friendly.

If one has a favorite client, I would have to choose *Gentlemen's Quarterly* magazine. Under the brilliant graphic guidance of art director Albert Greenberg, GQ was on the cutting edge of layout and design in New York's publishing world. My Seventh Avenue drawings had intrigued Greenberg, and I was asked to create a folio of drawings that could reflect the marvelous variety of the Big Apple's life. It was an unbelievable carte blanche assignment, and I was told that I could select those sites that seemed most revealing. Over a number of weeks I filled my sketchbooks with Ninth Avenue belly dancers; Shakespearean actors backstage in Central Park; off-Broadway theatergoers at the first night of *The Fantastics*; the arrival of the *Da Vinci*, a great Italian liner, at a Fifty-seventh Street pier; mounted police at their stables in Central Park; hot dog eaters at Nathan's on a teeming Broadway; and a street scene on my own adopted Seventh Avenue! The work was warmly received and mounted handsomely by Al Greenberg in the pages of GQ.

In subsequent assignments from GQ, I was to explore the French Quarter of New Orleans, a Yale-Princeton football weekend in New Haven, and the Dublin Horse Show. I never confessed to my Medici at GQ that for assignments like these, I would happily have done them for free. If someone had asked me if my cup was half full or half empty, I would have said, "My cup runneth over."

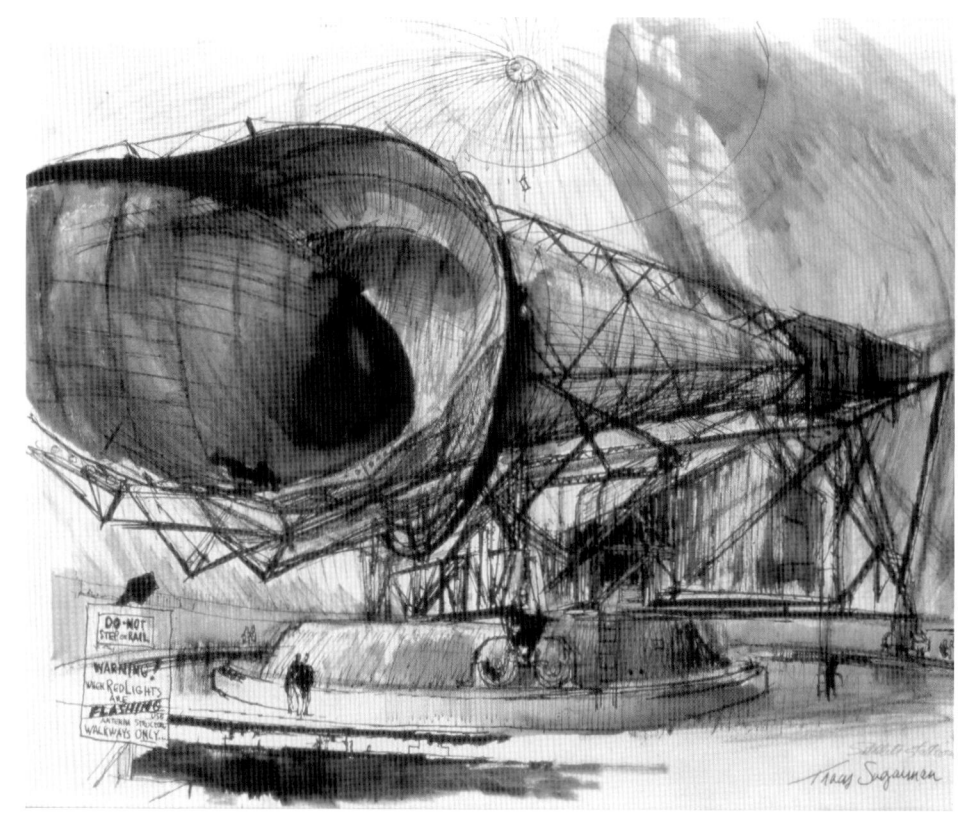

20. *Space Listener*

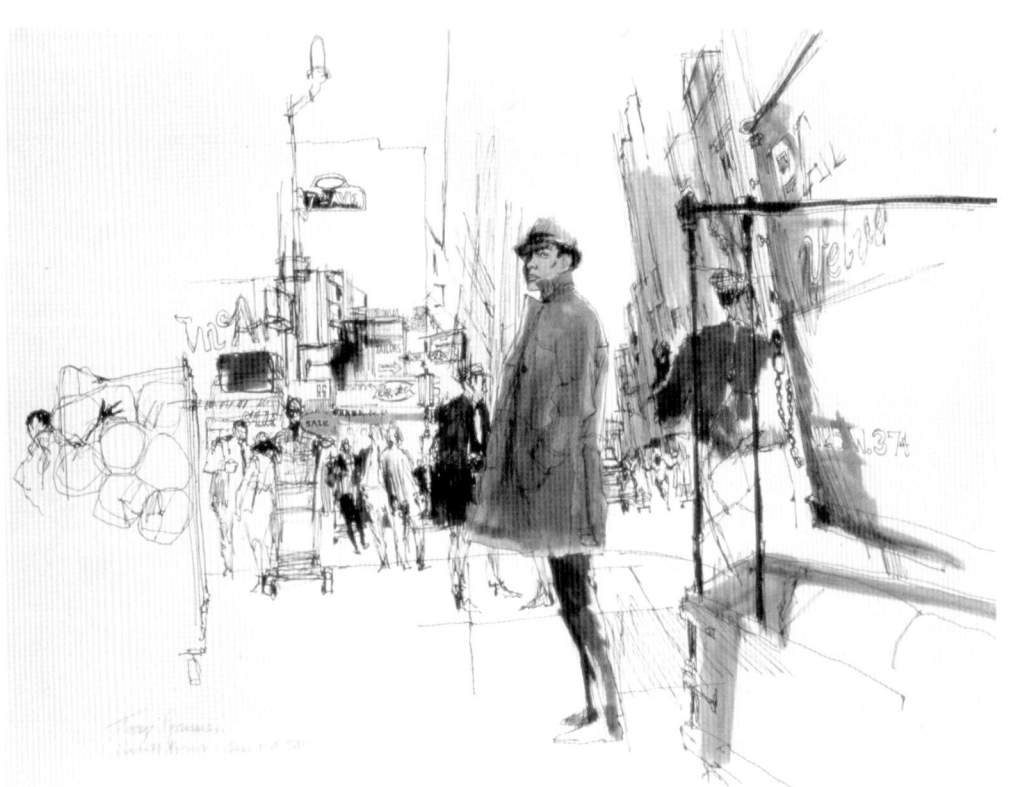

21. *High Noon on Seventh Avenue*

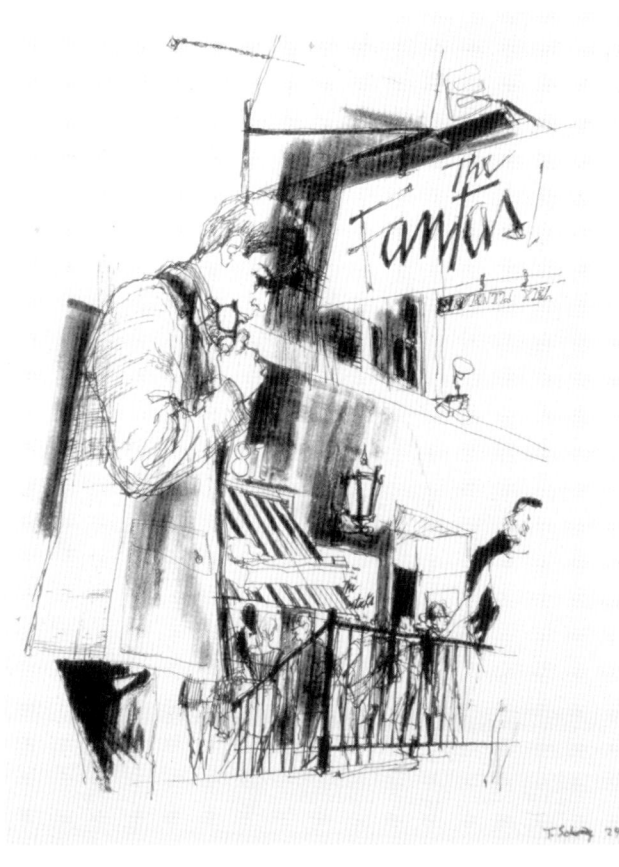

22. Off-Broadway Opening

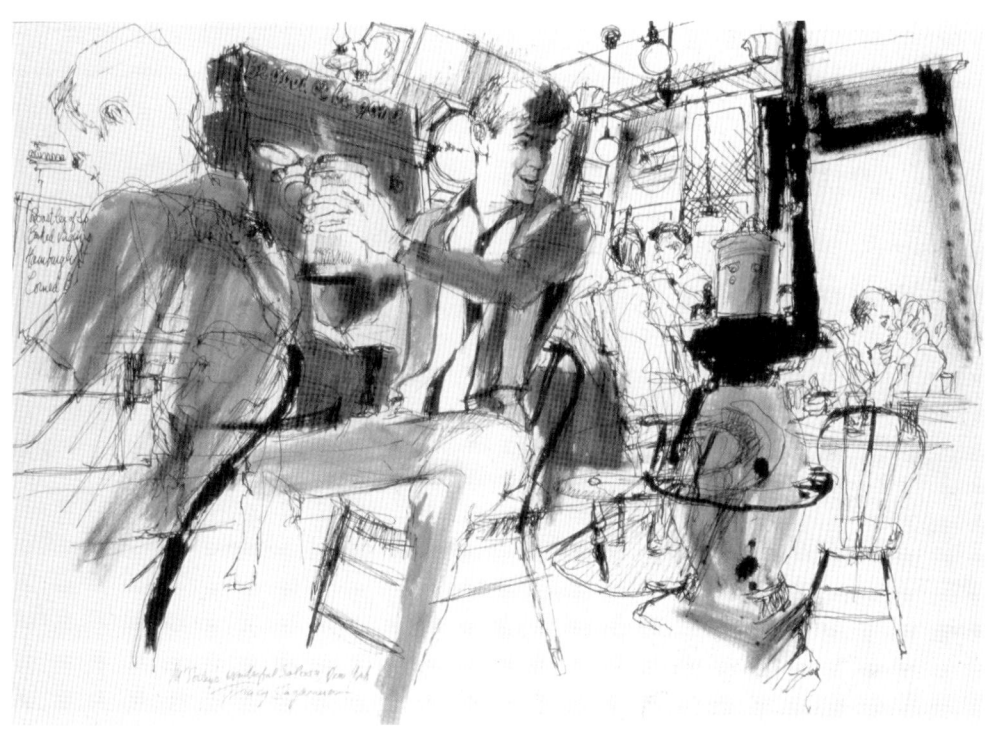

23. McSorley's Wonderful Saloon

8

Reaching Out

As our kids achieved more independence, fashioning allegiances and relationships with their peers, June and I both began to stretch out from our nest, eager to see beyond the predictable routines we had long enjoyed. A life when our children would be off on their own explorations at college or career suddenly was a horizon neither of us had really examined. June enrolled in a Seven Sisters curriculum that began to define the career possibilities for professional women eager to return to the world of work. And I decided to explore painting, not as a means to illustrate someone's manuscript, but for its own sake. It was a decision that has resonated in my life, opening aesthetic doors into rooms I had never before entered. It was a diminutive, gifted abstract painter, Reuben Tam, who handed me the key. I first heard his name at supper with a bunch of illustrators on a snowy evening in the winter of 1962.

A most informal and unbuttoned group of artists, photographers, designers, and art directors who lived in or about Westport would collegially meet for supper and drinks at infrequent intervals. Our name was, unsurprisingly, the Westport Artists, a loose "marching and chowder society," created only for getting together and kicking back. On some occasions we'd hang recent work or invite guests from New York to speak and be grilled by the locals. Mostly, it was just fun, schmooze, and Madison Avenue gossip. For two years I served as president, which meant I made the reservations at various restaurants and invited people like painter Ben Shahn to come and endure the often well-oiled questions of my hearty comrades, paying the guests with bonhomie and a decent supper.

On this winter eve, as the crowd began to head for their cars, a small bunch of illustrators still lingered at the bar. Ward Brackett's voice rose briefly in the now quiet room. "His name is Reuben Tam." His wife, Dolly Tingle, added quickly, "He's supposed to be a terrific teacher. And Ward and I are thinking of signing up. Tonight I heard that Coby Whitmore and Joe Bowler are going, too. The class is at the Brooklyn Museum."

"What in the world is Coby Whitmore doing going to study?" I asked, bewildered. "He's one of the highest-paid illustrators in the country and has been for a bunch of years. And you and Ward are going to go to Brooklyn? You're kidding, right?"

Dolly grinned. "It's only an hour each way. And the guy is supposed to be a hell of a painter. If Whitmore thinks he can learn something from an abstract painter, who am I to say he's wrong?"

Ward nudged me. "Why don't you come with us? There's room in the car."

"To Brooklyn?"

Brooklyn it was, and a small, hardy band of illustrators, the Bracketts, Arthur Shilstone, Ken Riley, and I, began an odyssey that would go on, once a week, for two years.

Reuben Tam, a short, bespectacled, witty, and wise Hawaiian, seemed ageless to me. His cheerful, optimistic manner made him appear young. Perhaps it was the barely suppressed merriness in his eyes as he moved silently about the room, saying very little. His head would be cocked to the side, nodding, his eyes searching each canvas with an innocent eagerness, seeming always to be expecting something really interesting. But it was in his critiques held once a month that the canny intelligence and long experience of a painter whose work had covered scores of years became provocative words for each of us. It was only later that I learned, not surprisingly, that Tam was also a poet. In a quiet, low voice that was humorous and reassuring, he became our gifted guide into a terra incognita, a finite world whose borders were the four edges of the painting.

For an illustrator who was always seeking to make intimate connection with the world around me, I was a wide-eyed tourist into an interior world that deliberately threw away any compass to the world beyond the picture at hand. It was a wondrous journey, and a frightening one. I had to learn a visual language summoned from my unconscious, responding to imperatives that made themselves evident only in painted gesture, in color, and in the relative proximity of shapes within my frame. The ideas within the painting were self-referential, abjuring the images that sought to re-create a mundane connection to the world beyond. Often bewildered, I stumbled on through the labyrinths of the paintings on my easel.

Tam's gift to me was a passport to a richer way of seeing. In the challenging two years I spent with him at the Brooklyn Museum, he instilled a confidence that I did possess the tools and had the interior maps that could help inform and enrich any drawing or painting I might attempt in the future. I learned that if I were to continue to explore my interior world, it would require my being a little braver than I had ever thought I could be as an artist. When I returned to my quest as a reportorial artist in the real world, a calling I still cherished, I knew I could now see with a greater clarity.

9

On-the-Spot Drawing

To me, the most significant aspect of on-the-spot drawing is the ability to get closer to man and the world he has made. I become part of the picture emotionally, and I often find myself having to reexamine assumptions and generalizations I held before being exposed to the real thing. It's a revelatory experience, one that invariably challenges my preconceived ideas. I feel fortunate in having the chance to touch life in a manner that few people have the opportunity to do. The experiences I've had, the pleasures I've derived, and the feeling of sometimes being able to make a contribution of value through my work continues to sustain me. Working only in my studio may increase my knowledge of materials, of technique, but not of the world. When I'm on-site, I meet people. We talk and trade ideas and opinions. I learn about them, and sometimes more about myself than I suspected.

The essence of successful reportage is capturing the meaning of a moment in time. I have often found myself in the pressured position of struggling to fix that instant on paper when the situation has been fugitive, uncomfortable, and sometimes hostile. It is an ideal that I have only sometimes been able to achieve. But it is in the attempt that I have found the joy of reportorial work. The facility necessary to translate the often transitory image to the hand and the pen is an acquired skill that grows over the years. But it is never simple.

The false starts, the nervous broken line, the drops of sweat that blot a passage of the drawing all echo the immediacy of the search. When one tries to pin down the touching heroism of black Americans as they brave threatening mobs in their attempt to vote in Mississippi, or seeks to capture the terrible helplessness of poor whites whose lives have been stunted in the forgotten corners of Appalachia, his drawing becomes only an incidental result of an emotional meeting. My thrust as an artist is to winnow from the scene the single true note. It takes more than agility and the capacity to draw rapidly. It demands an honesty of purpose, a relating to your subject that is less technical than human. If the moment is worth preserving, then I have the responsibility of trying to endow the drawing with the compassion that comes from understanding. It is only in this fragile dimension that the artist's gift to the viewer can be made.

Two extraordinary invasions did most to shape me as a person, and to set my path as an artist. In 1944, I was part of the naval amphibious force that stormed the Normandy beachhead on D-day. In 1964, I was part of the nonviolent civil rights movement that challenged the bastions of America's most shameful apartheid in Mississippi. In both instances, I found myself in a life-and-death struggle I could never have imagined.

In 1944, at the age of twenty-three, I spent months on that battered Normandy beachhead with the men in my charge. It was there that I discovered that through drawings and the writing I was sending to my new wife, I could come to understand and rationalize the tragic world I was in. That need to communicate and share is what kept both of us mentally and emotionally intact during those terrible months of separation. Remarkably, when those personal letters and drawings were published fifty-six years later in *My War: A Love Story in Letters and Drawings*, they found a whole new generation that could be touched by the memoir. Perhaps if a picture is worth a thousand words, a picture and a thousand words may tell the story even better.

10

My Two Invasions

Perhaps it was because I was transported as a child to the marvelous world of N. C. Wyeth and Howard Pyle. Perhaps it came later, when I was stunned by a folio of Goya's war prints, or moved to tears by the poignant insight of Käthe Kollwitz. At any rate, it has long seemed to me that the artist has helped save history from the dust of the archivist and the impersonal cataloging of the historians. Intensely sensitive to the peculiar chemistry of his time and place, the artist has often captured the essence of the moment, and preserved it for us. The unknown painter who used vegetable dyes on the cave wall breathed a moment of reality across the ages. The hunters still circle their prey, spears held at the ready; their ancient quarry race forever across the moldering wall. We marvel at the facility that pinned the fugitive moment like a lovely moth, displayed for our delight.

Whether in fresco, on vases, in illuminated manuscripts, or on the torn and sodden sketchpads of war correspondents, man has sought to preserve the great moments of his experience in pictures. At times his reportage has been inspired. Daumier and Goya did not merely record history. They succeeded in illuminating man's understanding of his society and himself. It is a tradition that seemed to ask the best of the artist, and I wanted to be part of that tradition. My desire to become an illustrator took me to the College of Fine Arts at Syracuse University.

During my junior year at Syracuse, the Japanese attacked Pearl Harbor on December 7, 1941. Like millions of others, I signed up to offer what help I could, enlisting in the United States Naval Reserve, expecting to be called up immediately. But the navy did not summon me until my graduation in May 1943, ordering me to Midshipman School at Notre Dame University. After four months of indoctrination, I was commissioned an ensign, United States Naval Reserve, and assigned the task of training sailors to be amphibious combatants for the coming invasion of Europe.

It was a sobering and frightening time. The free world was being torn in a savage war for survival. Europe and Asia lay bleeding, already prisoners of fascism and militarism. America was struggling to mount an assault for liberation, and all its energies were directed toward the invasion of Fortress Europe. I stored the skills of peacetime "for the duration" and began to use the tools of war. But even as I packed my seabag before shipping out for embattled England with my invasion crews, I stowed sketchbooks, pens, and brushes at the very top. For the next eighteen months I was at times a small boat officer and a gunnery officer in the United States Navy. But for my wife, who received a flood of filled sketchbooks, I was a war correspondent. Even without the memories stirred by those dog-eared drawings, I remember that first invasion vividly. It taught me so much, so quickly, about my country and about myself.

We had circled off the beach for hours. The landing craft staggered each time we came about, the flat iron ramp crashing awkwardly into the lead-gray swells. The ramp would lift drunkenly, and the swell would roll toward the blurred stretch of sand and seawall that was France. We were drenched and dizzy from the hours of pitching, but the enormity of the moment moved and exhilarated us. When the flag on the pilot boat dropped at last, we raced toward the beach. Each of us knew that he was part of the greatest armada in history. Waves of Allied planes roared overhead, the whine of their motors washing away the fear and the fatigue. The barrage from our cruisers was a bellowing "whoosh!" that seemed to lift the laboring crafts, hurrying them through the mined thickets of iron obstacles. A German 88 shell slapped a geyser of water in a crashing, choking wave that cascaded into the cockpit of the boat. When the sand ground hard under our keel, the ramp clanged down and we stared at Utah Beach. Smoke lay across the tortured strand, and the smell of cordite mingled with the sour odor of the turning tide. The training, the waiting, the agonizing false starts were done. The sweat and treasure of the West had broached the wall of the European fortress. Already, the army was fanning out from the seawall and moving into the murderous hedgerows of Normandy.

Two profound impressions moved me during those terrible days. The first was that the "soft" kids of rich America could, when tested, respond on a raw level of courage and dedication that vindicated their frontier heritage. The second was that an aroused America is awesome in its power. I have never since doubted that my country can accomplish anything in its defense of freedom once it makes up its mind to do so. Twenty years later, on a very different "invasion," those convictions were given a new dimension.

The death of fascism in Europe and militarism in Japan had heralded a new beginning. As if released by the shattering frenzy of the struggle, gusting winds of change raced through the postwar years. They altered the face of Africa and Asia, and buffeted a Europe that was struggling to stand. A surging tide of expectations touched the disinherited everywhere. In America, the Negro who had been waiting a hundred years for the death of "Jim Crow" shuffled his G.I. boots impatiently, and stared hard at his democratic society.

From the moment that the U.S. Supreme Court declared in 1954 that "separate but equal" schools were unconstitutional, the American Negro launched a sustained assault on

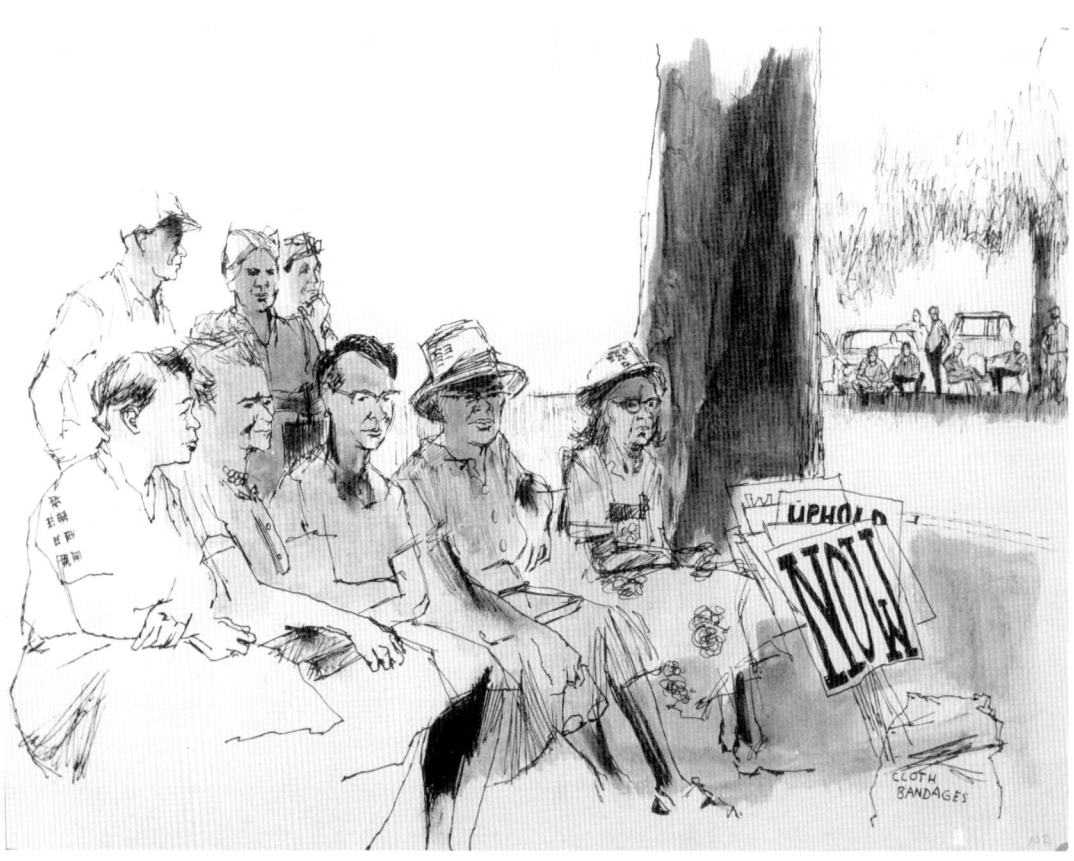

24. *Their Patience Is Infinite*

discrimination and segregation. Adapting the Ghandian tactic of nonviolence, he challenged his society with his cry of "Freedom now!" One hundred years after Appomattox, his "sit-ins" and "freedom rides," "wade-ins" and "kneel-ins," were defying the legal evasions and moral pretensions of America. Against police dogs and fire hoses, vigilante shotguns and torches, he placed his body in eloquent testimony to his belief in Christianity and the U.S. Constitution. Like so many others in the United States, I was moved by his sacrifice and appalled that in this land it should be necessary.

All hell seemed to be breaking loose in the American South. The nonviolent challenge to a centuries-old racial apartheid was being answered with state-sanctioned violence, the unbridled viciousness of the Ku Klux Klan, and the apparent collusion of the white establishment. Few white businessmen, congressmen, clergy, journalists, or professionals across Dixie raised their voices in protest even when the lynchings, the beatings, the burning black churches, the poignant pleas of preachers like Martin Luther King were news in every northern paper and featured nightly on television. In our household, the images of police dogs, hoses, and the four young black children who were killed in their Sunday classroom at church appalled and outraged all of us. We wanted to do something, anything, that would help to stop the cruel assaults on Americans who happened to be black. For me, who had been happily documenting the wonders of American industry, invention, and education across the country, the sudden revelations of a part of my country that seemed more like the horrors of fascism I had helped to vanquish twenty years before were sickening.

For years, I had been making drawings and paintings that celebrated this often astonishing country. Its marvelous hospitals, enormous productive factories, sparkling laboratories, and grand universities were my subjects for corporate annual reports and pages in *Fortune* magazine. The postwar years in America were something to celebrate. How, then, could such a good and diverse country permit such atrocities? I had tried to reflect the excitement and promise of the best in our society. I felt pride in who we were and what we represented as a free people and a democratic society.

Could I help now by documenting what was the worst? In family council we agreed that if a way could be found for me to go south where I could do my reportage, I should go. Perhaps my drawings could bring a better understanding to those in the North as to what was at stake for our whole society. If nonviolent protest was to be destroyed, the alternative was unthinkable.

The urgency of the racial crisis mounted, and President Kennedy urged a sluggish Congress to enact relief through the Civil Rights Act of 1964. As the proposals fought their way through committees and filibusters, the civil rights movement prepared an attack on the most inviolable fortress of segregation in the United States.

In the spring of 1964, we read that the Student Nonviolent Coordinating Committee (SNCC), an offshoot of Dr. King's Southern Christian Leadership Conference (SCLC), had issued a call to white students in the North to come join them in their struggle for the vote in Mississippi. Against the Klan, the White Citizens Councils, and the might of a hostile society's police, a thousand unarmed students prepared to move into Mississippi. They were to receive their orientation at the Western College for Women in Oxford, Ohio. I decided that their odyssey should be recorded in pictures. So twenty years after Normandy, I found myself on my second invasion.

It could not have felt more foreign if I was planning a trip to the moon. Racially isolated as I was by the circumstances of living in a community that was nearly exclusively white, I was eager for guidance on how best to conduct myself when I would arrive in the Delta. Should I offer to go to church with my Negro hosts? How should I dress? Should I buy the groceries? How could I make people who had never made eye contact with a white man, let alone shared their house with him, feel comfortable? I wanted to talk with some black people who could assist me, and I knew none.

It was then that I called for help to George Simon, the jazz critic and writer for whom I had illustrated *The Feeling of Jazz* in 1961. As a man who had spent years in jazz, George had countless friends among the black community. He smiled at my innocence, but was eager to help me with my mission. "Let me talk to Jackie and Rachel. There ought to be some generous soul to help a honky like you." He gazed at me over his glasses with a new seriousness. "You sure you want to go to Mississippi?"

The Jackie Robinsons, who were neighbors of Simon's in Stamford, Connecticut, also kept an apartment in New York City. It was the top floor of a brownstone house that was owned by their close friends Arthur and Marian Logan. And it was Marian Logan whom George urged me to visit when he called. "She's been back and forth to Mississippi ever since *Brown vs. The Board of Education,* working with women in Mississippi to keep the public schools open. Hell of a lady, Tracy. And she was a very good cabaret singer when she was Marian Bruce, before she met Arthur."

In today's parlance, the Logans were a "power couple" in the life of New York. Tall, blue-eyed, and light in complexion, Arthur Logan could easily have passed as a white man, but he was a person who bore his race with great pride and had the confident air of one who had long known who he was. The son of the treasurer of Tuskegee College, he had early been given privilege and status. After graduating from Williams College, he had gone on to become an outstanding surgeon and teacher, serving for many years as chief of surgery at Harlem Hospital. When we first met, Arthur and Marian had recently adopted their new son, Chipper. They made a handsome and loving family. Their house on Eighty-eighth Street in Manhattan was often the nexus where the white and black communities could negotiate when racial trouble threatened or political and financial support was needed to be cobbled together for struggles like those taking place south of the Mason-Dixon line. Often, in the years that followed, the Logan home was the setting for meeting black artists such as Charles Alston and musicians like Duke Ellington who were their close friends, and for a myriad of black and white political leaders who helped shape the progress of the civil rights movement. Justice Thurgood Marshall, Whitney Young of the Urban League, Harry Belafonte (who helped to support SNCC), and Jack Greenberg of the NAACP Legal Defense Fund were only some of those with whom we mingled at the Logans'. Marian was an active member of the board of the Southern Christian Leadership Conference and accompanied Martin Luther King when he went to receive the Nobel Prize for Peace. Being invited to be a part of that vital group was a heady and memorable experience for June and me.

Our meeting with Marian and Arthur Logan was the beginning of a friendship that both couples embraced, a bonding that would bring great pleasure to both families. The counsel of Marian about what I was likely to encounter was invaluable, and it was given in the earthy, direct, and caustic language that we came to expect and love from Marian. Tall, willowy, mahogany in color, and strikingly beautiful, one could easily imagine her as a chanteuse at Cafe Society Downtown. But when you came to know her, you recognized the high intelligence and keen understanding of people and events that made her a highly

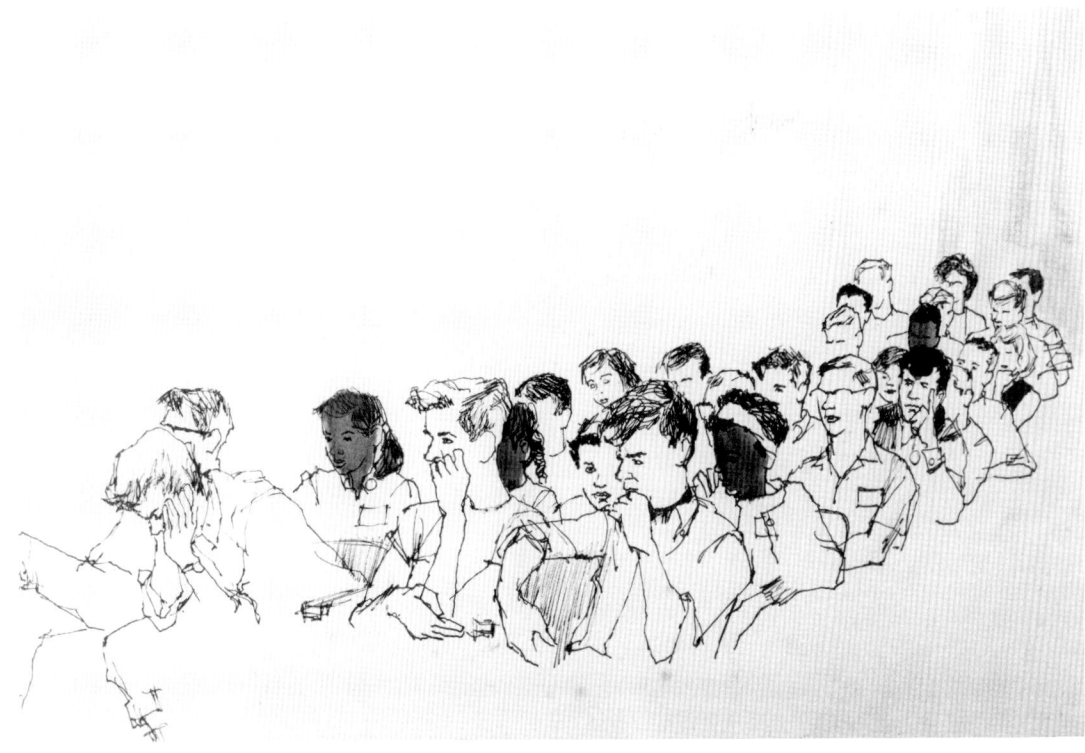

25. *You've Got to Expect to Be Afraid*

valued adviser to Dr. Martin Luther King and a confidante of some of New York's most influential political leaders in both parties.

Meeting the Logans through George Simon via Jackie Robinson had been one of the seemingly countless interactions that have woven my life as an artist into an interesting and sometimes mysterious fabric. Perhaps it is simple good fortune that has intervened in my life, but I have enjoyed so many remarkable coincidences that I sometimes feel there is a design that I am not aware of. Our treasured friendship with Marian and Arthur Logan was to last for the rest of their lives.

In June 1964 I joined the students at the orientation sessions for the invasion of Mississippi. The campus of Western College lay cradled in the spring green of the Ohio farmland. It was an idyllic setting for so sober and searching a course of study. For two weeks, lawyers, ministers, doctors, and young Negro leaders from the Student Nonviolent Coordinating Committee described the reality of race relations in Mississippi. It was a frightening picture of a society where both black and white had been assigned roles that were rigidly circumscribed. If one were white, to move beyond the historically permissible bounds was to invite censure and ostracism. If Negro, it could mean arrest without due process of law, economic reprisals, and violence. The rigidity of the social, economic, and political structure had permeated every aspect of Mississippi life.

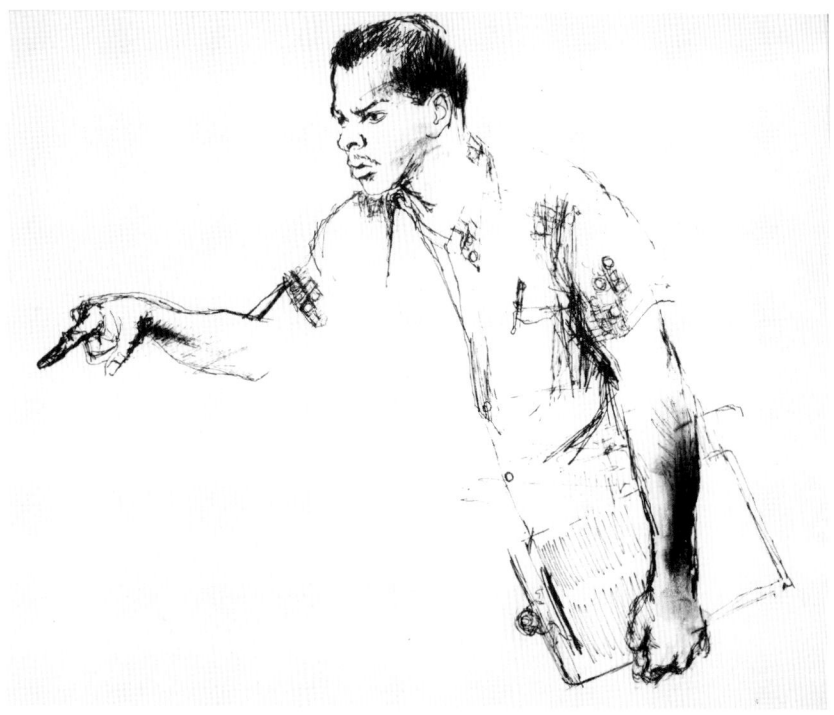

26. *Mr. Charlie Says "Run," but We Ain't Running*

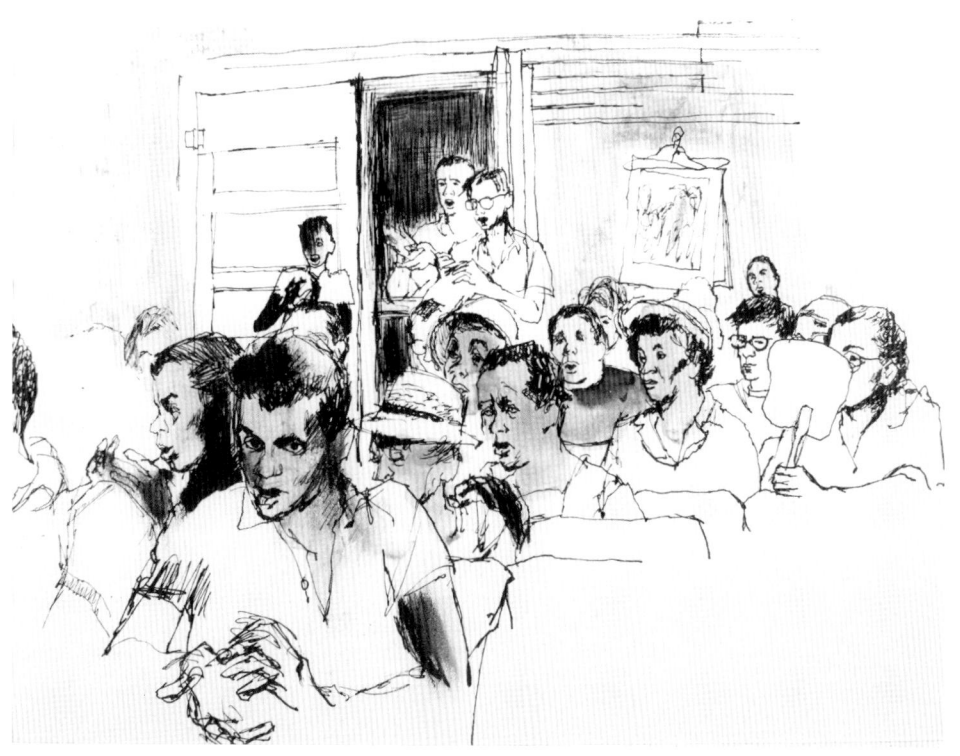

27. *Ain't Gonna Let Nobody Turn Us 'Round*

The students were cautioned that merely entering the state would be considered a provocative act by the state government as well as the Ku Klux Klan. If they were to come to Mississippi to set up libraries and Freedom Schools or to assist Negroes in attaining the vote, they could expect little protection from the local police, no support from the clergy or the press in the state, hostility from the congressmen and senators, and resentment from the white community. To the fresh-faced youngsters from America's colleges, the recital seemed unreal. It bore so little relation to their own homes that they might have been listening to descriptions of Stalin's Russia or Hitler's Germany. These were essentially the children of middle-class America, and they tended to be idealistic, curious, and confident. I shall never forget their incredulous faces as the young Negro leaders from Mississippi taught them how to protect their heads,

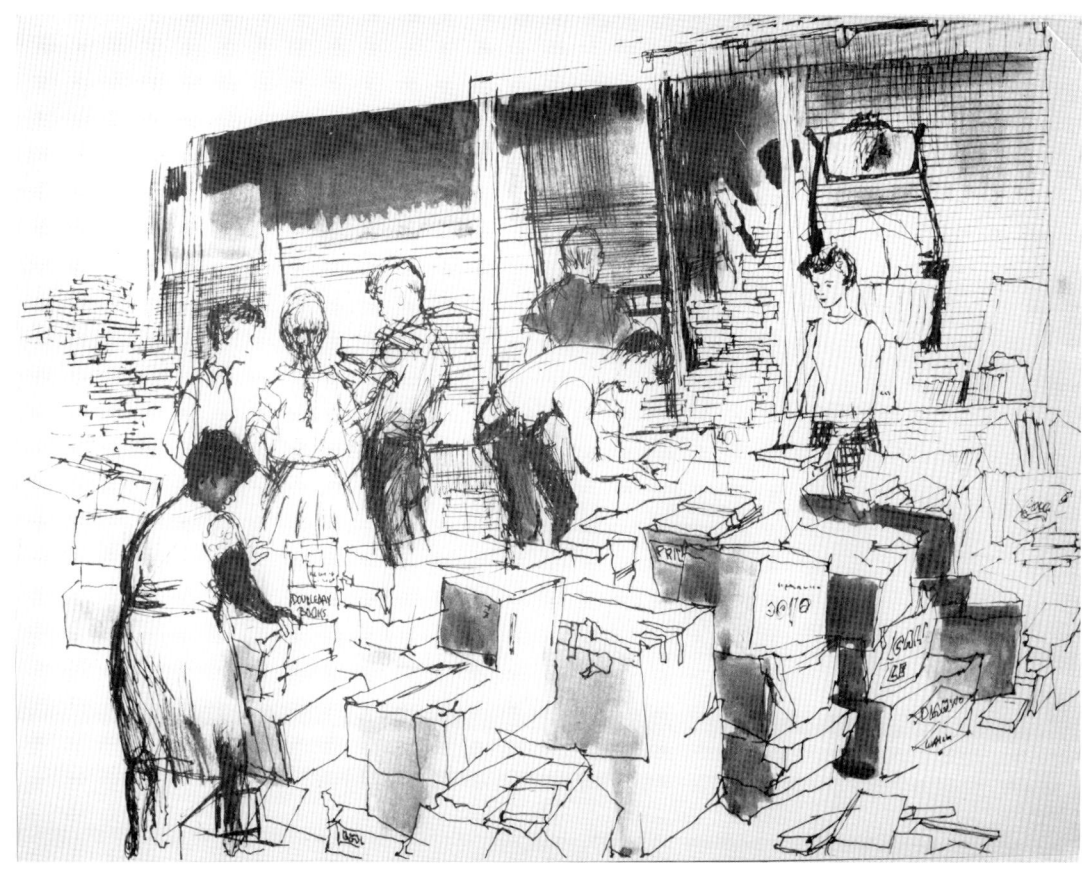

28. *Books for the Freedom School*

groins, and necks from police clubs and cattle prods. These Negro youngsters of twenty and twenty-one had been beaten, often in jail. They had survived the night riders and the police assaults. As they gazed soberly at these fortunate young college people who had come to join them, they seemed deeply troubled. One sensed the terrible responsibilities they shouldered leading these dedicated innocents into Mississippi.

Bob Moses, the gentle and scholarly young leader of the Mississippi Summer Project, addressed the students at Oxford. His words set the tone for the whole summer. "Don't go to Mississippi to save the poor black man," he said. "Only go if you understand that your democracy is being threatened there." By the end of the orientation, they understood. In cars and buses they trickled into the Delta, the red hills of central Mississippi, and south to the Gulf Coast. That first week, four hundred of them arrived, in blue jeans and cotton skirts. In the first forty-eight hours, three of them were murdered in Neshoba County.

As I packed my pens and camera at Oxford before heading south, I realized that on this assignment I would not be the invited guest of management. I would be an "outsider," an "invader," "one of them." There would be no sanctuary corner or empty stool in Mississippi. As had been the case in Normandy, the war correspondent had to function within one camp. I knew that I could warrant the trust and confidence of the civil rights

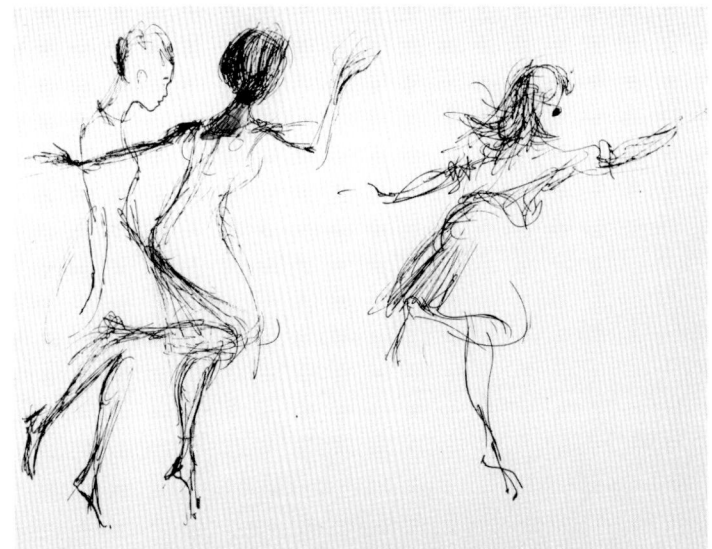

29. *Linda Davis's Modern Dance Class at the Freedom School*

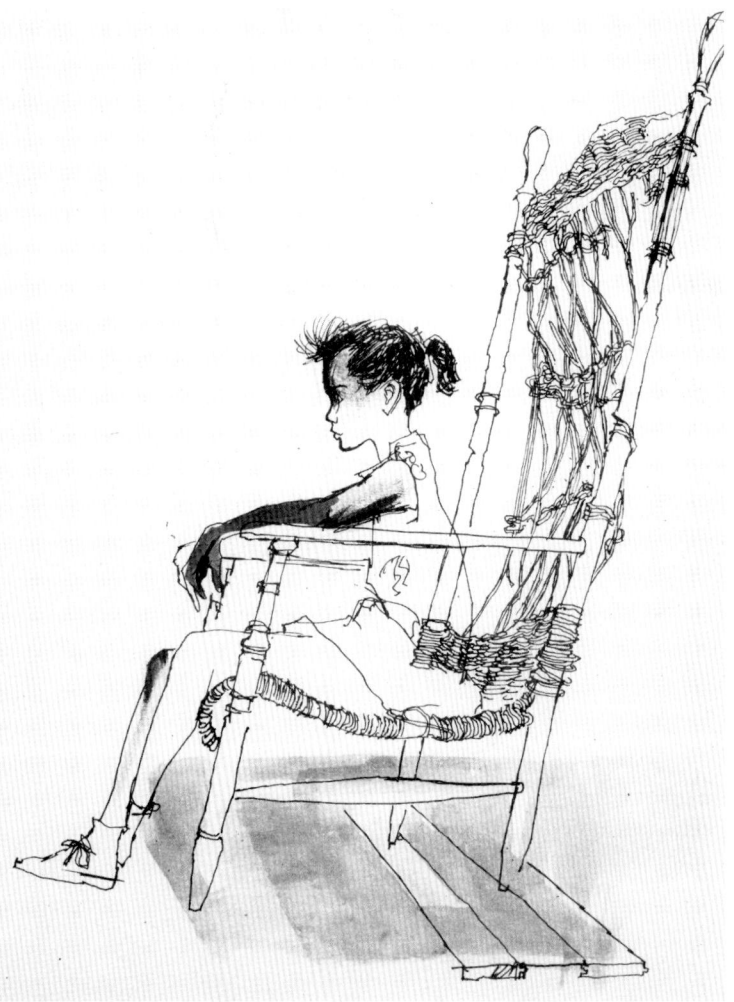

30. *Olivia at the Freedom School*

movement only if I shared their hazard and their fear. It was the only way of recording the reality of "the long, hot summer."

I joined a group of fifteen students who were going to the heart of the Delta, Ruleville, Mississippi. They were the ones who would establish contact with the Negro community and work on voter registration. One week later, another fifteen would join them from Oxford, and these students would start the Freedom Schools and community centers in Sunflower County.

It was a remarkable and exciting campaign to capture. My sketchbooks recorded most of it. Wherever I could, I drew directly. I confess that many of the accent washes were a mixture of sweat and ink. Large areas of tone I would add at night in the tiny bedroom of the house I shared with Mr. and Mrs. James Williams, an elderly Negro couple. Within the Negro community I soon became a familiar sight and part of the landscape. I could settle anywhere—at

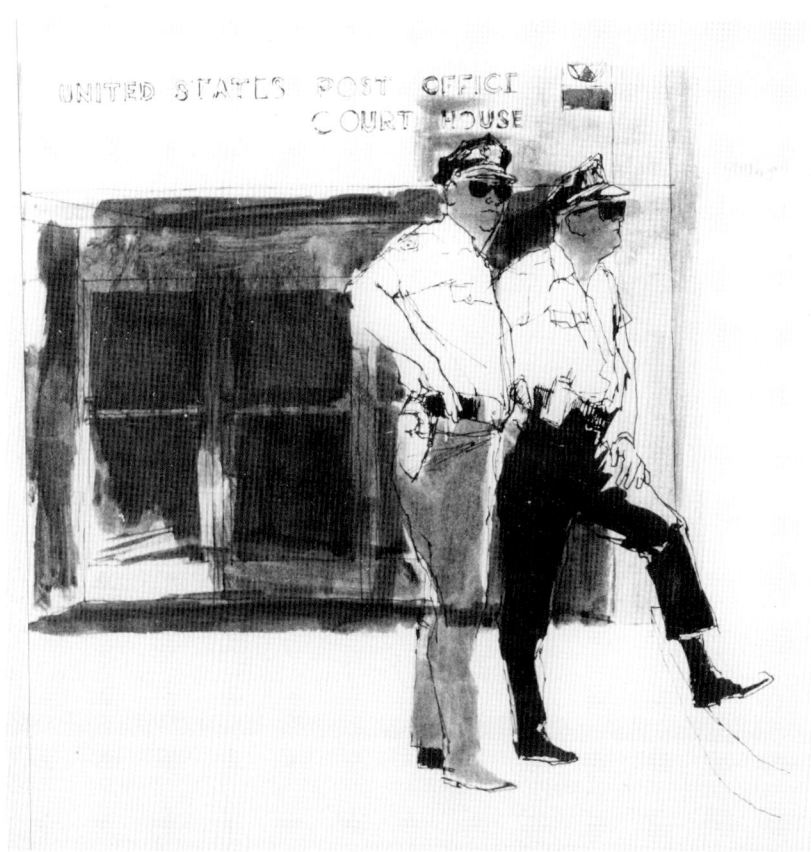

31. *Look at Them Niggers*
Marching with Those White Girls

a mass meeting in the tiny Williams Chapel, on the edge of the Freedom School class in American history at the community center, or in the dusty roads and yards of the Negro quarter. I was welcomed as part of the movement. When I accompanied the students to the county seat in Indianola to help register voters, or to Cleveland, Mississippi, for a Freedom Day demonstration, the sketchbook went with us. Even the hostile armed deputies of Indianola would succumb finally to curiosity and saunter over to watch as I sketched the great pillars of the courthouse. But at those times when I went with the students into the tiny rural towns that had never allowed a Negro to register, I contented myself with furtively taking pictures with my camera. One had to stay mobile and alert, and even my tiny Leica camera was an obvious target for the local toughs or the infuriated local police.

Each day was hot and long. Each night I crawled into bed bone tired. In five weeks I had made 115 drawings and taken nearly 1,000 pictures. What could not be recorded in the sketchbooks or on film was the incredible atmosphere within which the students lived and operated. You cannot draw the feeling you have as you watch unlicensed cars of whites with shotguns patrolling the dirt road beyond your bedroom window. Nor can one capture on paper the heartbreak of a poverty-stricken Negro community as it watches its church fired with gasoline bombs by night riders. And how can one re-create with pen and ink the courage of the selfless youth from the cloistered American campuses? They woke up every morning scared, went to their jobs scared, ate scared, prayed scared, and the next day did it all over again. And the next. Despite a cruel and unceasing harassment, they did their jobs with humor and skill, and none left to go home.

And how, as an artist, can one adequately demonstrate the sweet generosity and gentle forbearance of the Negroes who opened their homes to us? I wish I knew. Families that live on six hundred dollars a year shared what they had with their guests. Knowing that welcoming the "outsiders" could mean physical and economic reprisals, they never faltered. I made many drawings of the Negro boys and girls of SNCC, for I felt that in many ways they were the unsung heroes of the freedom movement. Cheated by their state of their national birthright of freedom, denied equality before the law, badly educated, and badly nourished, they persevered with a faith in democracy that ennobled all America.

The hidden face of "the southern way of life" was hideous. By the end of Freedom Summer, three civil rights workers had been murdered by a mob led by a deputy sheriff. Hundreds of student volunteers had been arrested, and many of them beaten. Sixty-six homes and churches had been burned by night riders. The violence was as color-blind as it was vicious. What was new was that the attention of the entire nation was now riveted on Mississippi. And the long-muffled voices of the Mississippi blacks were starting to be heard. I thought back to those first sessions at Oxford, Ohio, when Bob Moses's insightful strategy was still being argued about by the veterans of SNCC. Moses had known what would move America to action. The tragic events of that summer proved he had been right.

Like the volunteers who would soon have to return north, I felt uneasy and guilty. We would be abandoning our black friends in the Delta, knowing that because of our intervention in their lives, they would now face retaliation for their struggles for justice. But I knew that the only way I could continue to help them was to bring their story to as much of America as I could reach. When I left Ruleville, I carried with me more than 100 drawings, countless photographs, scores of taped interviews, and several crammed notebooks.

I was welcomed home by a loving and relieved family. While I was away, June had worked tirelessly with friends in Westport to raise thirty thousand dollars in vital bail funds because after Andy Goodman, Michael Schwerner, and James Chaney had been killed by the deputy's mob, we knew it was imperative to get any of our workers released promptly from jail. By summer's end in 1964, our whole family had become deeply committed to the ongoing struggle being waged in the South. Our fourteen-year-old daughter, Laurie, and nineteen-year-old son, Richard, had become eager partisans in the freedom struggle.

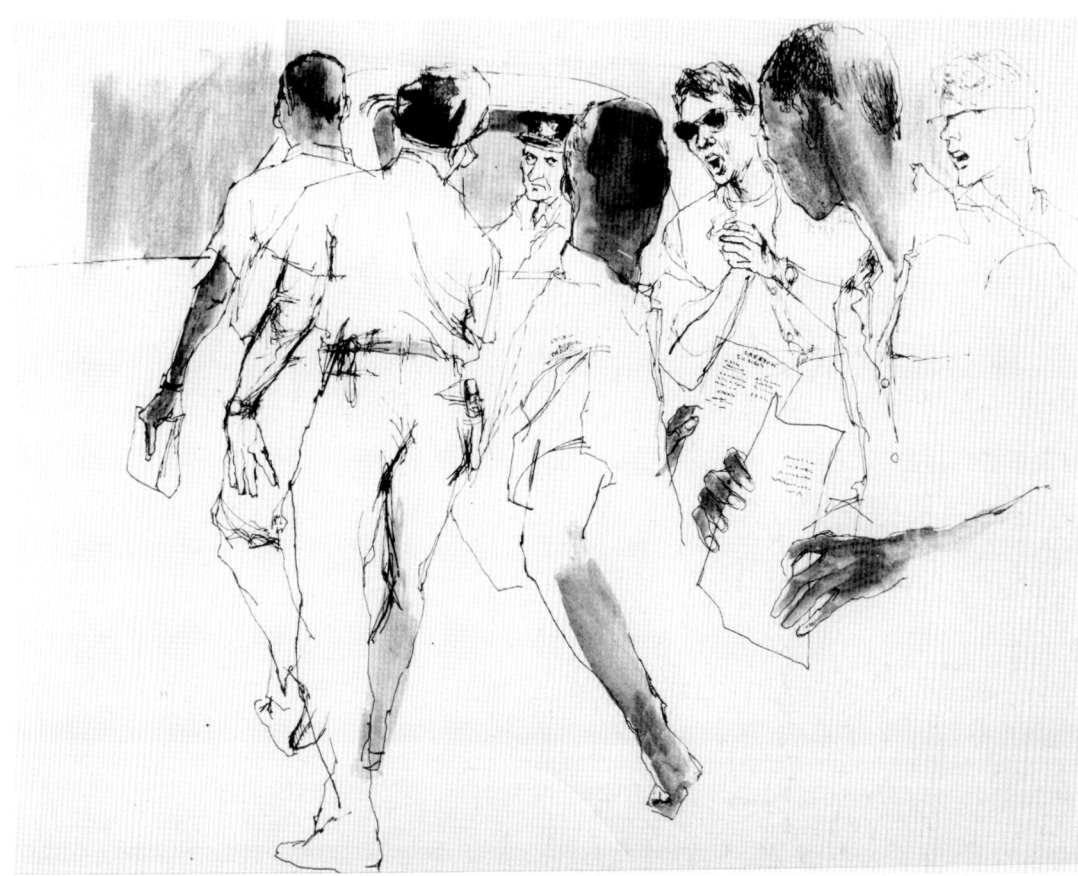

32. *First Arrests*
in Drew, Mississippi

Laurie would go on to work with disadvantaged minority kids in the inner city of Norwalk. As I started to plan for continuing my reportorial work in the Delta in 1965, Richard approached us with his desire to go south and work with SNCC on voter registration. It was a difficult moment of truth for us as parents and activists. In our discussions with our son we sought to make sure that his dedication to the hazardous work was not motivated by a desire to mirror his father. We pointed out that I had gone because I had a particular skill that I thought could be useful to the movement in telling its story. There was certainly injustice enough in the North, we said, to engage his idealism. But Richard was adamant. For more than a year our house had been a stopping place for many of SNCC activists from Mississippi, so he knew intimately the dangers of the frontline struggle being carried on by SNCC. He was determined to help. Life at Brown, he felt, was very removed, and he was eager to go where he could make a difference. He promised that he would be careful and would return to Brown in the fall. We gave him our blessings and held our breath because the white violence in the South was accelerating, as blacks were seeking the vote in ever greater numbers. We knew that if Richard was going south, he was going into harm's way.

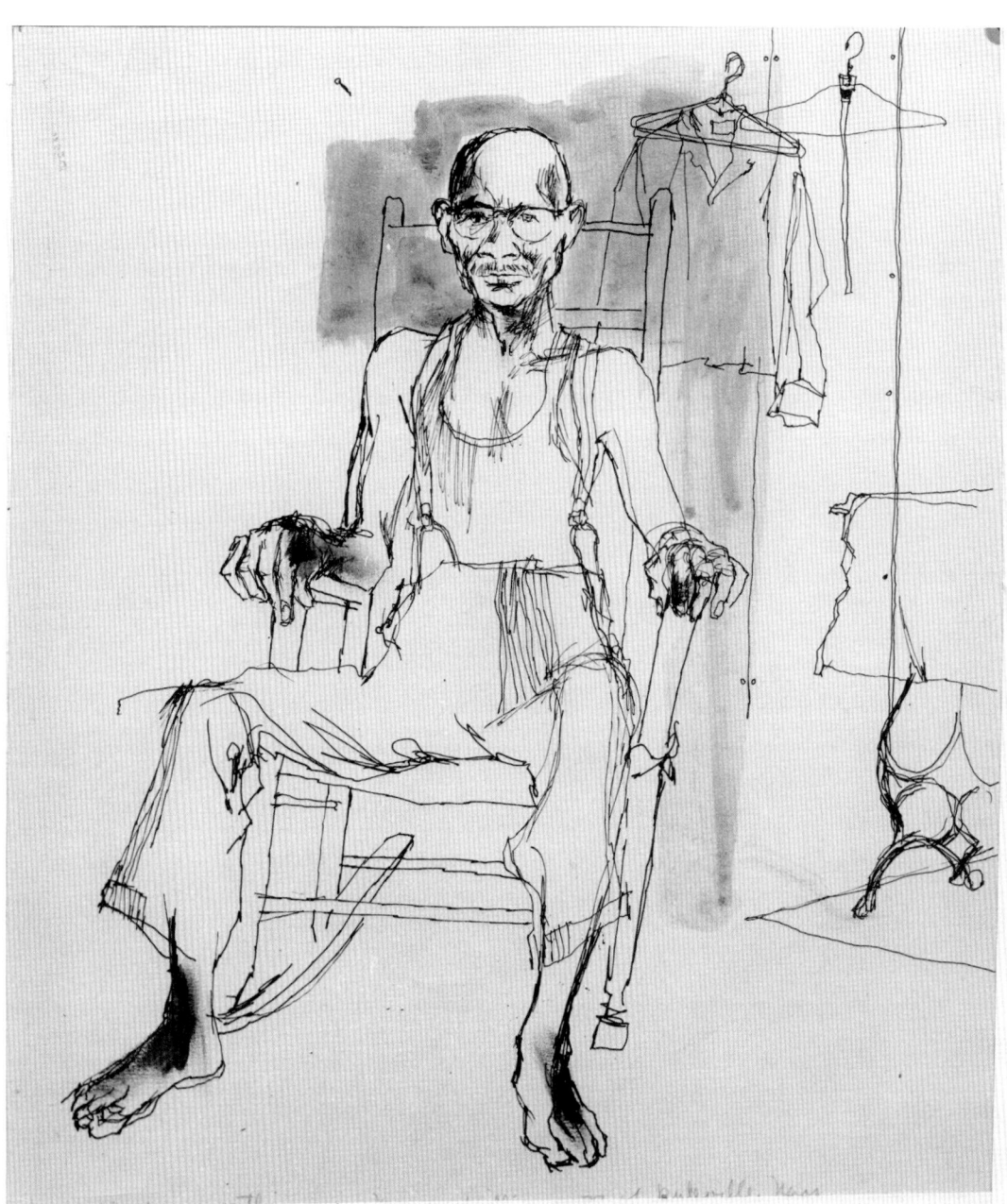

33. Mr. James Williams,
Ruleville, Mississippi

SNCC needed workers to help register black voters in Arkansas, where violence was constant, though largely unobserved by the media who had flocked to Mississippi once white civil rights workers had been killed. But Richard's territory was in Forrest City, a small Arkansas delta town rarely visited by outside reporters, where he and his co-workers were totally exposed to vigilante violence and police hostility. His room in the black undertaker's home was shared with the recently deceased, a situation that was more tolerable than the constant harassment of random firing that would strike the house or the repeated attempts by night riders to burn the place to the ground.

On his birthday I drove to the local hardware store in Ruleville and purchased a stout fire extinguisher that I presented to him after crossing the Mississippi and seeing the Delta from the Arkansas side for the first time. "Perfect, Pop!" he said with a grin. "We can sure use it."

When I called home I reported that Dick was well, looked a little older, but was eager to finish out the summer. June and I would not learn of the beating he received or of the repeated arson attempts on his house until years later. The resolute dedication to racial justice that we observed in both our kids remains a source of great pride.

My drawings from the Delta were almost immediately given national exposure by the *New York Times Magazine* and the *Saturday Evening Post*. The United States Information Agency (USIA) used my words and art to explain the civil rights struggle in its international magazines in Russian, Polish, Spanish, English, and Arabic. Tony Schwartz and I, with the enthusiastic assistance of producer Pamela Illot, created a documentary for CBS-TV called *How Beautiful on the Mountains*, which used my tapes and drawings to recount the heroic struggle being fought in the Deep South.

In 1966 our family presented the entire collection of drawings to Tougaloo College and all the photographs to Jackson State University, believing that the history should be enshrined in Mississippi. The work is now meticulously preserved and exhibited through the Mississippi Archives in Jackson.

11

The Concert

Like most of us who had been participants in the revolution taking place in the Deep South, I was repeatedly invited to gatherings at people's homes, churches, synagogues, schools, and colleges upon my return from Mississippi. Being white, middle-aged, and middle-class, I seemed a safe person to come report on what I had observed to those who wished to know. Filled with conviction about the urgency to build support for those individuals still struggling in the South, I went gladly as a partisan speaker for the movement.

It was on such an occasion that I went to the home of a good friend, Sonny Fox, who was a popular television personality. Sonny and his wife, Gloria, welcomed us and led us to meet friends who had gathered to hear about Mississippi. It was a chatty and enjoyable afternoon, and just before we were about to leave one of the guests approached me. It was Frank Brieff, the conductor of the New Haven Symphony Orchestra.

"I just wanted to thank you," he said. "I found your stories very moving, and I appreciate your coming to Weston to share them with us." He hesitated a moment, then said, "I'd like to help if I can. I think it's very important that we find the money to guarantee bail for those kids who are putting themselves on the line."

"I'm glad you feel that way," I replied. "It's vital. How did you want to help?"

"I've got a few ideas, but I want to check them out." He smiled and we shook hands. "I'll be calling you."

The next noon Brieff was on the phone, and his voice was excited. "Tracy, I called Lennie and told him I wanted to put together a concert to raise bail money. And he wants to come and be part of it!"

"How wonderful," I said. "A concert! Great! But who's Lennie?"

There was a pause at the other end, and then a small chuckle. "Lennie is Leonard Bernstein."

"Oh, my God! Bernstein! No kidding?"

"No kidding. But I have to make some other calls. I'll get back to you. Do you have a specific date in mind?"

My mouth was dry, and I stared at the telephone.

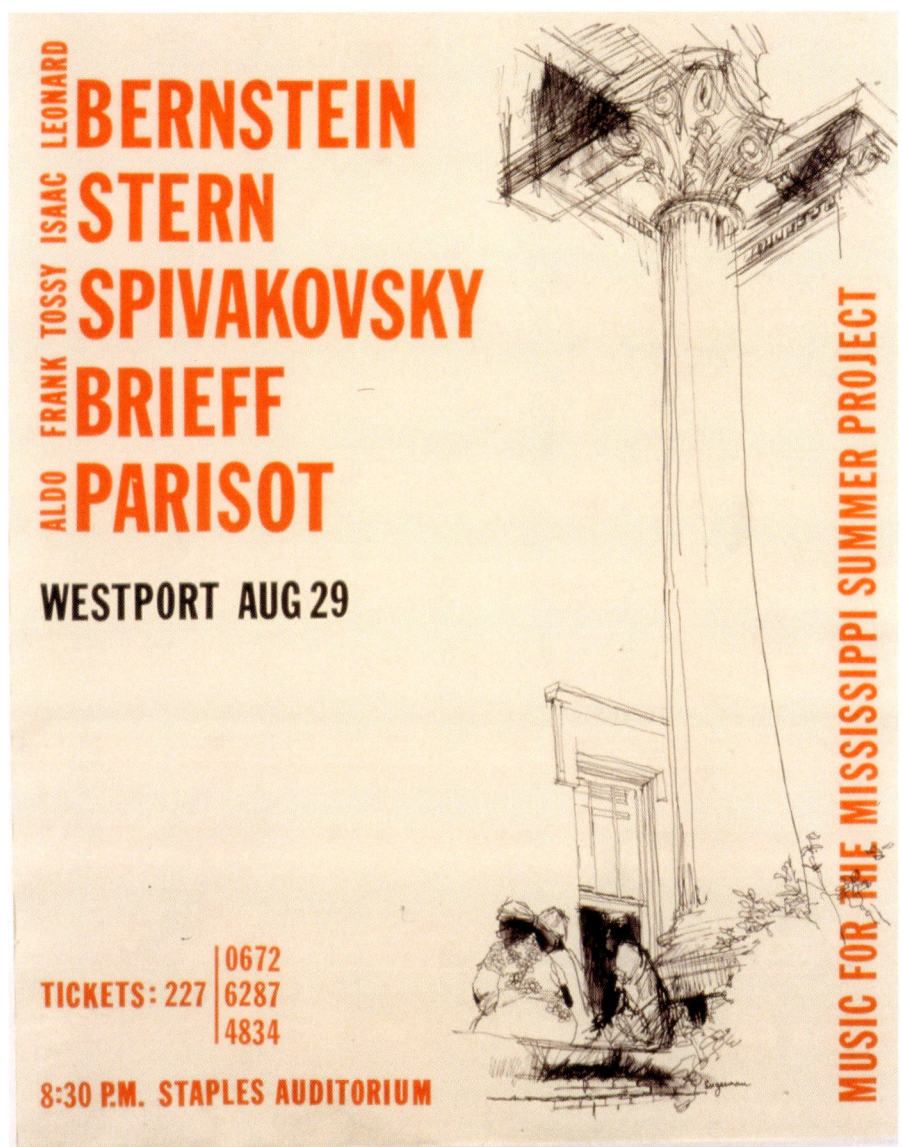

BERNSTEIN
STERN
SPIVAKOVSKY
BRIEFF
PARISOT

LEONARD
ISAAC
TOSSY
FRANK
ALDO

WESTPORT AUG 29

TICKETS: 227 | 0672 | 6287 | 4834

8:30 P.M. STAPLES AUDITORIUM

MUSIC FOR THE MISSISSIPPI SUMMER PROJECT

34. *Coming Saturday!*

"Are you there, Tracy?" Brieff's voice sounded concerned.

"Oh, yeah. I'm here. Just trying to figure out a time. And a place. That's all. Bernstein. No kidding, right?"

"No kidding. I'll get back to you." He was laughing as he hung up.

On the following days my phone kept ringing, and the deficiencies of my musical sophistication were nakedly exposed.

Monday:

"Isaac wants to come."

"Who's Isaac?"

"Isaac Stern." There was a pause. "He plays the fiddle, Tracy."

Tuesday:

"Tossy says he can make it."

"Who's Tossy?"

"Tossy Spivakovsky." Frank sounded a little weary.

Wednesday:

"It's all set! Aldo is joining us!"

"Who's Aldo?" My voice was unrecognizably weak.

"Parisot. Aldo Parisot."

"That all sounds great, Frank," I said heartily. "We have the high school auditorium for Saturday night, August 29. Eight o'clock."

"Good! Oh, one other thing, Tracy. Lennie will need a Steinway grand piano when he rehearses on that Saturday morning." The phone went dead before I could even thank him.

The ten days leading up to the concert made me appreciate, not for the first time, the energies and talents that live in our town and are willing to be enlisted in a worthy cause. Perhaps there are other communities that can, in ten days' time, put such a five-star cultural event together, but June and I were astonished by the frenetic industry and the resulting organization that emerged. Committees got formed, telephone trees got assembled, tickets got printed, and a fine graphics designer, Oliver Lundquist, used one of my Mississippi drawings for a handsome poster announcing the gifted musicians who were coming to town. Most important of all, the Steinway grand piano was found and delivered to the high school auditorium for Leonard Bernstein through the heroic efforts of Ruth Steinkraus Cohen, the doyenne of the musical community.

All seemed in readiness on that Saturday morning when we drove to the auditorium to be certain that Mr. Bernstein had what he needed. The resonant sound of a piano drifted through the open windows of the auditorium as we hurried inside. The morning sun brushed the rows of empty seats and glinted on the shiny raven surface of the Steinway's raised lid. As we moved quietly toward the absorbed player, I was struck by Bernstein's powerful shoulders and large head that might have been expected on a much taller man. The light played on his salt-and-pepper hair, and one could not help but observe the seeming melancholy on his expressive face. It seemed to echo the gravity of the passage he was exploring. When he concluded, he turned and beckoned us closer with a disarming smile. The sadness on his face had fled with the music, and the vibrancy in his persona made him appear more youthful than his years.

June approached him, thanking him for his generosity. "The whole town is excited that you and your friends are coming tonight," she said. "Please don't let us interrupt your playing. We just thought you might be getting hungry. It's almost noon. Can we bring you something?"

"Thank you. That would be splendid. How about three ears of corn?"

"Fine," said June. "Three ears of cooked corn. Anything else?"

"No," said the maestro. "Just the three ears of corn. But not cooked. Thank you very much. I want to get back to this." He turned back to the keyboard, and we retreated up the aisle.

We drove out to the farm stand on the Post Road, bought the corn, and raced back to the high school. Without interrupting his reveries, I placed the ears of corn beside him on the bench and went silently back to listen with June as the session continued. Minutes later, Bernstein paused, picked up an ear of corn, and denuded it. With hardly a glance, he tossed the huskings into the bed of the Steinway and swiftly ate every kernel. When he finished, the husk went sailing into the depths of the grand, and he resumed his playing.

"Oh, my God," I groaned. We sat, stunned, enraptured by the extraordinary music echoing through the hall, and unbelieving as we watched Leonard Bernstein finish his lunch as he started it. June's eyes met mine. "I think we should get the hell out of here."

There are mysteries one learns to live with. All I really know is that the concert was a great success. On the hottest night of the summer, our incredible stars made beautiful music. Starting in gleaming white jackets, they concluded gamely in their sweat-stained shirts. Ruth Steinkraus Cohen was applauded for her valiant efforts, and the Steinway, Lennie, Tossy, Aldo, Isaac, and Frank exited our lives as mysteriously as they had entered. The next morning I called Mississippi and told them that we were sending ten thousand dollars for the bail fund.

12

Being White

As a visible white participant in the civil rights struggle in the South, I tried never to turn down an invitation to speak about the struggle. I knew how important it was that as many of us as possible tell the truth about the courageous people who were fighting against enormous political and economic odds. Often after my return north, I was asked to write and illustrate articles that covered events in the black community. It was an awkward position to be put in. They were often stories that ought to be told. Sadly, in the sixties, many white editors were not yet comfortable having black journalists tell their own stories. It was a subtle kind of racism, and one that most reasonably enraged very capable black writers and illustrators.

In the fall of 1964, I began to write *Stranger at the Gates: A Summer in Mississippi*. The sweat-stained diaries I had inscribed every night in my Delta bedroom became the spine of my story, and the hundred drawings brought vivid recall of the days and nights I had spent with the movement. Eager to evaluate what progress was being made in the Delta, I returned to Ruleville in 1965. It was an opportunity to visit Freedom Schools, help Mrs. Fannie Lou Hamer and the civil rights workers in the Delta to register voters, and to observe the emerging fight to organize the long-exploited black tenant farmers. At the end of that summer I resumed working on *Stranger at the Gates* and completed the book. After the memoir was accepted by Hill and Wang for publication in the following year, I finally returned to my role as a reportorial artist who covered a wider spectrum of the American experience.

One night in the late summer of 1965, shortly after returning from Mississippi, Marian Logan called to ask if we could join them the following Friday evening. In typical Marian style she came straight to the point. "I need your help, Tracy. We've got a bunch of people who are so uptight with all this talk about 'black power' that they need someone who's been there to explain without bullshit what Stokely Carmichael and Rap Brown are all about. And bring June."

When I hung up, I said to my wife, "You'll never believe what we're doing next Friday night."

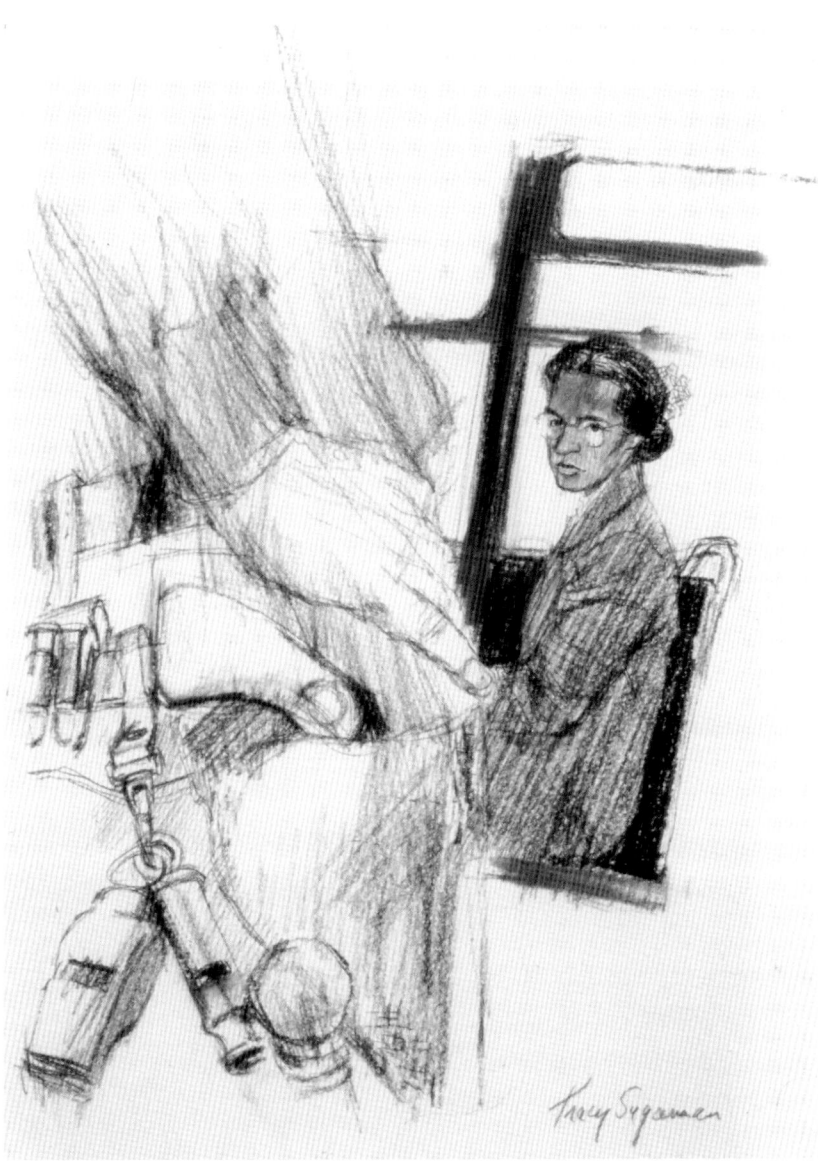

35. *Rosa Parks*

The light from the Logans' brownstone spilled out across Eighty-eighth Street as we approached in the dusk. The large windows facing the street had been opened wide to get the evening breeze after a long, hot August day, and the excited chatter and laughter from the living room were inviting. We paused at the bottom of the stairs. "Just another Marian Logan evening at home, Snoon. Probably no more than thirty close friends!"

She pushed past me, grinning, and headed up the stairs. "Just mind your manners, or Marian will have your head."

I paused at the door and watched my wife be enfolded in the arms of Arthur Logan. From our first evening together before I left for Mississippi, Arthur and June were like kin. Arthur's long experience in community organizing across New York City intrigued June, and his natural generosity and warmth made for long discussions every time they met. Her desire to get involved in community organizing was ignited in those heady dialogues and helped lead to her work as an organizer in the inner city of Mount Vernon.

The first faces I saw as I entered from the landing were those of a very sober Jackie Robinson and his beautiful and vivacious wife, Rachel. Robinson was taller, grayer, and heavier than I remembered from the newsreels and the sports pages, perhaps as a result of his ongoing struggle with diabetes. People milled into their orbit, carrying on lively conversations with Rachel. Jackie stood quite silent, a very dignified presence, watching with quiet amusement the animated chatterers and gossipers who eddied about.

The living room was filled with people, only some of whom we had met before. An energetic, bright-eyed sparrow of a woman, an adviser on racial affairs to Governor Rockefeller, spotted me and gave a welcoming wave, and two horn players from Duke Ellington's band with whom we had shared a birthday party at the Logans' home beckoned me to join them at the piano where a dwarf of a man was quietly evoking echoes of the Duke's endless treasury. A Broadway arranger with whom we had had long convivial evenings with Arthur and Marian made his way through the crowd. "You made it back from Sunflower County in one piece. Welcome home!" His black musical was making a historic and most successful run on Broadway. It was a typical Logan gathering of professionals from Arthur's medical friends at Harlem Hospital, musicians from Marian's world of cabarets where as Marian Bruce she had made her earlier career as a blues singer, and politicians who found this brownstone to be where black and white New York power brokers could talk shop and cement relationships. It was a mixed crowd racially, but preponderantly black. It was, as always, a fascinating mix of bright and talented New Yorkers.

But I could not take my eyes off Jackie Robinson. He had been a hero of mine ever since he broke the color line and joined the Dodgers in 1948. I knew of no one who had shown more personal courage in confronting racism than he. I had never met him in the flesh, and when Marian approached, I seized her arm with alarm. "Jesus, Marian. You want me to explain black power to Jackie Robinson?"

She grinned wickedly and kissed my cheek. "Yes, Tracila. You know more about it than he does." She moved to the piano and whispered to the pianist, who stopped playing. The room grew silent. "As some of you know, Tracy just got back from the Delta where he's been working with Fannie Lou Hamer. Some of you may have questions he can answer." She looked at Jackie and then at me. "Some of you want to know particularly what 'black power' means."

"Or doesn't mean," added Arthur. "What does Stokely Carmichael mean when he says whites are the problem, not the solution, that it's time for blacks to be the rightful and only decision makers in the fight for equality?" Arthur's troubled eyes searched the room. "Everyone in this room knows that the Congress was moved to pass the Civil Rights Bill after

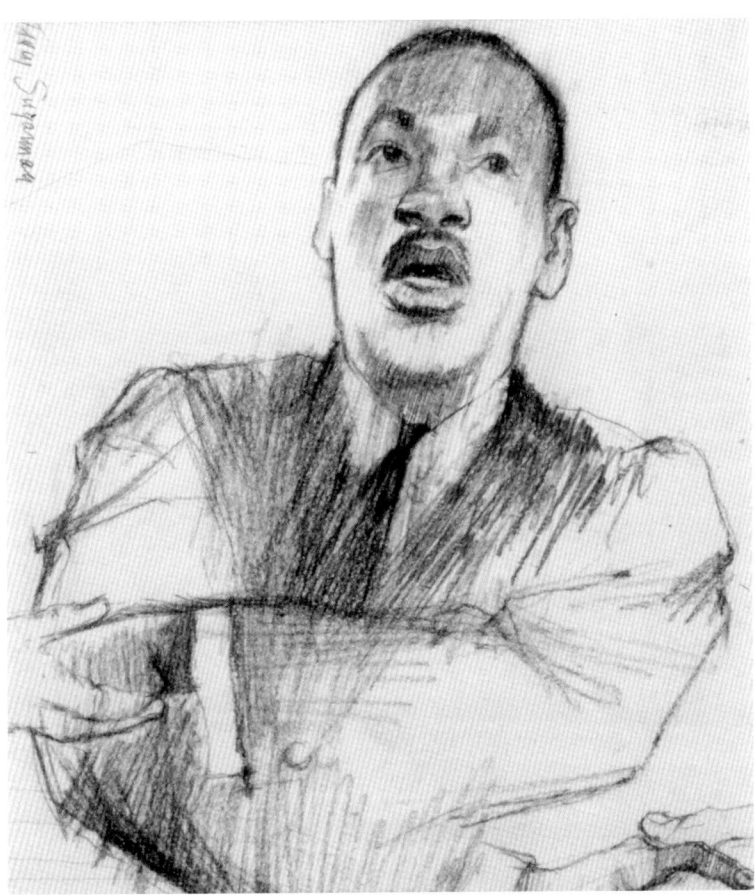

36. *Rev. Martin Luther King, Jr.*

all these long years of struggle because Andy Goodman and Mickey Schwerner were white. It wasn't because James Chaney was black. In the U.S. Congress some people are more equal than others. We need powerful partners, and Stokely can't bring that kind of power to the table."

For the next hour I found myself leading a spirited discussion about "black power." As I gazed at the attentive faces, I knew that they, like me, were committed to the principle of an integrated civil rights movement.

Most particularly, these were people who knew how vital it was to retain white financial and political support if the civil rights movement was to survive. Many in the room had devoted years to that cause, and now they worried that the movement was rejecting its white supporters. Some, like Robinson, who were now entrenched in the white corporate structure were finally able to bring powerful resources to a racially integrated movement.

"A number of us remember singing 'Black and white together, we shall overcome' in this very room," said Marian, "the last time Martin was here in New York for our board meeting of the SCLC."

Robinson nodded. "Black and white together." His eyes held mine. "Not exactly the same as black and black together." The tension in the room was palpable.

I tried hard to bring some context to the phrase as it was understood in Mississippi by quoting Mrs. Hamer. "'We have been black, powerless people for four hundred years. What we mean by "black power" is we mean to have a say in our destiny. We want to know about our own history. We want to have a voice in the education of our children. And we want to vote for people we can trust.' It's hard to imagine in this handsome room, in this

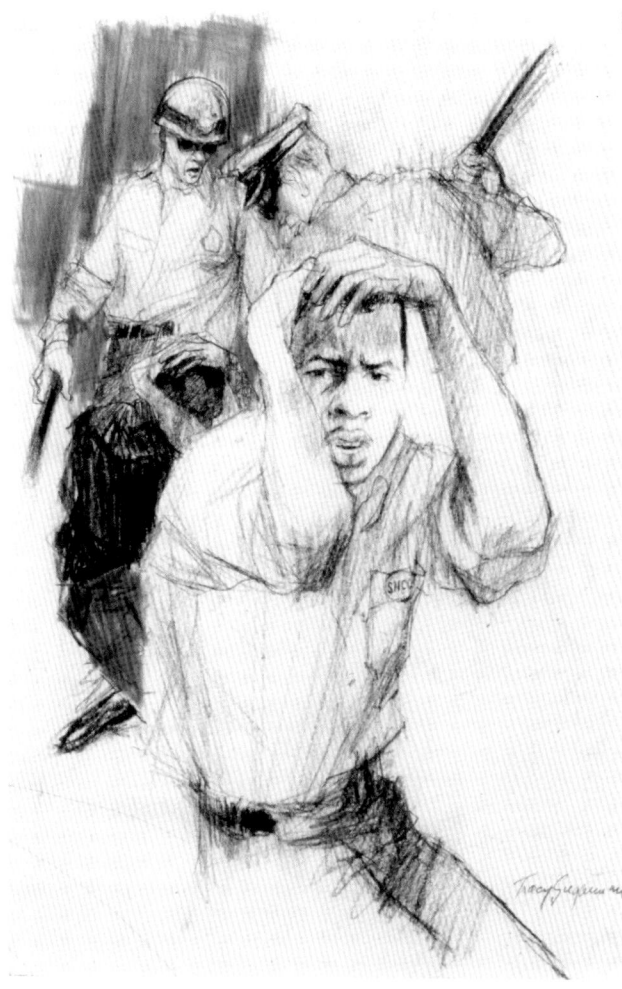

37. John Lewis

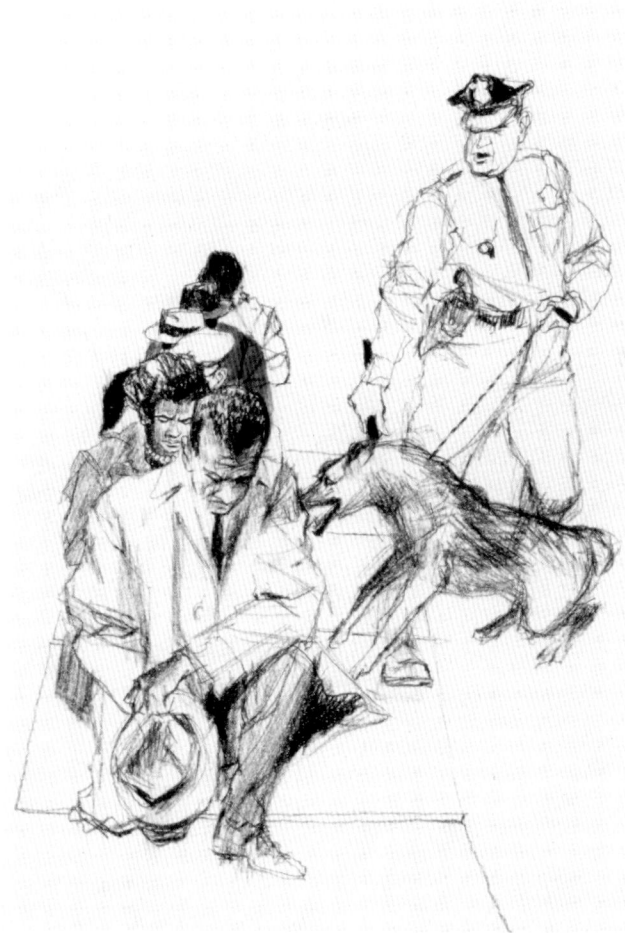

38. Rev. Fred Shuttlesworth

incredible city, how frustrating and demeaning black powerlessness is when one is systematically and brutally denied the assumed rights of other American citizens. Militants like Stokely, deeply religious Christians like Mrs. Hamer, and the underfed, underrepresented, underpaid millions of blacks no longer trust the white power structure to keep its word. They've been lied to for too long. When Carmichael declared, 'We want black power and we want it now!' it was a cry from the heart that all black people in Mississippi recognized and embraced."

"And how did you feel when they asked you to move over, Tracy, and get out of the way?" Arthur's voice was soft and sympathetic.

"I hated it, Arthur. But I tried to understand where it came from. Most of the student volunteers who were working in the Delta were white like me. Some of those kids had been beaten, and a lot of them had been arrested. Mickey, Andy, and James, who had been with us at the orientation, had been killed. These white kids had paid some dues. But the truth is that I don't know a single one of them who did not understand and sympathize with the idea of the necessity for 'black power.' It was time."

We lingered as the crowd slowly drifted down the stairs and out into the humid summer night, reluctant to leave the Logans. Jackie and Rachel, who had an apartment on the floor above, were unwinding on the couch, and the piano player was softly exploring "Lush Life," seemingly unaware that we were even in the room. Arthur moved to the little bar and brought each of us a nightcap. Jackie Robinson raised his glass and nodded. "To us. All of us."

It was a long, quiet ride home to Connecticut. It was nearly dawn when we reached home. We both felt that we had shared an astonishing evening that somehow signaled an end, or perhaps a beginning. Looking back I am happy remembering that it happened as it did. It was important that the context for "black power" be given, for in the time immediately ahead, tragic racial confrontations in the northern cities would cause the integrated civil rights movement to evolve into a black movement. Many friendships and alliances were painfully torn apart, and the "loving community" seemed to be in tatters. A racial polarization emerged that would weaken and finally destroy the remarkable coalition that had changed history. Whites like our family would retain and cherish the friendships forged in the sixties. We would continue to support the aspirations for justice that had motivated so much sacrifice in the movement, aspirations still tragically unfulfilled. But we would do so from the sidelines.

13

VISTA

Shortly after the publication of *Stranger at the Gates* in 1966, I was asked to come to Washington to meet with Arch Parsons, the editor of the *VISTA Volunteer*. Parson's magazine chronicled the challenging projects throughout the country that were being tackled by the young men and women who joined Volunteers in Service to America.

When President Kennedy had urged young Americans in his inaugural address to "ask not what the country can do for you, ask rather what you can do for your country," he touched a particularly responsive nerve among thousands of idealistic college students. Some had flocked to join the new Peace Corps to bring their "can-do" enthusiasm and skills to third world countries that often lacked both expertise and capital. Others were intrigued by a challenge closer to home and enrolled with VISTA. VISTA's mission was to seek out those corners in our own country that were similarly impoverished.

Arch Parsons, a slender black man in his early forties, greeted me with a smile. He held up a well-notated copy of *Stranger at the Gates* and waved me to a chair beside his cluttered desk.

"I'm glad to meet you," he said. "Hell of a good job, Tracy. Been a journalist for enough years to recognize a writer who's tuned in to his subject." He paused for a moment, and then continued. "Particularly when it's a white guy writing about poor folks who look like me!" He settled back in his chair, and a mischievous smile moved across his face. "How tuned in can you be writing about poor folks who look like you?" We both laughed.

Parsons explained that five hundred college-trained VISTA volunteers were going to spend their summer vacations serving in one hundred of the most isolated communities in Appalachia. They would bolster the efforts of the nearly three hundred volunteers who lived and worked in Kentucky, West Virginia, Virginia, and Tennessee. "If Appalachia is something that would interest you, I'd like you to go with the volunteers who are going to Fonde, Kentucky, and tell their story in our magazine."

I responded that I would love the opportunity to write about an area that I knew only from books and films. Parsons grinned and said, "I hoped you would say that. I'll get you the schedules and logistics. Just don't forget to pack your sketchpads with you when you go!"

Kentucky Highway 25E winds crazily skyward. The road snakes ever up, coiling and uncoiling as it seeks its way up Clinch Mountain. At the summit you lose the jagged rocks and sheltering trees, and suddenly you discover the Cumberlands. The great, green hills turn blue, blue-gray, then dissolve into charcoal smudges as they march west. Cars halt to stare at the vast panorama, and the tourists' kids race to the coin telescopes that can sweep the far reaches of the mountain.

"Hey, Ma, way down in that clearing, past where the sun is shining on the river—I can see a house! And kids!" The telescope pauses, sweeps past, and in that moment the youngster has probably seen all he will ever see of the hidden Americans in Appalachia.

For many of the 500 young Americans who went into Appalachia in the summer of 1966 as VISTA associates, Clinch Mountain was the first eagle's-eye view of their new home. Wrestling duffels and books, sleeping bags and bulky guitars, they move on through the Cumberland Gap, push into the heartland of the region. Soon they move away from the macadam and tailored tar roads, and up the rutted dirt trails and streambeds that lead to the hollows and coal camps in the fastness of the Cumberlands.

When the spattered cars of the eight volunteers who are to work in the coal camp of Fonde move across Fonde Mountain in June, they leave behind an America that is confident and affluent. Middle-class kids from cloistered campuses in California and Colorado, Massachusetts and Kentucky, stare for the first time at the sooty, unwashed face of poor America. Dirty towheaded children sit listlessly on sagging porches or scramble over the rusty corpses of cars that are wheelless and useless. Torn, endlessly mended black-and-gray tar-paper roofs top the unpainted shacks, a melancholy mosaic of desperation. The encroaching forests of Fonde Mountain move between the hovels, mercifully hiding the corroding iron that spills like dried blood down the gullies. Scrub growth and sun-touched foliage clothe the stark skeletons of abandoned coal tipples. A great brooding silence lies on the mountains.

As they ascend, the volunteers overtake the awkward, humpbacked coal trucks that labor with crashing gears, fighting their way up the grades and around the hairpin curves. Now there is only forest and sky, skittering glimpses of misty vistas beyond, and then a sudden break in the woods and the first shocked sight of the strip mines. Like angry wounds, red earth and spilled surface coal had been gouged from the mountain's side. With unbelieving eyes, the associates spot the wanton, ravaged signs on still another ridge, another ledge, and another. Fallen, rotten timber, naked and torn earth—the scars are hideous on the long, verdant sweep of the hills. Now, for the first time, they see that the stream that raced their cars down from the mountain's crest is blown with mud, fouled by the runoff from the strip equipment tearing into the mountain's side.

The road suddenly descends to a clearing at the base. In a brambled field at the fork in the road stands a brown cement cross. "Jesus Is Coming," it proclaims to the silent hills.

The cars turn left at the fork. Half a mile beyond is Fonde, their home and mission for the next ten weeks.

My home in Fonde, Kentucky, is in a small, dilapidated house that I share with volunteers Jim Cope and Steve McCurrach. Sketching their daily activities, I soon begin to feel the heartbeat of this hidden community. From the beginning, I am troubled by Arch Parson's sly question: "How tuned in can you be with poor folks who look like you?" The truth is that the honest answer is hard to find. The pervasive malaise I feel everywhere shocks me so deeply that I have to struggle to remain nonjudgmental of the life I am recording with my drawings and words. What I am seeing in Fonde, I have never witnessed before.

Only one year before, I had left the cauldron of racial apartheid in the Mississippi Delta after sharing the lives of the desperately poor blacks for a "long, hot summer." Even with the continuous threat of violence and the dehumanizing effects of segregation, there was a bubbling and unmistakable vitality among the blacks. Perhaps it was partly the result of the freedom movement that animated them to heed Mrs. Fannie Lou Hamer's exhortation to "keep on keepin' on," or perhaps it was the result of centuries of denial in which they had learned how to live as well as to survive. What was triumphantly clear was that they refused to accept defeat as a final judgment no matter how high the price they would have to pay for being poor and black.

How very different is Fonde, Kentucky. Cradled in an elbow of magnificent mountains whose beauty seems to shame the shabbiness of the little town, this is a shattered community in spirit and seemingly resigned to a future that will never equal its past.

In the third week of August the coal camp of Fonde nestles under maples, seeming to slumber in warm, moist air. A raucous, metallic crash of gears and the piercing scream of a locomotive whistle tear the silence, as an engine backs along the track, pushing three empty, echoing coal gondolas. The sweaty engine pushes past the weary houses beyond the single store at the edge of the hollow. Soon it is lost in the green branches, but can be heard racketing its way along the iron rails to the one remaining coal tipple in Fonde.

An old man, a gray work shirt buttoned neatly about the thin, seamed neck, leans on the gate of his yard and stares at the school beyond the tracks. The pale-blue eyes never acknowledge the passage of the train. A gaggle of barefoot boys is racing from the entrance of the fieldstone school, following in the wake of two tall young men who are carrying heavy wooden seats. Long metal chains trail from the seats, bouncing through the rutted turf of the schoolyard. Excited, laughing voices bubble in the quiet air.

"Now, Jim? Now? Are we really putting them up now?"

The group pauses at the shiny red stanchions, suddenly hushed as the tall young men secure the chains. When Jim Cope and Steve McCurrach step back to survey their handiwork, the kids race whooping to the swings. Till eleven that night, lines of children wait for still another turn. Judy Stewart, an Appalachia volunteer whose family in Cincinnati had come from just such a Kentucky hollow, watches the skinny, soiled youngsters pumping joyfully in the schoolyard. She sits on the dusty rail of the tiny home that houses the six girls in the project. Her soft Kentucky voice is musing. "Folks here have been tryin' to get swings for their kids for almost ten years." The wide eyes glisten behind her glasses. "Ten years. Bake sales. Church suppers. All that. Somehow enough money and enough will never got together—before now." A huge truck with coal chunks grinds past the sagging wire fence of the schoolyard. Judy's voice sounds small in the silence that follows the passage of the truck. "There aren't any big victories down here."

At Fonde's request, the eight VISTA workers spend the summer working on programs of enrichment for the village children. They move simply and quietly into the worn fabric of Fonde life. A once thriving coal-mine town that boasted during World War II that more than five hundred of its men were on the local mine's payroll, Fonde now has only fifteen of its men working in pits in the area. Ten years ago the local mine sealed its shafts and ceased operation.

"Many of the best 'git up and go' families left," says Tom Murray, the school principal. "They went where the jobs were. But some of our poorest families stayed. It's reflected in the school population. We only have a quarter of the students we had ten years ago. And we're down to only three teachers to teach the eight grades. We have more than our share of slow or retarded children, too. My own theory is that it has to do with malnutrition during pregnancy. Reason I say that is that in a number of the real large families, the first children are right smart, and the later ones are much slower." His eyes are troubled behind the wire glasses. "The same amount of food comes into the house, but the number needing it gets bigger and bigger."

The sad shacks of Fonde house a population that is preponderantly unemployed or retired. A federal program designed to give employment to those still able to do physical labor has been dubbed by the local citizens the "happy pappy" program. The work provided is dull and unchallenging. Men who once cut coal or ran complicated rigs in the pits are now listlessly cutting brush in the lots where abandoned homes have been pulled down. Instruction for the discouraged men in developing skills that might tear the shroud from the stricken community is simply not available. Fonde fathers are either too weary from the work in the remaining pits or too broken by the dead weight of failure to have much left to give their children. Fonde mothers, weighted with the demands of too many children born too close together, struggling to keep the family fed, clothed, and together, have little energy left to devote to curious young minds. Too often the youngsters drift, rudderless, sighting no horizon beyond the bend of a muddy stream. As I sketch them, I can see that the children have found some of the trust, warmth, and inspiration they hunger for from the volunteers who have come from beyond the mountains.

An old man who was a miner for thirty-seven years has grandchildren who haunt the steps of the volunteers all summer. "We older folks know that we ain't done enough, not near enough for these kids, or to help these young people who've come down here to work with the children. We're too plumb tired at the end of a shift, and on the day we're not workin' we have to do all the chores for the house that have waited all week." He pauses, and his eyes follow two of the volunteers who move down the road, hand in hand with two little children. His voice is husky when he speaks again. "We're gonna just hate to see them go. We love these people. And our kids love them."

For the volunteers, the total provincialism of the Fonde children has been a shocking reality. "Do you know," one exclaimed, "we took this eleven year old over Fonde Mountain for the first time in her life! She'd never seen a store or a neon light, let alone a library or a movie house."

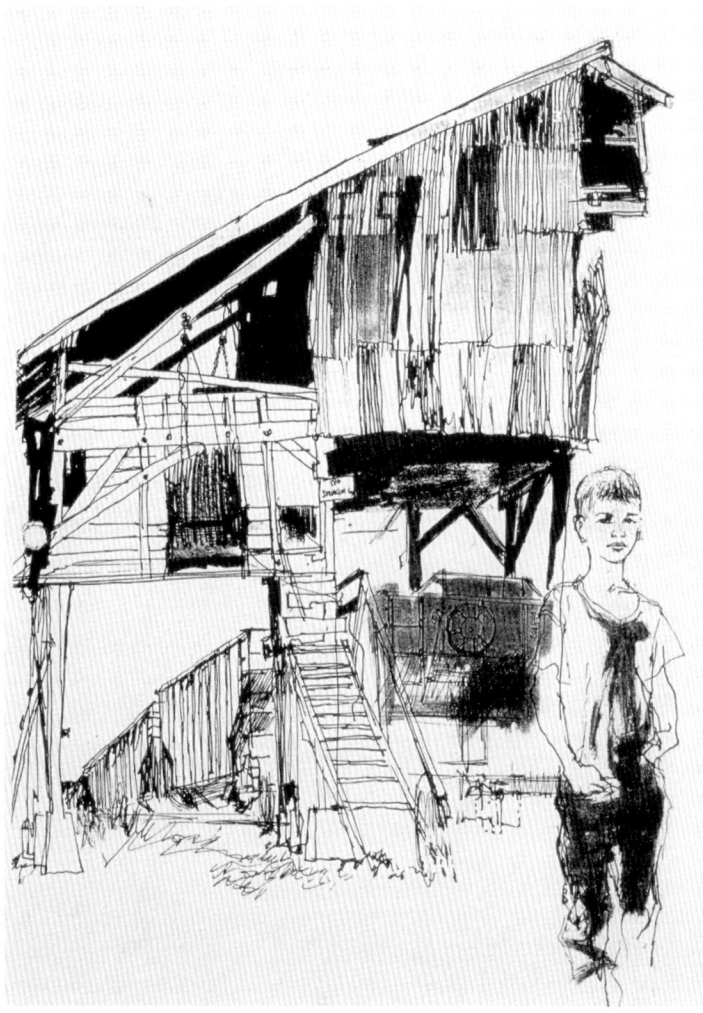

39. *Boy and Coal Tipple, Fonde, Kentucky*

Even if there had been no field trips, no biology hunts for snakes and insects, no carefully crocheted place mats for a newly created "to scale" dollhouse full of furniture, rugs, and curtains, no art classes for children who had never before seen a crayon, the very fact of the young volunteers would have been enough to justify that remarkable summer. The creation of the long-dreamed-of swings, the scrounging for parts, the painting, the carpentry were not important for themselves. But for the first time in their lives, Fonde kids were working with young people who believed in themselves and had a stake in the future. Most wondrous of all, these students from far away seemed to believe in them.

Steve McCurrach, whose skills as a mechanic and carpenter make him a pivot of much of the activity of the summer, shakes his mane of blond hair. An outgoing, happy twenty year old who radiates confidence, he is horrified by the attitudes he has found in the Fonde

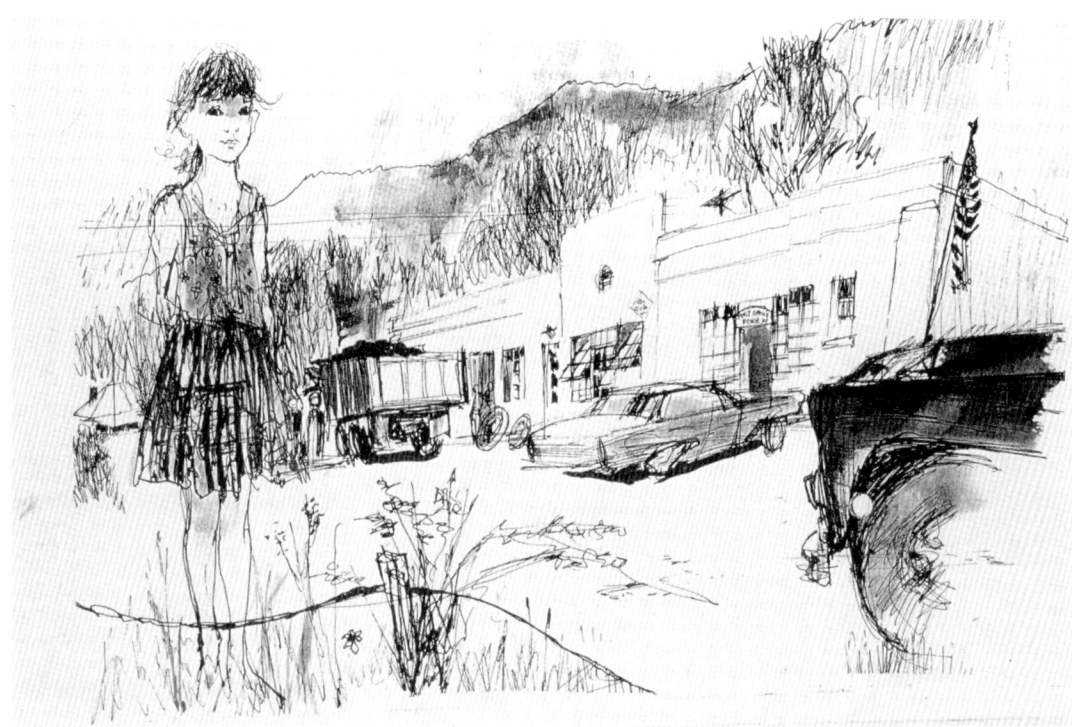

40. *Girl on Main Street, Fonde, Kentucky*

children. "Even kids who are 'with it,' good, smart little kids, tell you, 'Whatever you want is okay with me,' or 'I don't know how,' meaning 'I can't learn.' It's depressing as hell to find kids who don't believe they are capable of anything—who think that nothing ever is going to happen to change the way things are."

Through the long, patient summer days, the friendship of the volunteers and the Fonde children deepens. In a town that lingers longingly in an unredeemable past, seeds of curiosity and perception are planted looking toward the future. Whether the green seedlings will root in a soil so long arid remains to be seen.

In 1966, Fonde folk speak most of "how it used to be . . . when the houses were good and the land company that owned them took care of them . . . when the labor union gave a damn . . . when the strip mines weren't ruining the mountains, drowning even the minnows by the silt in the streams . . . when the school had eight teachers for eight grades." An apathy born of past exploitation and hopelessness has made any real assault on the present obstacles almost impossible.

On my last day I meet with Tom Murray, the principal. He sits in a classroom, his large bulk straddling a small stool. A volunteer's insect collection from the summer rests on a dusty desk, waiting for the first science class of the fall. Bright sunlight filters through the new batik curtains that have been sewn by the Fonde girls. Crayoned images of melons and vegetables have been ironed into the beige fabric, and the cheerful colors light the shabby room.

Murray frowns as he gazes past the gay windows to the hills rising beyond. "We're so isolated," he says. "The world all around us has left us behind. Folks here think that if they feed their young ones and clothe them, that's all they got to do." He shakes his head in exasperation. "If we're going to make it, we gotta get these kids educated."

Judy Stewart's eyes shine when she tells me, "Two girls, and maybe a third, have decided now to go on to high school!" More than Tom Murray, she knows that eight grades in a three-teacher school are not adequate preparation for twentieth-century America.

Steve McCurrach sits late on the porch one night, talking with the other Fonde volunteers. The summer is waning, and the desire to understand what they have experienced moves the conversation. "I guess we all correlate reality with what we have known. A lot of us bring big-city reality with us when we come into the hills." He pauses for a moment, staring into the soft dark. "But maybe there are ways of seeing things that are truer here than we know. There seems to be time here, time to develop real relationships. You don't seem to have the time or that chance in other places. And that doesn't seem to have a thing to do with money. Or poverty." He shifts his weight on the scarred rail of the porch. "I want to spend two more years here."

For the volunteers, the summer has been a tapestry of impressions. "It doesn't mean much to say it's been a good summer," one volunteer says. "There have been good things and bad things, and frustrating things." For most, the summer brought initial impatience with local attitudes that had been warped by despair. Later, an accompanying compassion had led to understanding. For all, it has been a testing ground for old values and myths, and for some the opportunity for new insights. For a few, the summer has brought anger, and for more it has brought new resolve. "Greedy corporations and absentee landlords have robbed this region," one volunteer says bitterly. "And self-serving politicians and school superintendents have kept it hidden. But in hills as beautiful as these, with tall timber all around you, a wealth of minerals under your feet, and the good people we've gotten to know this summer, there must be a way to make it all work."

At the top of Clinch Mountain I pull my spattered car to the side of the road. My eyes search for the last time this sweet, sad piece of America. And yes, in that clearing, past where the sun is shining on the river, I can see a house! And kids!

14

The Great Society

My work with VISTA was deeply satisfying, although I discovered a whole new dimension of despair and poverty. Before going to Appalachia I believed that the racially chaotic landscape of the Mississippi Delta had established the very limits of willful exploitation. The generations-old deprivation of human rights that a racial minority of whites had inflicted on the black majority seemingly would have destroyed their capacity for joy, humor, or faith. Yet my work with the blacks in the movement in the sixties showed me a spirit that was quite unquenchable. Many believed that they could effect revolutionary change through a courageous nonviolence, a determination to "keep on keepin' on," and I saw them begin to win that struggle. But in Appalachia, no such vitality seemed to have survived the economic pillaging that had raped the now abandoned coal towns. Even as I saw the pinched children relishing the simple magic of a new set of swings, I watched their elders, staring blankly at the once verdant hills, rocking and rocking on the sagging porches of Fonde.

I had hoped that the portfolio of drawings telling the VISTA story would create similar opportunities to draw and write about other social programs being announced by the president in his plans for the "Great Society." One could sense a stirring in the heart of many of the northern inner cities, a tentative, not-quite-believing hope that finally change might come to their stunted ghettos. The South from which so many had fled was being altered before their eyes. It was happening. You could see it every night on the TV. Not dogs and hoses and police clubs. Black kids and white kids going to the schools together! Why not here in Harlem? Why not in Bedford-Stuyvesant in Brooklyn? I, too, was caught up in the escalating excitement, watching some of the most benighted communities struggling against the bigotry and darkness that had so long maimed them. When I heard that there was a meeting in Bedford-Stuyvesant to organize their community to effect real change, I hurried to Brooklyn to record the historic evening.

It was an excited gathering, and you could see neighbors greeting neighbors with a look of happy surprise. A pick-up jazz group was pounding out a groove on "Sunny Side of the Street," and the kids were swaying and clapping. The older folks kept filing in,

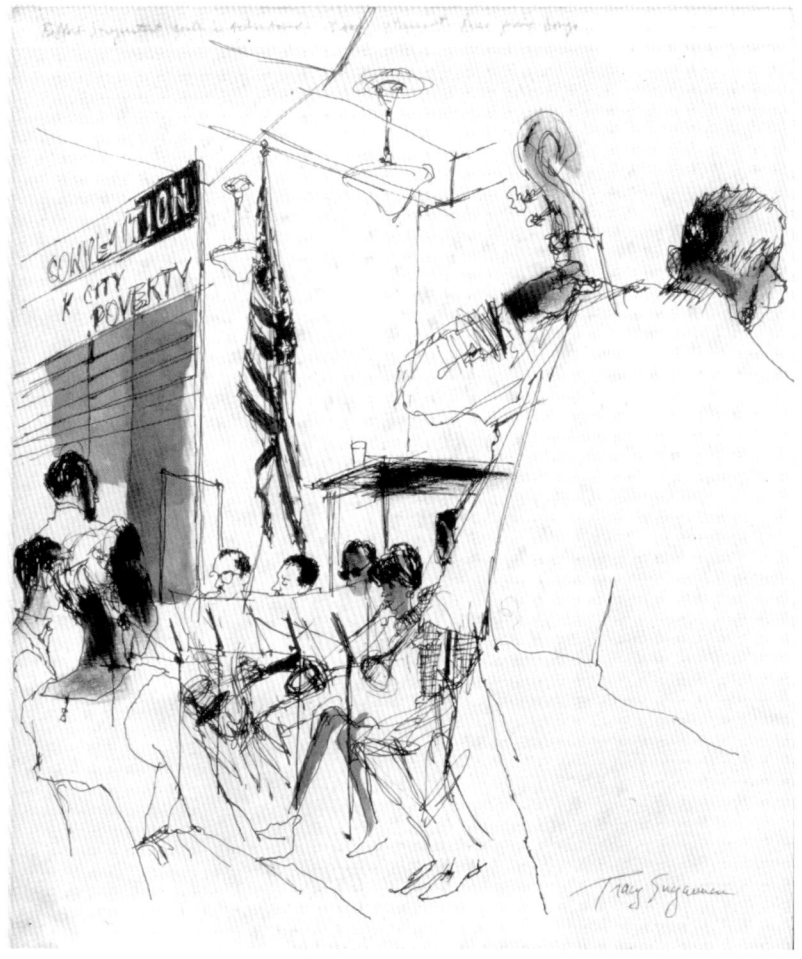

41. *Jazz in Bed-Stuy*

settling in their folding chairs, their heads nodding, their faces half-smiling. Nothing quite like this had happened in Bed-Stuy before. "Supposed to be a meeting about politics and organizing? Hell, this feels more like a church supper back in Georgia! So where do we go? What do we do?" The fat was in the fire that night, and everyone there thought, "Hey, why not? Why not us? We know this community better than the politicians who've milked it almost dry."

When I'd filled my sketchbook and driven up into Connecticut, it was near midnight, and my heart was full and racing. Let it be, President Johnson. Let it be, Congress. Let it happen!

The United States Information Agency used my folio of drawings in its overseas magazines to demonstrate that America was addressing its problems by empowering the people. Those dreams of progress may have inspired the Russians, South Americans, and Africans who had a chance to read those glossy advertisements of American idealism to organize on their own. But they had little shelf life here. Those dreams faded before too many dawns had broken over the weary streets of Bed-Stuy.

It was not the last time that I learned one choreographs the future at his own peril. Who could have written the nearly Elizabethan tragedy of Lyndon Johnson, the domineering, take-no-prisoners, raw Texan whose arrogance would both courageously midwife a revolutionary blueprint for a "Great Society" and perpetuate, out of hubris, a tragic war in Vietnam that would destroy his dreams and maim the country? "I'm not going to be the first American president to lose a war."

Who could have predicted that this most pragmatic and politically savvy puppet master from the South would proclaim "we shall overcome," bully his social engineering through

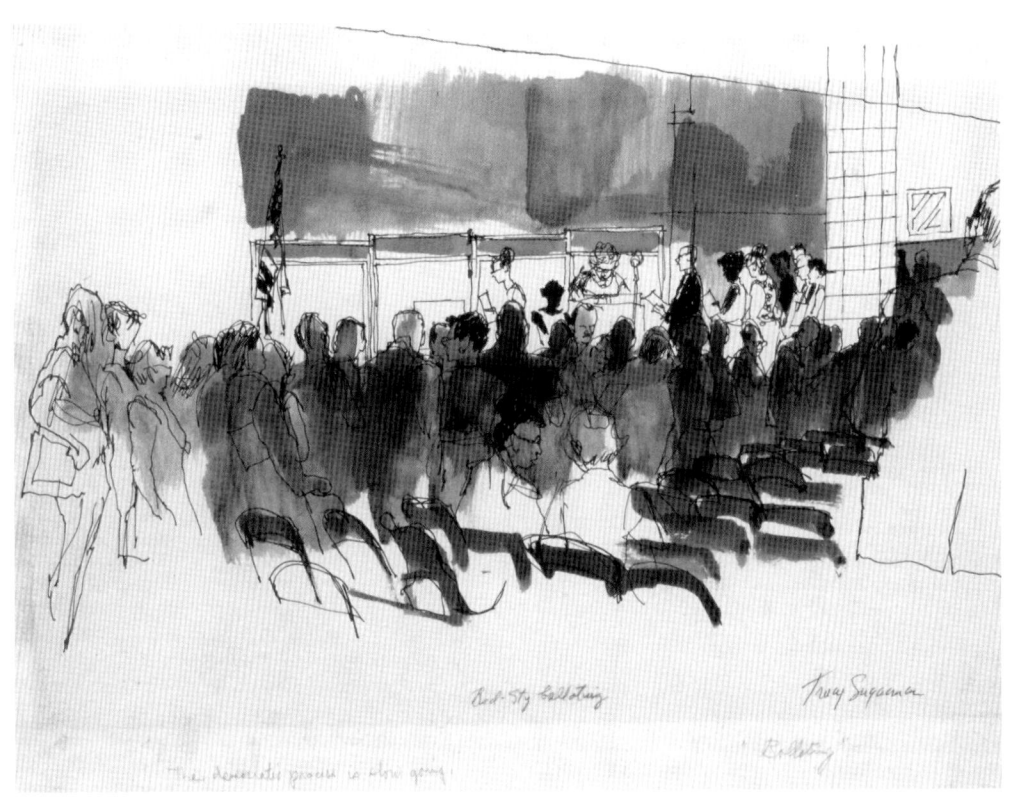

42. *Signing Up*

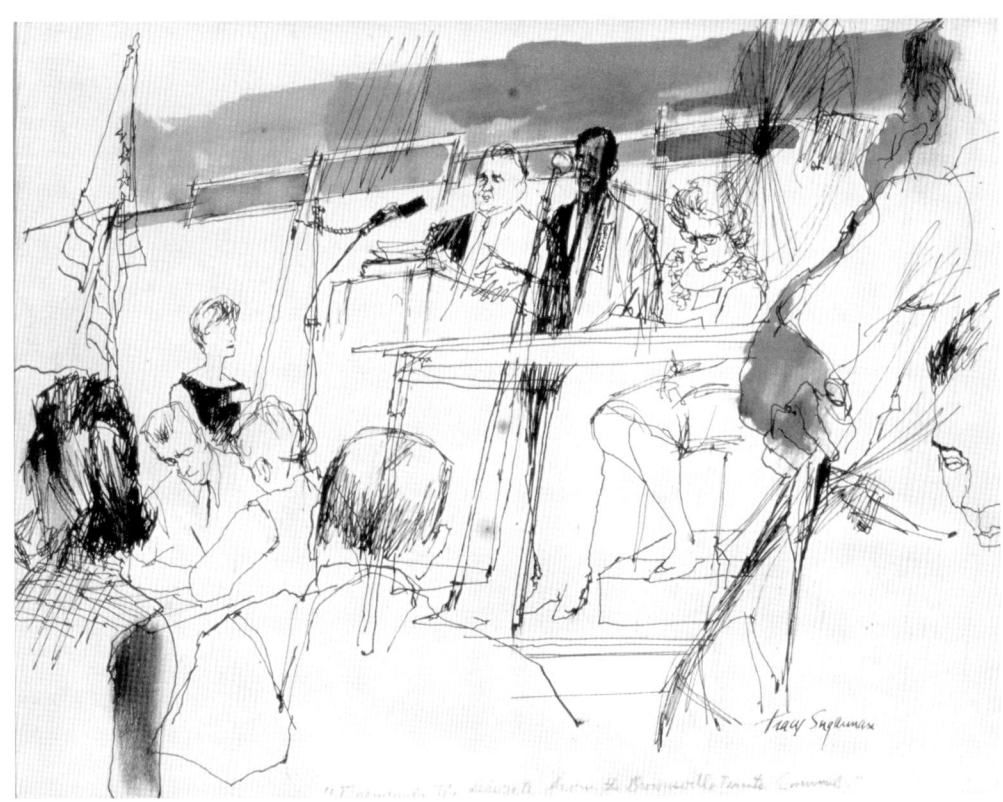

43. *First Meeting in*
Bedford-Stuyvesant

a stunned Congress, and, in the end, retreat from the political stage, discredited and alone? The escalation of the conflict that raged in Vietnam grew at a pace that galvanized the whole country into discord and confrontation. On campuses across the country students were speaking "truth to power," and the stern police and National Guard responses at Kent State and Jackson State resulted in deaths and widespread arrests. The inner cities of Newark and Watts in Los Angeles erupted in lethal civic revolt, and the fires of fury were illuminating whole sections of Washington, D.C. Like a cancer in the bloodstream of the body politic, disillusionment, cynicism, and despair replaced the heady promise of King's "I have a dream" or John Kennedy's "Ask not what your country can do for you. Ask rather what you can do for your country."

The resources necessary to sustain the promises of the "Great Society" went instead to prosecute the endless war in Vietnam, and the replacement of Lyndon Johnson's relentless energy with President Richard Nixon's hostility and uninterest nearly destroyed any possibility that the ghettos of the nation would be transformed. Only the intervention of personal wealth and influence like Robert Kennedy's efforts in Bedford-Stuyvesant encouraged a halting but determined march forward to achieve a vibrant sense of community for its black citizens. But in the desolate streets of most of America's inner cities, one witnessed the ascendancy of a rampant drug culture and its attendant violence, nourished by the rank despair of shattered dreams.

Looking back at those last lost years of the bright and promising decade of the sixties fills me with a sense of melancholy and loss. So many dreams for a more just and equitable society were lost in the smoke from burning ghettos in the North and from the distant war that was bleeding America.

15

U.S. Tour

In the late summer of 1966 I was asked by American Express to be their resident artist on a tour of five hundred European travel agents and journalists. Twenty-two cities were to be covered by eleven tours in the most ambitious travel promotion ever undertaken in the United States. In conjunction with the U.S. Dept. of Commerce, the U.S. Travel Service, the Civil Aeronautics Board, and the International Air Transport Association, an ambitious odyssey, "See It for Yourself," was being designed by American Express to encourage the flow of tourists from Europe. It was an assignment that I welcomed because I had toured coast-to-coast six years before with my family, and the recollections of the trip were still sweet in memory. Each of us had fallen deeply in love with the wonder and beauty of this great and abundant land. Like most parents on a family trip, I had contented myself with film records of our explorations and discoveries. Now I would have a chance to make my own personal sketchbook of people and places, and an opportunity to witness our foreign guests discover America in all its diversity.

But the timing of the trip seemed ironic, for in many ways it was a deeply troubled time for our country. The assassination of John Kennedy seemed to have drained much of the optimism and youthful vitality from the nation. The sense of invulnerability that was so definably American was replaced for many by a wary skepticism as the news of discord at home and abroad seemed to accelerate. Our involvement in Vietnam was becoming mired in the rice paddies and jungles, and the heartbreaking sight nightly on television of body bags was demonstrating how costly the misadventure was in American lives. Our own son, Richard, devoted to the nonviolence he had practiced in the civil rights movement, was prepared to resist any draft, and as a family we were prepared to support his moral position. The nonviolent civil rights movement, which had raised such buoyant hopes in so many of us, had seemingly run out of steam, replaced now by dispiriting violence in the northern cities. The angry voices of confrontational Black Panthers, and alienated students who were protesting the war and challenging the establishment, seemed to fill the very air. What a strange time it seemed for showing the face of our nation to the critical gaze of foreign visitors.

But politically involved as we were in both unresolved issues, this tour seemed like a benison. My head, my hand, and my heart that had so long been invested in focusing on the unfinished business of our society could once more be focused on the beauty and bounty of America. And I would have a chance to rediscover the country with men and women who longed to come here and see "the fruited plain" and the "purple mountain majesties."

My mission was to make a sketchbook of impressions of my assigned tour, which when reproduced at its conclusion could serve as a personal souvenir for the foreign guests. It was a role I could play easily, for on this journey there were no hostile presences in the wings. My attention could be set solely on the wide-eyed visitors gaping at the scale and breadth of our prairies and mountains and the modernity of our cities. What was less certain was the role I would often find myself playing as a spokesperson for America, being the only one in our caravan who actually lived here.

The group that I accompanied included travel writers from Denmark, Ireland, Italy, Sweden, and Germany. They were enthusiastic and curious men and women, and almost without exception first-time visitors to the United States. There was a shared sense of adventure, and I found my companions to be remarkably open and humorous guests.

In the cacophony of New York's traffic (which reminded the visitors of Paris, Rome, and Berlin . . . "London is much worse!") the austere grace of Lincoln Center seemed a haven. We first met in the elegant cavern of Lincoln Center's home for the New York Philharmonic, and it was predictably awesome to the travelers. But the sweep of the plaza and the lovely use of mirrored pools of water evoked memories of home. For many, Lincoln Center seemed the very best of the sophisticated East. There was a noticeable reluctance about leaving the Big Apple before they had a real chance to savor the delights promised on a Broadway that they had always fantasized about. One sensed that appetites had been stimulated and that revisiting New York would be on many agendas.

As they made their way among the noisy family groups crowding into Philadelphia's Independence Hall, I noted that my group was uncharacteristically quiet. When they inspected the historic Liberty Bell, they did so with a hushed respect. But the animated discussions in the buses afterward revealed an in-depth appreciation of the extraordinary changes that the American revolution had brought to the world. They knew a great deal about American history, and I could not help but consider how little previous historic knowledge I could bring were I to visit the countries of my companions.

The notes I scribbled on the margins of my sketches, however, revealed their very human responses to the particular rigors of travel in the United States. To this American, they were often amusing and invariably surprising. The lady from Denmark: "I must say that the bathrooms in New York and in Philadelphia are not terribly clean. I'm shocked because I've so often heard Americans discussing European bathrooms and not

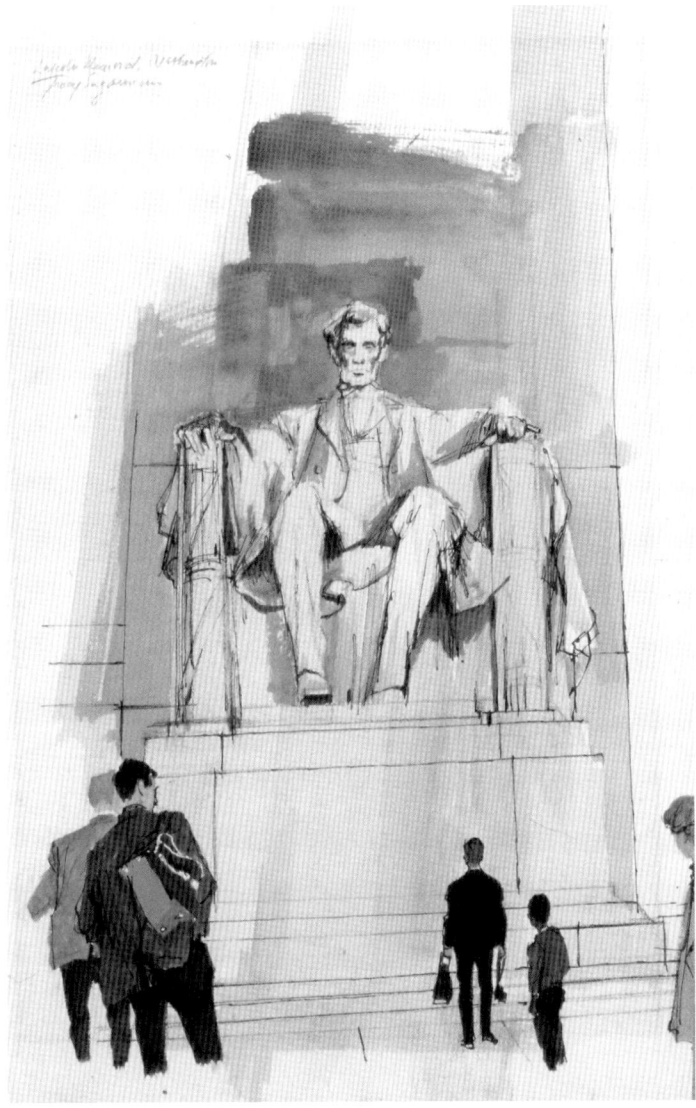

44. *Lincoln Memorial*

being very kind." The lady from Belfast was charmed by the sense of history that she found in Philadelphia, and aghast at the central heating at the hotel. "Jasus, I think I'm being strangled!" The gentleman from Copenhagen was simply disoriented by the coffee service. "The waiters bring coffee to the table while I am eating my soup. Now, I like a cigar with my coffee. And I can't have a cigar with my soup!" All three missed the presence of beer or wine with the meals, and were astonished that in so cool a climate they should constantly be served ice water! Not surprisingly, there was a great, shared anticipation of our next-day visit to Washington.

Touring the Capitol with the visitors provoked a series of images from my past. I remembered the awe I felt as a child when my parents had first brought me here to the great avenues, the White House, and, most particularly, the Lincoln Memorial. Now I gazed down the Mall where I had watched Martin Luther King make his historic speech in the shadow of that memorial during the March on Washington, and I retraced my steps where I had marched with hundreds of thousands of my fellow Americans protesting the war in Vietnam. I could still remember the smell of tear gas that fouled the air on the side streets leading up to the Capitol during that war moratorium. And I could see again the sad tent cities that had covered the bright grass of the Mall during the Poor People's days of demonstration. I had known my Washington in many incarnations. But now I was simply proud of my city. Its monuments to the unknown soldier and to the raising of the flag on Iwo Jima were as moving to me as they were to the teary visitors. Not for the first time, I found Washington to be handsome and wonderful, and I was eager to show it off.

Pristine and marvelously simple, President Kennedy's grave in Arlington, the Lincoln Memorial, and the Tomb of the Unknown Soldier were most moving to the Europeans. What shocked and astonished them most was a sign posted at the base of the steps ascending the tomb: "NO PICNICKING IN THE CEMETERY." One by one, they filed slowly up to the sign, obviously committing the words to memory. Would Americans really picnic on these hallowed grounds? I could only shrug.

It was not the gleaming boulevards and handsome monuments, however, that were to linger most vividly in the memories of the hundred foreigners I accompanied to the White House. It was the astonishing informality and welcoming bonhomie of the vice president of the United States, Hubert H. Humphrey. The second most powerful man in the United States invited us in with the gracious smile of welcome he once would have extended to kinfolk dropping in on him when he was mayor of Minneapolis. It was an endearing and totally democratic happening, unlike anything any of the visitors had ever witnessed at home. For twenty-five minutes the business of state was put aside, and the vice president told the guests how happy we all were to have them here. "How I wish I was going with you! It's a great country out there." Standing in the very back of the crowd, I found myself beaming. Thank you, Mr. Vice President.

For the voyagers from Europe, the stops along the way in the East were interesting but not far removed from the historic cities of home. But by the time we had visited Phoenix and shared the glitz and comfort of a Sun Belt city, "Like Baghdad in the West! Those attendants are running for the cars!" there was a palpable eagerness to get to the real West, the Wild West. Each of our visitors had childhood memories of "westerns." And the West did not disappoint them. If the Indians were fewer and less fierce than they had imagined, and the cowboys seemed to do their wrangling from dusty jeeps, the land itself was more theatrical than they could have dreamed. The plains and the mountain ranges were simply staggering to behold. Where in Europe or Scandinavia were there vistas like these? They were enchanted with the enormity of the skies and the brilliance of the colors. "I'm coming back with the family!" was the refrain heard daily as our odyssey continued westward.

But it was in the very civil and domesticated Salt Lake City that I first was confronted by my fellow travelers. After a long and remarkable choral concert at the Mormon Tabernacle, we had ridden our coach to the parched shores of the Great Salt Lake. The heat by the salty lake was stifling, and tempers were beginning to fray. By the time we were back at our hotel, the weary journalists were ready to repair to the bar to quench their monumental thirst. It had been the only topic of conversation in the bus since we headed back to the

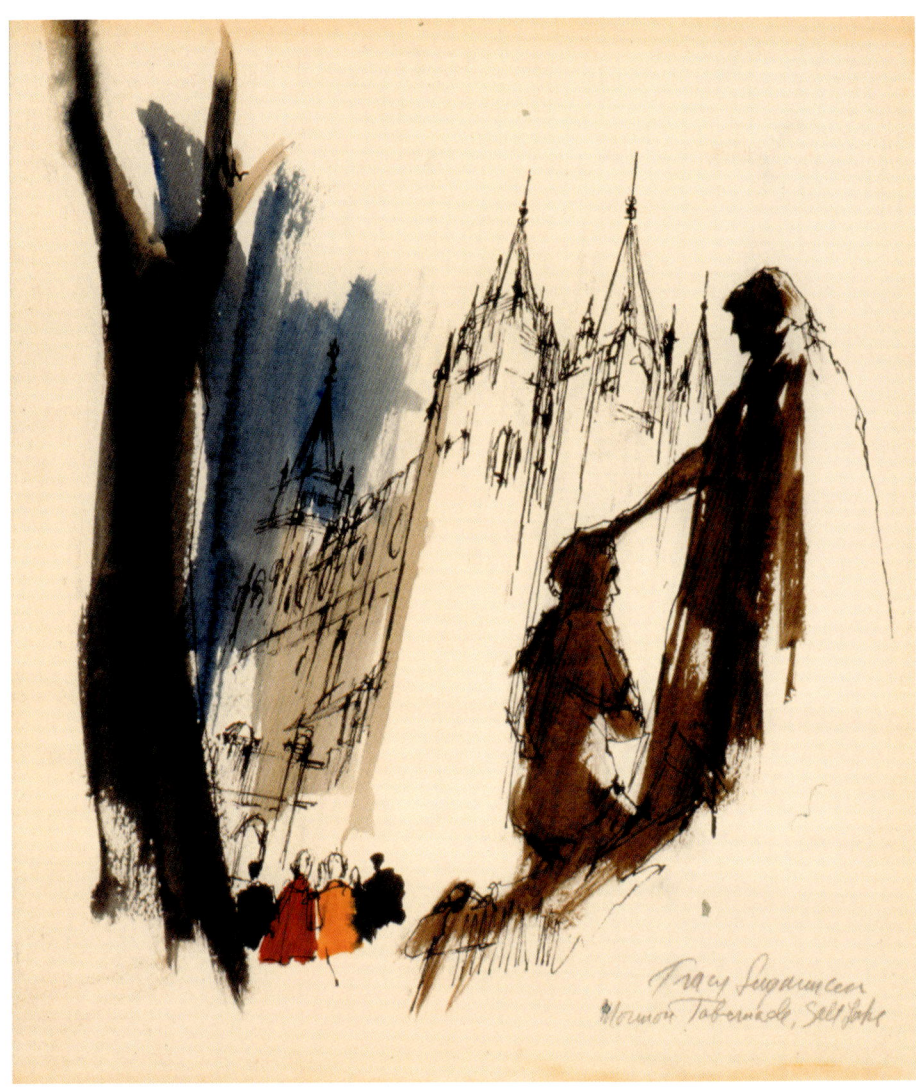

45. *Mormon Tabernacle*

city. As they descended from the vehicle, there was the cry of "See you in the bar!" My heart shrank, because I alone knew that there was no bar. There was no booze in the whole city. Salt Lake City is a dry city. The Mormons want it that way. I skulked to my room, hoping against hope that no one would find me. It was a foolish hope.

When the loud banging on my door would not cease, I opened it to find five overwrought men, an Irishman, a German, a Dane, an Italian, and a Swede. Their eyes were wild with disbelief and potential mayhem.

The Irishman seized my arm and stared deep in my eyes. "We've heard a terrible story, Sugarman," he croaked through parched lips. "A terrible story."

Slowly, the mob was edging into my room, and I found myself sitting on the edge of my bed, surrounded. "What terrible story, O'Hara?" I asked in a small voice.

"That there is no bar, Sugarman. That there is no booze. Now that terrible story can't be true." His eyes searched mine, then widened. "Can it?" he whispered. The room was now totally silent.

I cleared my throat and answered, "It can. It is. It's a terrible story. And it's true. The Mormons want it this way."

The Swede said, "But it's not credible! We're not any of us Mormons!" He glanced at his fellows. "Are we?" There was a furious silence. "In your great land," said the Swede in a voice filled with sorrow, "in the year of our Lord 1967, they can do that?"

I nodded. "They can. In this great democracy, they have the right to be terribly wrong." In the silence that greeted my words I composed my thoughts. "But all is not completely lost," I said with a bravado I did not feel. "I have a drop I'm happy to share, but it will not be enough if anyone else hears about it." In a trice, the door was closed and locked. A call to the porter for a bucket of ice was placed. And from my Val-Pak I extracted two pints of Johnnie Walker. A deep sigh sounded through the room. When the ice arrived, my small United Nations stretched out on the floor as the bottle passed from hand to eager hand.

O'Hara's voice was quietly merry now. "God bless you, Sugarman." And the Swede concluded the toast. "And God bless America."

But the next morning O'Hara sat speechless, staring at the grapefruit placed before him, as I joined him for breakfast. His eyes, slightly florid from the Johnnie Walker of the previous evening, moved up to mine.

I was startled by the agonized look of the man. "Are you alright, O'Hara?"

"Is it a Mormon plot?" he asked.

"Is what a Mormon plot? What are you talking about?"

"The grapefruit," he whispered. "It's hot." His eyes darted around the room, seeking out the conspiracy. "They served the grapefruit hot." There are only so many ways one can defend his country, and I had exhausted all of them.

"O'Hara," I said enthusiastically, "try the French toast!"

Our escape from the pristine goodness of Joseph Smith could not come fast enough for me, but our explorations of the marvelous ski areas and old mining towns in Utah were happy highlights for the foreign guests. But it was the majestic silence of the Grand Canyon that was the trump card of the whole journey west. Having been there before and been so moved by the awe-inspiring chasm, I could hardly wait to watch the reactions of my new friends. They reacted as I believe everyone must who encounters this extraordinary and beautiful cleft in nature. They acted as they would have in a great cathedral. Their voices were quiet and their eyes often filled with tears.

The greatest single asset of the Grand Canyon other than its moving beauty and fugitive color was our guide, Swede Larsen. To every European visitor, Larsen was the living evocation of the West they had imagined. He seemed part rawhide, part wagon master, part Will Rogers. "He's so authentic!" exclaimed the German journalist. As with most tourists in any strange land, with very few exceptions contact with the natives for our group was confined to bell captains, guides, and waitresses. Impressions gained from these people tend to make the picture of "Americans" that our eager group would carry home to Europe. It was pleasant to realize that Swede Larsen would soon be at center table in all those living rooms.

It was only with the greatest prompting that they returned to the bus for the trip to the airport for our flight to San Francisco. Their reluctance to leave the presence of the Grand Canyon was a tribute to one of the most exquisite displays of nature. It was not, certainly, a hesitation about proceeding to the great City on the Bay. As was evident in nearly every conversation across the country with the journalists and travel agents, the single most anticipated city in every European's itinerary was San Francisco.

On the flight the talk was animated. Everyone had stories they had been told about the city, restaurants they had to dine at, museums they had to visit, concerts they had to hear, neighborhoods they had to wander, vistas they had to enjoy. I could only shake my head in wonder at the childlike anticipation of what was about to be revealed. I, too, loved San Francisco. But this was beyond belief. We landed at the airport amid the mud and dishevelment that attends every construction job. The airport was under redesign, and it was an unholy mess. Yet even while dragging their valises down muddy corridors and crossing roads awash with a rainstorm that was hitting the city, the mythology remained triumphant. Before even reaching the confines of the waiting hotel, voices were echoing their praises of San Francisco. "Now," they crowed, "this is a real city!" I could only conclude that the art of public relations in Europe was even more effective than here in the States where it was invented.

After the rich tapestry of San Francisco, the scrubbed unworldliness of Disneyland made you smile in disbelief. A cartoon of America, invented by a cartoonist, was shining through the smog of Los Angeles, beckoning to the child in every grown-up. "Castles? We've got castles! Fantasy? We've got fantasy! And spotless streets! And smiling guides! And Pluto! And Grumpy! And all the dwarfs! And there's Mickey! Yes, Mickey!" I watched our foreign guests as they joyously embraced this cartoon dream of the future. On one level I was pleased that they were having a good time. But somehow I felt disturbed. On our travels we had shared a reality of this country that was so rich, so diverse, so provocative that I wanted those images to be stored in their baggage, not this make-believe, charming though it may be.

But that was not for me to choose. My mission was completed, so I packed up my drawings, wished my friends a fond bon voyage, and took a plane back to Connecticut. It was great timing. I arrived home for that most American of all holidays, Thanksgiving, and everyone was going to be there.

16

1968

For any adult American who lived through the nightmares of 1968, that year will be etched in memory as a time of almost unremitting grief. The very skin of the republic felt so tightly drawn that one shuddered at any new tragedy that might tear it apart. Vietnam slogged on, disaster compounding disaster, yet there seemed no one who had the political or moral clout necessary to reverse the adventure. Protest had moved rampantly into the streets, shattering the comity of the National Democratic Party Convention as students demanded an end to the war in Vietnam. And the police of Mayor Daley of Chicago attacked them in an assault that was found by the courts to have been a "police riot." Shock after shock was registered on the dismayed and frightened public. And the killings raged on. The unbelievable assassinations: Bobby Kennedy. Martin Luther King. Malcolm X. The center was not holding, and often during those desperate days there seemed to be no center.

Like most citizens, we hunkered down, praying for an end to the madness. On Saturday mornings we would join the antiwar vigil in the center of town, constantly being surprised at the animosity the peaceful vigil generated. Old friends and neighbors would walk coldly by, pretending they had never known us. It hurt in a way that all the epithets I endured in Mississippi as part of the movement never had. But I knew that our protest was seen as an affront by some who had sons already in Vietnam, and others who had kids who were about to go. There was no one to hate, I thought. We're all victims. Only the war was hateful.

17

Malcolm X

I have often thought of the drawings and paintings I have made as my other children. Like my kids, once they have left my home they are out there in the world, making their own way, and you hope that, as a parent, they are not embarrassing you. And sometimes they become your emissaries, making friends you might never have met. That has been particularly so in the case of drawings that were somehow my most personal drawings, work often done because I, not a client, desired it done. That is how I came to meet Asger Jerrild, the art director of the *Saturday Evening Post.* Shortly after returning from Mississippi in 1964, I received a call from the *Post,* inviting me to come meet Mr. Jerrild. A tall, kindly Dane greeted me warmly as I entered his office.

"I'm happy to meet you," he said. "Please," nodding to a waiting chair, and settled his large frame comfortably behind his cluttered desk. "We share a very good friend," he said. "Eric Blegvad." We both smiled, equally enjoying the thought of the genial friend whom we both admired. "He's my countryman, you know." He cocked his head. "He's a great admirer of your work."

"Thank you. It's certainly mutual. I love his book illustration. And Eric helped me lay out my book on Mississippi. As you must know, he cares very deeply about injustice, and he wanted to help." Eric's loathing of the Nazi occupiers of his country when he was a child was known to all his friends. It had deeply shaped his political and moral sensibilities, and the racism he saw in America was a repulsive reminder of the past. I nodded at the recollection and smiled. "I guess we share the same prejudices. Maybe that's why we've been good friends for all the time he's lived in Westport." I paused, watching Jerrild's attentive face, not certain why he had summoned me.

Jerrild smiled. "He took me to see your Mississippi drawings at his wife's little gallery. He was right. They're very good." He paused, then shoved a sheaf of papers across the desk to me. "I think they are good enough to illustrate this wonderful piece by John Hersey."

I glanced at the cover page: "A Life for a Vote." "This is about voting in the South, Mr. Jerrild?"

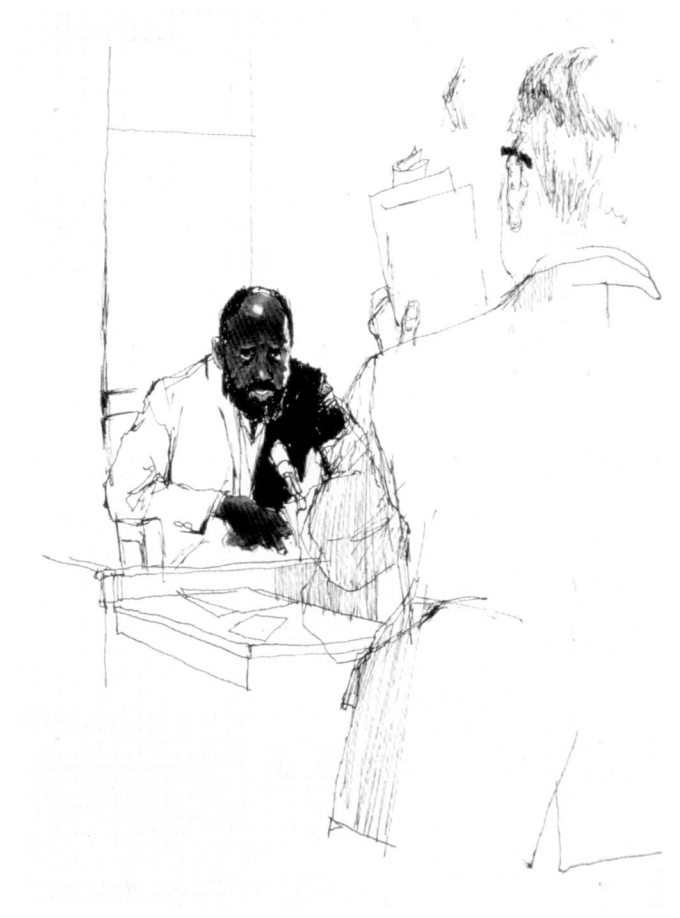

46. *The Witness Stand*

"It's about trying to vote in Mississippi when you are black. You're not black," he grinned, "but you do seem to know something about that situation. I'd like to use at least eight of your drawings. It will make a very strong piece, Tracy. And please call me Asger."

Hersey's insightful article was the perfect vehicle for the drawings I had made in order to bring the truth about Mississippi to a wide national audience. And it was the beginning of a professional relationship that five years later would result in being commissioned by the *Saturday Evening Post* to cover the trial of the alleged murderers of Malcolm X. Jerrild had been pleased by my contribution to the Hersey piece. Convinced that I had the racial sensibility necessary to handle the charged atmosphere of the trial, he secured permission from the court to have me record the entire scenario in drawings. It was a remarkable opportunity for me because there was a "no photography allowed" ban on the press. Presumably, an artist sitting in the corner would be less intrusive to the proceedings than a photographer prowling the aisles. The drawings that I made during those fraught days of the trial are now an archive of the Schomburg Collection of the New York Public Library.

I recognized the importance of the assassination of Malcolm X and the impact that such a catastrophic event would have on the black community. It was the death of a folk hero to countless Afro-Americans. Malcolm's passionate preaching had brought many a new sense of racial pride and a surging sense of personal value. His murder was the beginning of a legend that has continued to grow, and his life has been memorialized on film and in opera. Malcolm's searing autobiography has taken its place as one of the significant documents describing race in the United States.

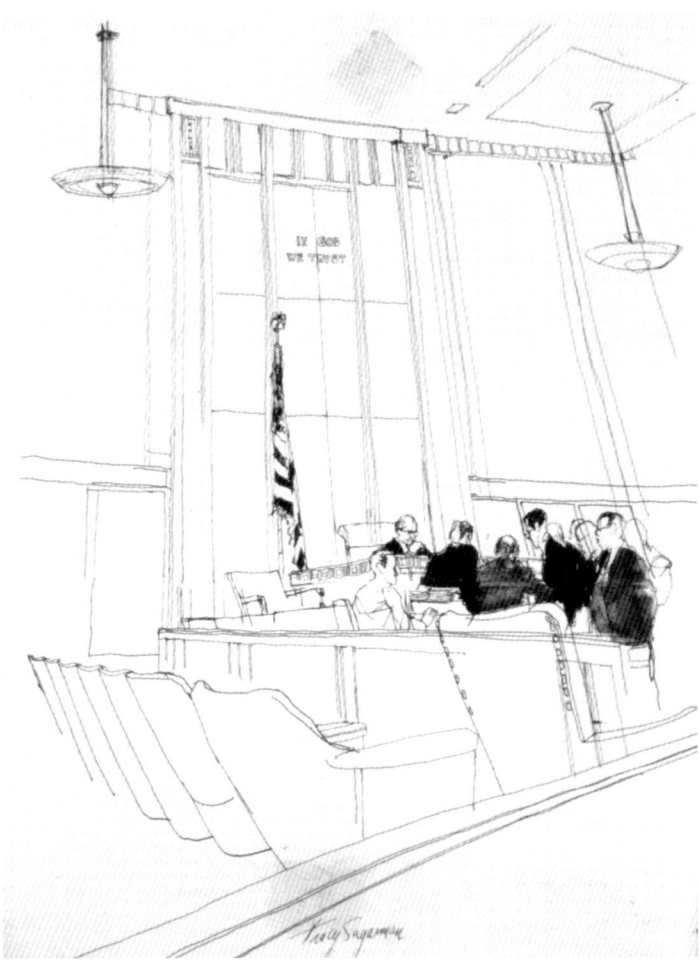

47. *Meeting at the Bench*

Although Malcolm had been hostile to the integrated nonviolent civil rights struggle of which I had been a part, I was intrigued by his bravery and by his capacity to evolve his philosophy and politics as he explored the various levels of his Muslim religion. I knew that as a result of his hajj to Mecca, he had come to understand that all whites were not "white devils," that color alone could not be the yardstick for measuring a man. Many whites had accompanied him on his road to Mecca, and he was in serious pursuit of a new paradigm in race relations. What had become visible to the public was that his new revelations had caused a deep schism with his spiritual mentor, Elijah Mohammad. Now Malcolm, the man who had defined so much of the nation's conversation about "black power," was dead, and men close to Elijah Mohammad were being tried for his murder. It promised to be a fascinating trial.

There are few dramas in contemporary life that are as arresting as a murder trial. Even as one watches the accused and the accusers, measuring their responses and evasions, one has to remind oneself that the stakes are years of a person's life, and the actors are real. I was never certain when a witness would be dismissed or if a defendant would be recalled. Consequently, there was an unrelenting urgency in making my reportorial drawing. For the weeks of the Malcolm X murder trial, before, during, and after the court was in session, I filled the pages of my sketchbook with the images of the unfolding drama. Sometimes I would sketch the architecture of the courtroom before the entrance of the presiding judge and then populate the picture with the spectators, attendants, and principals of the trial as the day wore on. Since the outcome of the trial could not be foreseen,

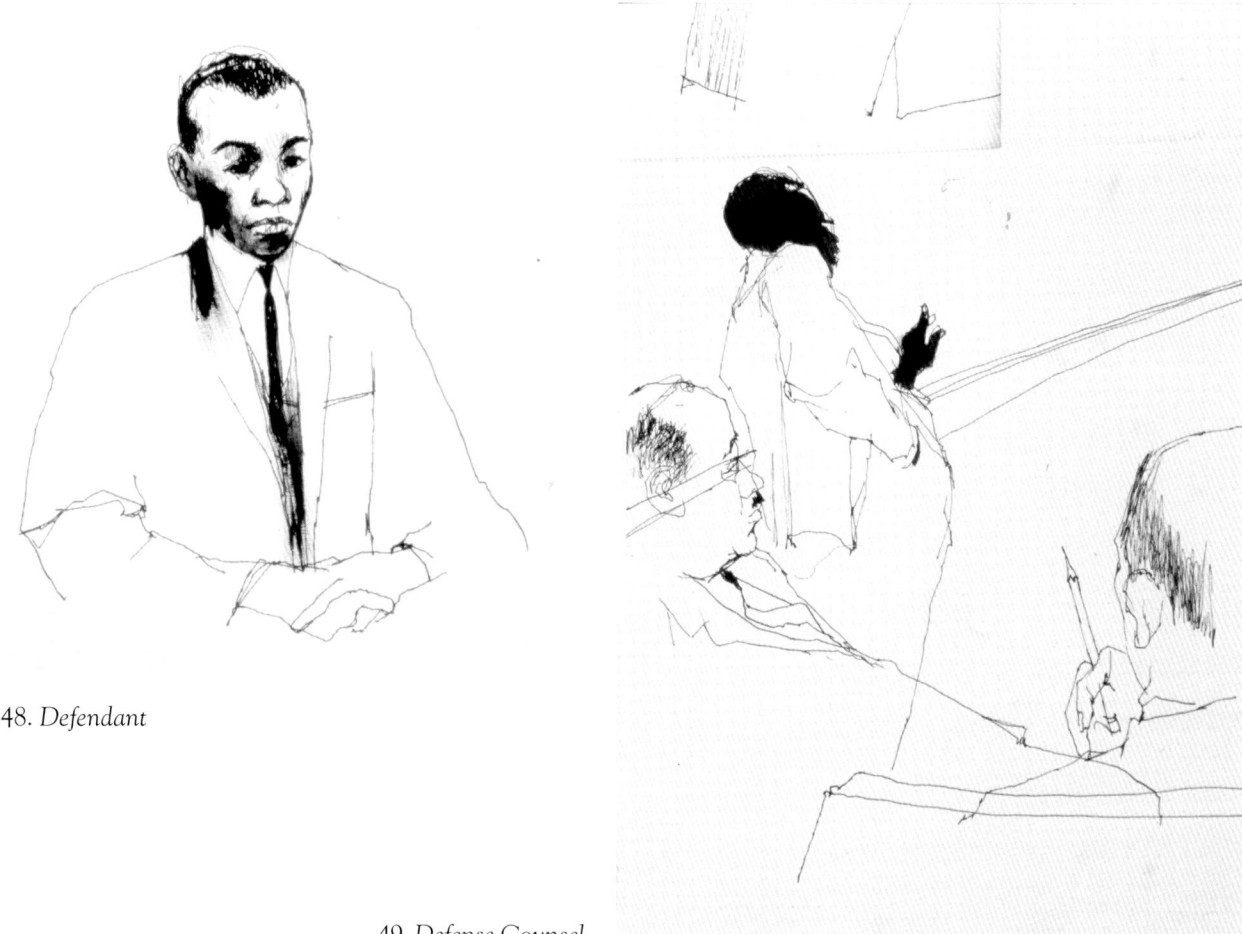

48. *Defendant*

49. *Defense Counsel*

each witness had the same potential of becoming central to the deliberations. I felt it imperative, therefore, to try to isolate his particular quality and style on my page. To me, the essence of successful reportage is capturing the fact and the meaning of a moment in time. At the trial I often found myself in the pressured position of struggling to fix that instant on paper when the situation was fugitive, even hostile. It is an ideal that I have only sometimes achieved, though it is in the attempt that I have found the joy of reportorial work. But the meaning of that moment can't be known until the jury returns with the verdict. Therefore, the total trial, the sum of all those moments and personalities, was the canvas I had to fill. My thrust as a trial artist was to winnow from the mass of images the truest ones that could tell the story.

The facility necessary to translate the visual image, sometimes in flight or in transition, to the hand and the pen is an acquired skill that has grown with the years. But it is never a simple chore. The false starts, the nervous broken line, the drops of sweat that

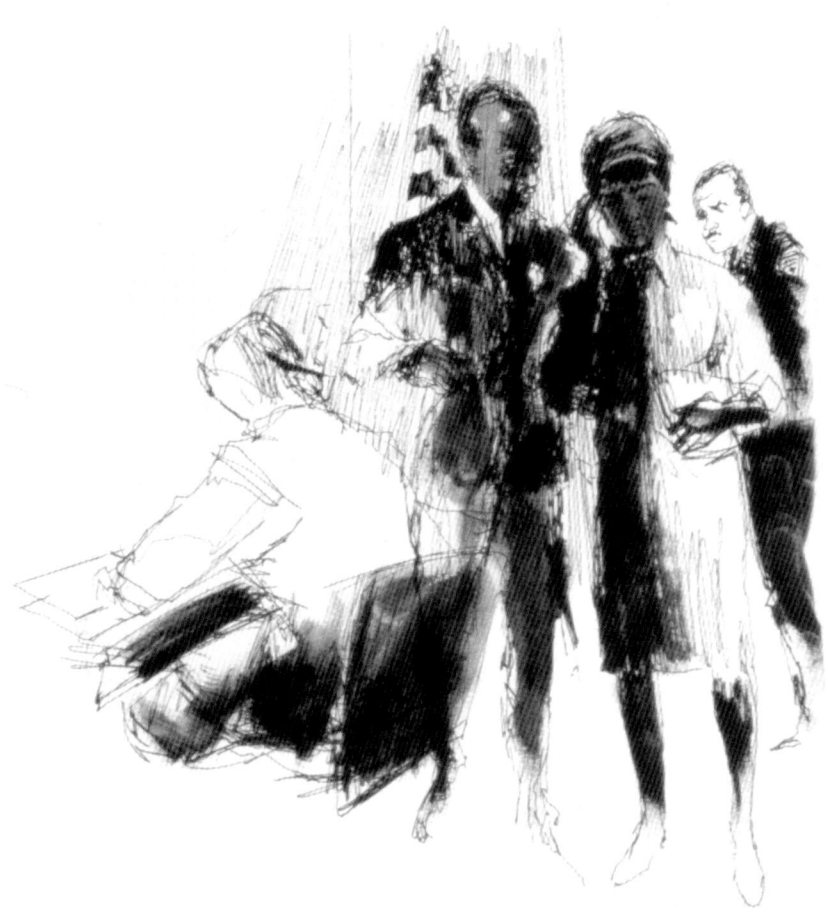

50. *Malcolm's Widow*

blot a passage of the drawing all echo the immediacy of the search. But particularly in a grave situation such as a murder trial, you are dealing with vulnerable human beings, and your drawings demand an honesty of purpose and a relating to your subject that is less clinical than human. If the moment is worth capturing, then I have the responsibility of trying to endow the drawing with the compassion that comes from understanding. It seems to me that it is only in this fragile dimension that the artist's gift to the viewer can be made.

Most difficult of all for me was demonstrating through body language, gesture, and facial expression the animus and tension that pervaded the courtroom. Those seated in the courtroom were not passive spectators. They were temporarily immobilized but active participants in the drama that began before the murder and was continuing in the court and out on the street. Half of the crowd was passionately supportive of the defendants, whereas the other half was in full cry, eager to avenge the killing of their leader. It was not irrelevant

51. *Spectators*

that every morning before entering the courtroom each of us was frisked and patted down by the nervous police. The two factions were separated by the center aisle like two hostile camps. I never recognized a single spectator. My friends in the black community were invariably men and women with whom I'd worked in the civil rights movement. At that point in time, Malcolm had not yet been embraced by the wider black community. Though he was very much respected, he had been such a harsh critic of the integrated struggle that it was not surprising that my friends were never in attendance. Those in the courtroom, however, were passionate in their love or hatred for the murdered man.

Early in the trial I became aware that my presence as a white man was not welcomed by either faction. It became clear that they resented being made the subjects of my drawing pen, and that somehow they felt I was compromising them. I regretted that this was so, but continued with my reportage. When there was a recess and all the spectators would collect in steamy patches of humanity in the crowded corridor, angry glances and muttered curses were sent my way as I would make my way to the reporters' room for a break and a cigarette. But my presence soon became as familiar and unthreatening as the shiny spittoons that adorned the hall, and I became simply part of the furniture, one more spittoon.

Over the years much of the fury and passion that I witnessed at the murder trial has leached away, and I hope that those whom I infuriated by my role as a recorder of that piece of history can now see the work I did there with some objectivity.

Ironically, the drawings were never given life by the *Saturday Evening Post* because the magazine ceased publication. It was a great disappointment to me. But the entire portfolio of drawings was purchased by my brother Marvin and given to the Schomburg Collection of the New York Public Library. The art is now part of the wonderful archives of that extraordinary Harlem institution, a home to preserve a complete record of the black experience in America. It is an honor to have some of my children living there.

18

The Men's Clubs

There is an ancient Chinese curse, "May you have an interesting life." Presumably, the recipient of the curse will be subjected to all kinds of unexpected troubles and dire calamities, never finding the calm waters of a tranquil life, but will forever be the victim of the stormy torrents of raging rivers and wild winds. What I have spent sixty years as an artist discovering is that "May you have an interesting life" is not a curse. It is a simple description of what life can be as an artist engaged in his time and place. If I had wanted a tranquil and predictable life, I would never have become an illustrator, and certainly never a reportorial artist. And think of the "interesting life" that I would have missed!

It is hard to imagine a more different canvas to paint than the one I encountered soon after the convictions of the three accused came down in the Malcolm X murder case. *Esquire* magazine was going to publish a story about the men's clubs of New York to be written by an author I had long admired, George Plimpton, and commissioned me to do the drawings. What a kick! No more skulking down smoky corridors in a draughty courthouse, no more nasty looks and smothered curses, no more being just another spittoon in the "real" world. My beat would be the Upper East Side of Manhattan, Park Avenue, Madison Avenue, and Fifth Avenue. I felt more debonair at the very thought.

But when I met George Plimpton in his glorious pad overlooking the East River, I started to learn what debonair really was. I wasn't debonair. Debonair was George Plimpton. Tall, charming, civilized, humorous, and immensely warm, he was every inch a gentleman and a delightful companion. It was at the conclusion of a leisurely lunch with Plimpton that he handed me a personal card. "You may want this when you go to make your drawings at the New York Yacht Club," he said. "A wonderful trophy room. You'll love it."

After he loped down the street I glanced at the card. It was the personal card of Commodore Alfred Vanderbilt. I tucked it reverently away in my wallet. Of course, I thought, Commodore Vanderbilt. How yar.

The assignment that meandered through the next weeks was a revelatory visit to the other side of the tall glass windows where, just beyond a good sight line from the street, men of wealth, in clouds of expensive blue cigar smoke, lounged among their own kind. It was a nirvana of worn good leather, heavy drapes, marvelous hunting prints, large and heavy brandy glasses, sparkling white linen, hushed voices, and well-oiled attendants who responded with alacrity to a raised finger or a silent nod.

Over drinks beside his crackling fireplace, Plimpton counseled me about the variety of character that I would find in my research into these dens of privilege. Some of the distinction, he said, was traceable to the original charters that carried a vague background of athletic endeavor. "The Links," he noted dryly, "was formed in 1916 'to promote and conserve throughout the U.S. the best interests and true spirit of the game of golf,' whereas the Racquet and Tennis Club was created 'to encourage all manly sports among the members.' But the New York Yacht Club," he announced with a faux reverence in his voice, "is perhaps the most prominent of all those which echo an interest in *la vie sportive*."

With crisp flair he expanded on the subject. "There are many members of these clubs whose athletic activity is limited to rolling the dice out onto the backgammon tables." He leaned back in his chair and grinned, his eyes mischievous. "I think of the membership as running to a type: a large element of young executives, bankers, members on the Exchange, almost all of them golfers." He rose and replenished our drinks. "They are confident men, club bands on their straws, who lean nonchalantly against the door of a Jaguar, their backs to the polo match, and occasionally have a short word or so to say to the pretty girl with the bamboo cut—at least that's the natural habitat they'd like to find themselves in and, regretfully, of course, rarely if ever do. They have to settle for excellent seats at the hockey matches at the Garden."

I applauded. "Scott Fitzgerald could not have said it better, George."

If my journey through this socially upward Oz seems to have been seamless, I have not said enough. When I spotted the galleon-like facade of the New York Yacht Club, I bounded down Forty-fourth Street with great anticipation. A dozing attendant at the marble stairs seemed too content to be roused, so I hurried past, eager to view the legendary trophy room that Plimpton had described to me with loving detail. And it did not disappoint. It was a marvelous room where members could drink among glass-encased models of great sailing craft that had won their niches in history. I was soon in a corner with a great view of both members and models. Drawing pad comfortably in my lap, I was off and away, having the time of my life.

Very briefly. With a start, I felt myself being lifted to my feet and then farther as I clutched my pad to my chest. My toes never touched the carpet or the marble steps again as I was noiselessly swept up by the now totally awake attendant and a fellow ruffian and deposited on the side of Forty-fourth Street.

"But, wait. Wait! I've got Commodore Vanderbilt's card. I'm supposed to be in there." I fumbled in my pockets, totally forgetting it was safely ensconced in my wallet.

But it would have availed me of nothing. My glowering attendant never favored me a glance. He merely turned on his heel and headed for the entrance. "Nobody is allowed to take photographs or make pictures in the trophy room," he barked to any of the startled people on the crowded sidewalk who might be listening. He turned to his companion before they headed up the stairs. "And who the hell is Commodore Vanderbilt?"

Were the membership committees of these delightful fraternities ever eager to expand their demographic base, I would be an enthusiastic appendage. My own favorite, were I to be invited to join, would be the Knickerbocker. It was elegant, smaller than several of the others like the Union Club and the Harvard Club, and an easy stroll down Park Avenue to Grand Central Station, were I to wish to go visit my family in the country. Yes, definitely. The Knickerbocker.

The transient dream of that Oz on Park Avenue was delightful but, like all dreams, evanescent. Too soon, the gritty reality of that turbulent year's politics reasserted itself. Vietnam was a presence that seemed to suffocate ordinary civility and discourse.

Two Democratic heavyweights, Senators Eugene McCarthy and Robert Kennedy, the heir apparent of the Kennedy mantle that had been shredded with his brother's assassination, were challenging President Johnson for the party's presidential nomination. Both were demanding that the war in Asia be concluded, and that the troops be called home. Nothing less, they argued, could bring the bitterly divided country together.

Like many of my fellow liberals in town, I was totally dedicated to the idea of electing a peace candidate, and we were working to make our views felt in the state's political decision making. But all the agonizing efforts to build an alternative choice for the voters seemed to rupture and crank to a painful halt when Bobby Kennedy was shot to death on the campaign trail in California.

19

Keepers of the Flame

In our corner of Connecticut, there was a stalwart cadre of men and women who tried to be keepers of the flame when it came to national issues with moral weight. In the late 1950s we began to band together to oppose atomic bomb testing, fearful that the strontium 90 level was rising at such an alarming rate that it could poison the milk of our children. We opened a small office off Main Street where people could come and get literature discussing the nuclear threat and find a variety of opinions about America's role and responsibility in the cold war being waged with the Soviet Union. By the early sixties we had named our often embattled storefront the World Affairs Center. With other local artists, I created drawings that could assist in raising funds to sustain the center.

Sensitive to the escalating struggle for civil rights taking place in the South, our efforts were being increasingly engaged in planting support for the movement. Our little community proved to be fertile ground. The center became the channel through which a wide range of people in the region could help. Housewives and playwrights, businessmen and painters, musicians and teachers, these were the folks in our town who boarded buses at night to join the March on Washington in 1963; who, during the "long, hot summer" when civil rights workers were being lynched in Mississippi in 1964, raised more than thirty thousand dollars in bail funds and sent some of the town's lawyers, doctors, writers, artists, and students to work with the civil rights movement in Mississippi; who filled trains to go petition our government in the Moratorium on the War in Vietnam, stood vigil in rain and shine to make our community awake to the need to stand up and speak out. These were the people who had the courage to join the Memorial Day parade, a signature patriotic event in Westport, walking silently, wearing black armbands, bearing witness.

Westport was but one of innumerable pockets of moral resistance that surfaced during those trying years. How hard it was to make our voices heard. But the often lonely efforts from coast to coast did finally help crack the resistance to the idea of peace, and help move the country to a conclusion of the war. It was a time of moral testing, and many

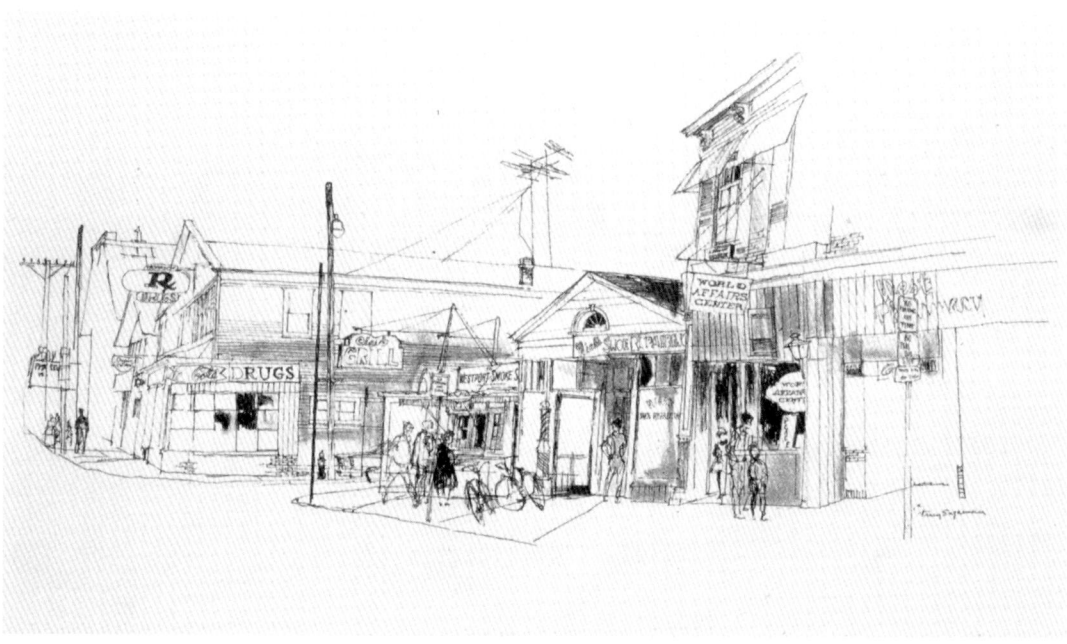

52. *The World Affairs Center*

of us came to cherish those who were always there to cover our backs and reinforce our determination.

At one of the recurrent crisis meetings at the World Affairs Center, my friend Sidney took me aside. "Interesting guy I want you to meet," he said. "He's a documentary filmmaker, and he was asking me about your work in Mississippi. Come on. He's the tall guy in the plaid shirt." As we made our way through the crowded room, the man spotted us and smiled.

"This is Sugarman," said Sidney. "And this big rube from Vermont is Bill Buckley."

"Not William F.?" I asked.

He grinned and held out his hand. "No. I usually have to throw my hat in the room and see if anybody shoots. Particularly in a room like this!" His eyes crinkled, and he laughed. "No. Not William F. I'm the real Bill Buckley." It was the beginning of a great and lasting friendship.

It was the brutal killing of Bobby Kennedy that first brought us together as a creative unit. Bill had been absorbed in the production of a corporate film, and I, too, had been busy making drawings of a manufacturing facility for a Seventh Avenue fabric house. Neither project could compete for either of us with the enormity of the drama unfolding in American politics. Meeting at the Society of Illustrators in New York for a sorrowful lunch on the day Bobby was buried, we brooded over the sad state of the world, wondering aloud how anyone could make the slightest difference in making things better.

Who, I wonder, first broached the idea of working together? Bill, who had meticulously weaned himself from a youthful overindulgence in alcohol, stuck to his Cokes

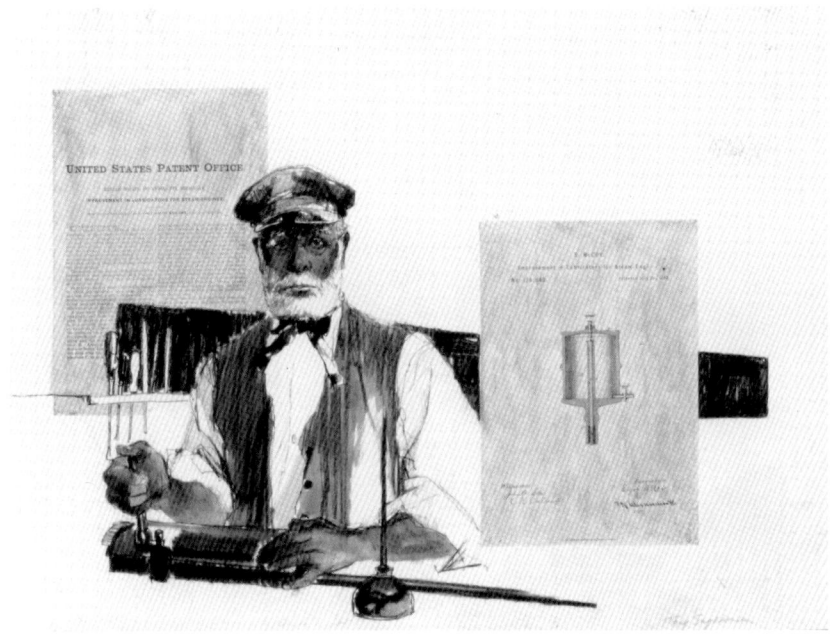

53. *Elijah McCoy, Inventor*

while I consumed several beers from the inviting bar. The odds are that it was I, therefore, who planted the idea of a collaboration. By the end of that long, exploratory lunch, it became clear to both of us that if we were to work together, the audience we needed to reach would be kids. Where else could you start to build? And the specific focus we wanted to achieve was to make films that spoke clearly and honestly about black Americans.

"Too many black kids don't even know they have a history," I lamented. "They never see themselves in the textbooks. And when they see black people at all in the movies, they're dancing or serving, or being a clown. No black cowboys, and there were lots of them. No explorers, and there were some. No scientists, no poets, no artists, no successful businessmen. And when they turn on the TV, everybody on the screen is white."

Bill looked thoughtful, tilting back in his chair, his eyes traveling slowly around the crowded and well-appointed dining room, settling finally on the lone black figure of the bartender. "It's not just black kids that we have to make the films for, Sug," he said softly. "Look around. We inhabit a society where whites don't even see black folks on their radar. If you polled this room, how many of these guys would know there used to be black cowboys or black explorers? And a lot of these fellows are the ones who are making those all-white commercials on television. And it's not necessarily out of malice—the most popular guy in the room is Frank, the bartender."

That afternoon Bill convinced me that if I could write a book like *Stranger at the Gates*, I could write documentary films. He'd show me how. But about what?

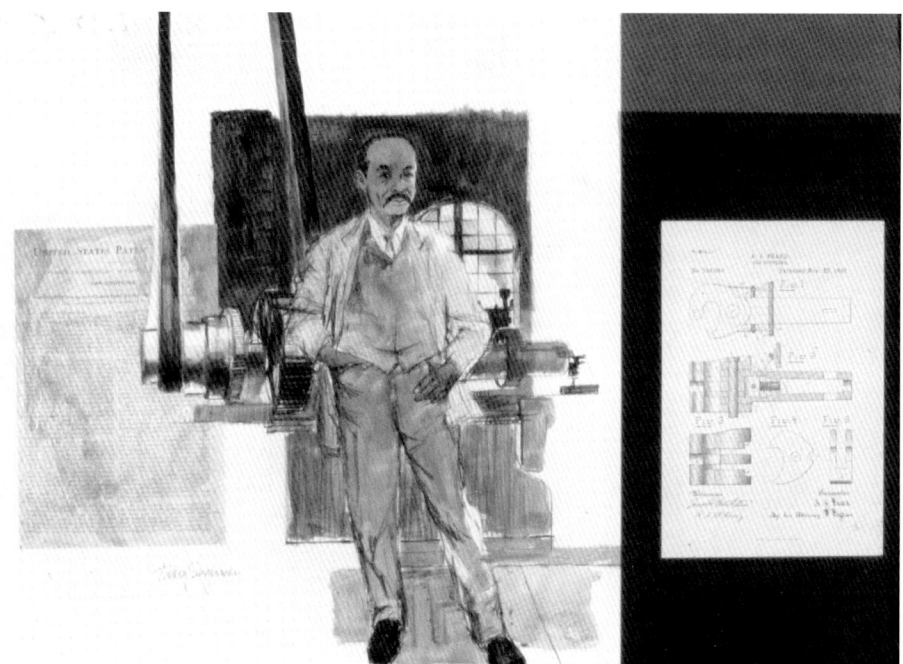

54. *Andrew Jackson Beard,*
Inventor

"Black history," I said firmly. "From what I saw in the South and from what I remember from the schools in Westport, there's nothing worth a damn about black history for kids. And there's a hell of a history to discover."

His eyes lit up. "Black history. I like it, Sug. I can make the films. You can write them, even illustrate them if we have to do that. Can we afford you?"

"I work cheap, Bill. But I don't know a hell of a lot about black history."

"You'll learn. We'll both learn."

I began to read voraciously about the true history of the Negro in America. The investigation was like peeling an exotic onion. The more I read, the more I wanted to read, and the more convinced I was that we had all been cheated. The selective Anglo perspective on who we are as a people had created a noninclusive history that had leached too many uncomfortable truths from our past, and so much of the humor, tragedy, pathos, and originality of our people of color had been papered over. Without studied scholarship, black history as it was lived could scarcely be detected in our films, our textbooks, or our public discourse.

My adventures in black history research became the subject of spirited, ongoing discussions with June, Bill, and his wife, Ellie. My exotic onion was now being shared with three inquiring minds that eagerly joined the search. A common resolve began to build about the necessity to ferret out these long-denied truths and present them honestly in documentary film form. There was a searing and remarkably American history to be told about Negro contributors to our national life. We were inventing nothing. We were simply discovering what was always there. By the end of 1969, Bill Buckley and I incorporated a fledgling documentary film company called Rediscovery Productions, Inc.

As an artist, I had long been comfortable with solitude. I had enjoyed the opportunity to delve unimpeded into my subject or assignment. That one-on-one dynamic had often proved challenging, frustrating, inspiring, or all the above. But it had been a conversation with my own work that had continued through all my adult life. Now, in 1968, at the age of forty-seven, I was a parent at the birth of Rediscovery Productions, Inc., and I was to rediscover for the first time since working with Tony Schwartz the great pleasures offered by the world of collaboration. I was redefining my role as an independent operator and learning how to appreciate and interact with other team players in a shared, common undertaking. I was constantly surprised by the special gifts each player brought to the table. It was as humbling and rewarding as it was revelatory.

We soon realized that we were launching an enterprise that would require many more skilled hands than Bill Buckley's and mine. Bill could adroitly cover directing and producing, and after some overly ambitious false starts I found that I could cover writing and art directing. But who could supervise the intricacies of putting together the disparate parts of the physical production? Ellie Buckley had previous experience during their early filmmaking days in Greenwich Village, and she soon came aboard. Ellie's innate modesty was deceptive. I soon observed that Bill's longtime partner had hidden steel that made her believe she could learn anything, and that she had the courage to plunge right in and try. Raised as a foundling, she had endured the rigors of being an outsider, and had a deep compassion for those who had been victimized in our society.

While Rediscovery was lurching toward its first production, it became clear that we needed someone who had a feel for historical research, an appreciation of the civil rights movement, and an instinct for organization. It was Bill who first suggested that June be invited to sign on. For a year, she had been pursuing her fellowship in intergroup relations at Columbia University, and was thriving in her reentry into the world of academe after twenty-five years as a successful suburban wife and mother. As the wife of one civil rights activist and the mother of another, her emotional credentials were impeccable. She was doing fieldwork with the black community in the inner city of Mount Vernon, looking optimistically toward a future of community organizing with America's minorities.

When she was approached by Bill and me to bring her talents to Rediscovery instead, she embraced the idea immediately. Perhaps more than any of us, she appreciated the need for authenticity in creating tools that could be helpful in race relations. Without a backward glance, she committed herself totally to the success of a company that had yet to make its maiden voyage.

The good personal chemistry among the four principals that became evident almost immediately was a source of wonder to all of us. Perhaps it was the urgency of our

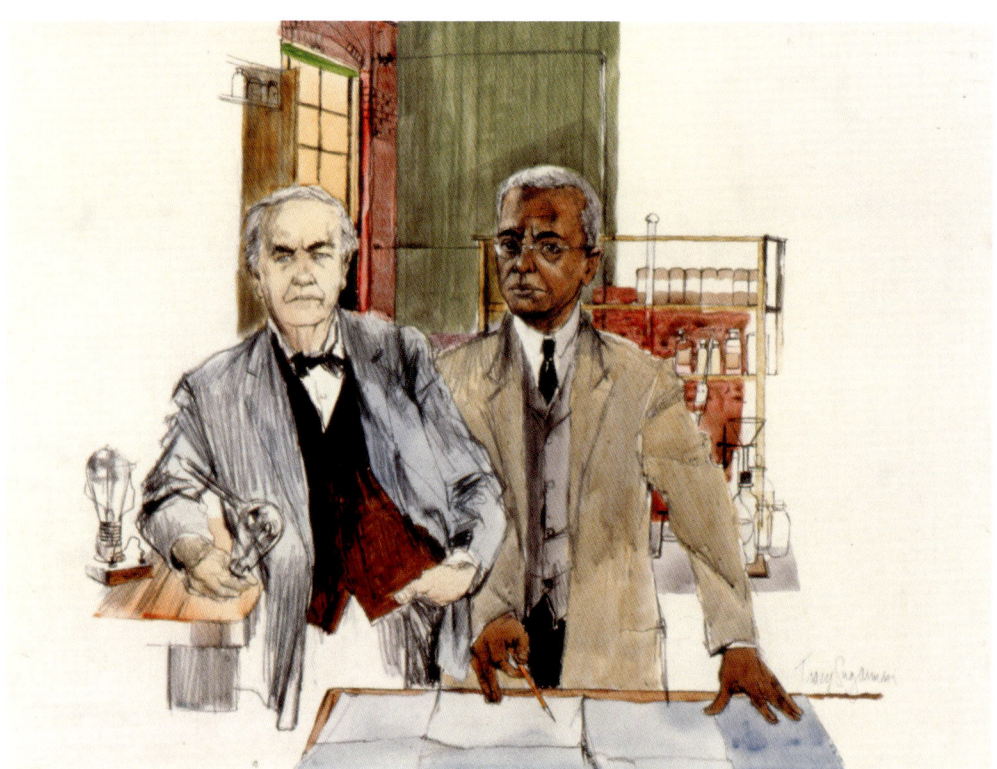

55. *Thomas Edison and*
Louis Latimer, Inventors

common goal that lubricated the wheels of our new vehicle at the beginning, but the trust and love that grew so effortlessly later kept Rediscovery moving over many financially challenging years.

From our first days of decision about starting Rediscovery, we agreed to confront and reshape the racial parochialism of our creative team. How could two white men in a white suburb make films about the black experience that would be persuasive to a black audience? And how could we make films that would be illuminating for white audiences who had rarely seen blacks as more than stereotypes? These were not simple questions, but they demanded answers that were creative.

Through an introduction from Dr. Arthur Logan, we were able to meet with John Henrik Clarke in his beautiful Harlem home, which was crammed from floor to ceiling with thousands of books about the black experience. This eminent Afro-American historian was searching and demanding in his discourse with us when we sought to involve him in the preparation of our scripts for Rediscovery.

"You must invent nothing!" he said. "Our history is fascinating and compelling enough if you simply tell the truth. The whole truth. If you agree, I can help you do that." Working with Dr. Clarke was an exhilarating and challenging experience, and he shared the satisfaction we all felt when our films won film festival awards and glowing critical reviews.

Once Dr. Clarke came aboard, Bill Buckley began a series of forays back into the film world of New York City, ferreting out, one by one, the black cameramen, soundmen, writers, lighting technicians, musicians, and actors who could complement the fine white players we had already recruited. It was a great learning experience for all of us, and our very visibility as an integrated racial team sometimes opened doors that would have remained barred.

Over the years our Rediscovery crews worked in Bedford-Stuyvesant in Brooklyn, the Mississippi Delta, and on the campus of the Naval Academy at Annapolis. We shot in white courtrooms and black churches, but we were not always welcome.

In the red clay country of Georgia, an armed, enraged plantation owner threatened our integrated crews. Our crime was that we wished to shoot an interview with a black Methodist bishop from New York whose family home had been on this plantation. Remembering the confrontations I had witnessed in Mississippi, I quietly invited the plantation owner out of earshot of the others and explained our situation. Our filming could be done quickly, and we would leave. The bishop, I explained, had traveled all the way to Georgia for this film. With a furious scowl at the bishop standing before his shabby ancestral home, the plantation owner climbed back in his pickup. "You got ten minutes," he growled, and sped off down the dirt road.

The shaken minister told us later that the plantation owner and he had been friends on the plantation when they were children. That friendship stopped when the plantation owner had gone on to the white high school. He, himself, had gone on to the black high school, to the seminary, and then on to a successful career in the Methodist Church. "I'm not sure my success in the North gave him much joy," he said drily. "I think we'd better get this done quickly."

It was only when we looked at the rushes of our filmed interview when we returned to Connecticut that we saw the jittery footage. The Methodist bishop was not the only shaken person at the scene.

For many of our documentary films, I made original drawings and paintings to be integrated with reality footage. Under Bill Buckley's direction, we devised new and innovative ways to meld the two kinds of images as we used camera movement on the art. We found that these transitional graphics could add a significant dimension to the viewer's understanding. A dissolve from an interpretive drawing to a shot of live action made both the abstraction of the drawing and the actuality of the live footage more effective for the watcher and increased his capacity to see in a richer way.

In the first several years of Rediscovery, researching and shooting films on the black experience in the United States was almost our exclusive interest. We all believed that we were creating meaningful documentaries that could deepen and broaden racial understanding, and we were heartened by the number of awards the films were getting in

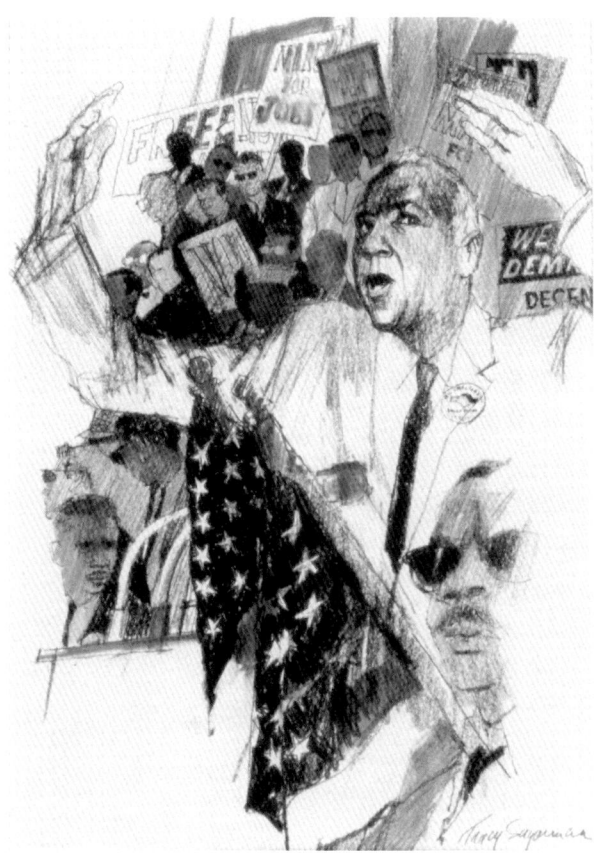

56. A. *Philip Randolph at the March on Washington*

festivals both here and in Europe. And we were enjoying the ride. It was only gradually that we came to recognize that although a small company can, indeed, do good, it is imperative that if it is to survive, it must also do well. We knew from the critics in the educational journals that Rediscovery was doing good. But we were not doing well enough to exclusively support two families. It would be necessary, we all agreed, to broaden the territory we wished to document beyond the minority landscape we had been exploring.

In the seventies, minority filmmakers began to surface, and companies such as Blackside in Boston began producing excellent films about the black experience. Their arrival made it easier for Rediscovery to focus on films and subjects of a less parochial nature. The intense, passionate commitment to dealing with the black experience that had initially motivated us to pursue film no longer had its urgency. Rediscovery would continue, but our subjects became more diverse.

Gender equality in the navy. The biography of a patron of science. A series on all aspects of fire. The running of a great medical center. The life of a university. The diverse voices of a modern city when it seeks civic harmony during racial strife. A provocative series on aging. There was no lack of fascinating subjects. But the intensity of the commitment seemed to be changing.

June was now spending more time in marketing the old films than in researching new films. When not engaged in a Rediscovery project, Bill and Ellie began to explore a whole new area of films about the victims of malpractice. Working with lawyers around the country, the venture was proving to be lucrative and challenging. It was not an area that June and I found of personal interest, but we were happy to see that the Buckleys had a successful project under way. As for me, I found myself doing more and more reportorial drawings for clients outside of the world of film.

But it was a heartbreaking call from Fannie Lou Hamer's husband, Pap Hamer, from the hospital in Mound Bayou in 1977 that made me realize I still had unfinished business in Mississippi. "Mrs. Hamer is dying, Tracy. I think if you want to see her, you ought to come down real soon."

20

Never Turn Back

During the summer of 1964 I had come to know Fannie Lou Hamer. Perhaps because our ages were much closer than the ages of the other volunteers who arrived in Ruleville, she had felt more comfortable in sharing her thoughts and concerns with me. I felt equally at ease sharing mine with her. It was the cement that bound our friendship. The time we spent working together in Mississippi in 1964 and 1965 and on her trips north at our home in Connecticut was a rich gift to me and to our life as a family. June and Fannie Lou shared a special bond of affection and mutual respect, delighting in hours of conversation. Richard and Laurie came to treasure the times we broke bread with her and heard the marvelous stories of a life that would always be an inspiring example to them of what one remarkable spirit can accomplish. To me, she was the bravest, single most formidable person I met during my years with the freedom movement, and the most memorable.

The hushed and sorrowful voice of Pap Hamer lingered in my mind as June and I hurried to Mound Bayou. The message was shocking but not really surprising. It had been months since we had last seen her, and we knew that she had been in declining health. Our friend Dr. Arthur Logan had examined her and reported that the long years of the struggle had taken a heavy toll on her strength. The courageous spirit that had sustained so many of us was in the end no match for the cancer, diabetes, and failing heart that were laying siege to her. We prayed that we would reach our dear friend in time.

For two days we were at Mrs. Hamer's bedside, sharing happy memories when the fog of her palliatives would lift, holding her hand when she would drift to frightening places. On the day we had to leave, she was propped up in bed, seemingly at peace and looking calm.

"Be careful driving up to Memphis," she said. The deep resonant voice that once could fill a cathedral was soft and weak. Her large eyes turned to me, and a smile lit the luminous, expressive face. "I know you know the way, Tracy."

We were both remembering how many times I had driven Fannie Lou Hamer—to church, to register voters, to organizing meetings, to services in Harlem, to bail-fund lectures in Connecticut. Those conversations we shared I would never forget. They revealed a mind that was always seeking a deeper understanding of history and of the human

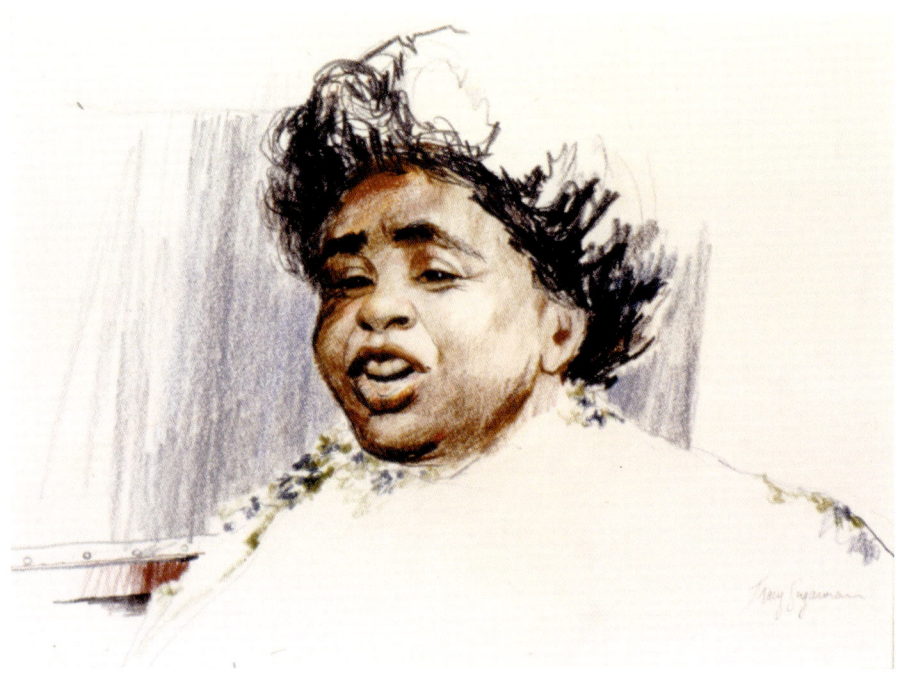

57. *Keep On Keepin' On* (Fannie Lou Hamer)

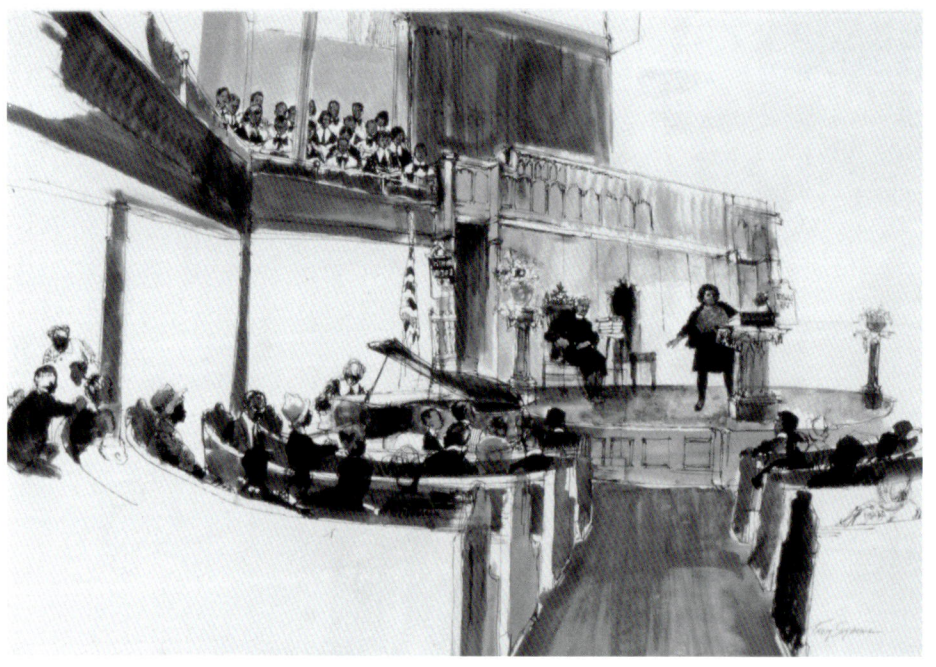

58. *Fannie Lou Hamer Preaching*

condition. And most unforgettable was the abiding love and faith that sprang from her Christianity. I knew that I would probably never again meet a truer person of faith than Mrs. Hamer.

She reached for June's hand. "And June, send my love to Dick and Laurie." They embraced, knowing it would be for the last time.

When we left the Delta, Mrs. Hamer's presence filled our silent car. We knew so well how extraordinary her life had been. This nearly untutored black woman, the seventh child of a sharecropper's family of twenty, had grown to become the voice and soul of the freedom movement. And now at sixty, much too young, that voice was about to be stilled.

On March 20, 1977, only days after we were back in Connecticut, our friend Charles McLaurin, who had been Fannie Lou Hamer's staunchest comrade, called from Indianola with the grievous news. "She's gone. Mrs. Hamer has gone."

At Mrs. Hamer's funeral, leaders from every corner of the civil rights movement, from the government in Washington, from the United Nations, and from the humblest houses in the

Delta, came to pay her final tribute in the tiny Williams Chapel in Ruleville. These men and women knew better than anyone else the precious legacy that Mrs. Hamer had left behind, and many spoke of how important it was to keep her story alive.

In Connecticut we pledged to make a documentary film that would celebrate and fittingly memorialize the woman we so loved and admired. It was a pledge we were determined to keep, but there was no way at the beginning to know it would take five years of effort to keep it.

From the very beginning, I knew in my heart how I wanted to start the film.

It is night in the Sanctified Quarter of Ruleville. There are no streetlights, and the residents of the shotgun shacks and the small, needy houses are sleeping. Before dawn the lights will start to flick on, and the men, women, and children will shuffle out to the highway for the trucks that will carry them to the fields. But now silence and darkness own the quarter.

Only the light from the pale sliver of August moon reveals the pickup truck, its headlights dark as it moves through the patterned shadows of the trees. The truck moves closer, and now one can hear the growl of the motor as it eases ominously through the quarter. In the blue moonlight there is the sudden glint of steel as it touches the barrel of the shotgun hanging behind the driver.

As the truck eases to a halt on the dirt road in front of Fannie Lou Hamer's house, the sound of the motor ceases, and one can hear again the wiry hum of the cicadas. Two men silently step from the truck and are quickly lost in the moon's shadow of the pecan tree that fronts the Hamer property.

Our camera tracks across the dim lawn and moves up the torn screen door. We cut to the watchful face of the woman on the porch.

NARRATOR: "She knew the night riders would come. When you had grown up in the Mississippi Delta, you knew it. You knew it in your bones. They came whenever a black stood up and said: 'No more.' And she had done that. So now the unmarked trucks with the shotguns were coming again. Every night during the angry times, in the early days of the movement, they had moved ominously through the quarter where Fannie Lou Hamer lived. She'd watch them from her darkened porch and sip a long, cool glass of cold water. And now the students were here, and the faceless men at the gas station knew they were here."

FANNIE LOU HAMER (Voice-over): "Although I get threats, I still feel great, knowing that for the first time in my life that I can stand up with dignity. I feel more free than some of the worst segregationists down here, because I can go to bed and sleep. But they're restless because they're studying up another scheme, and wondering what they can do next."

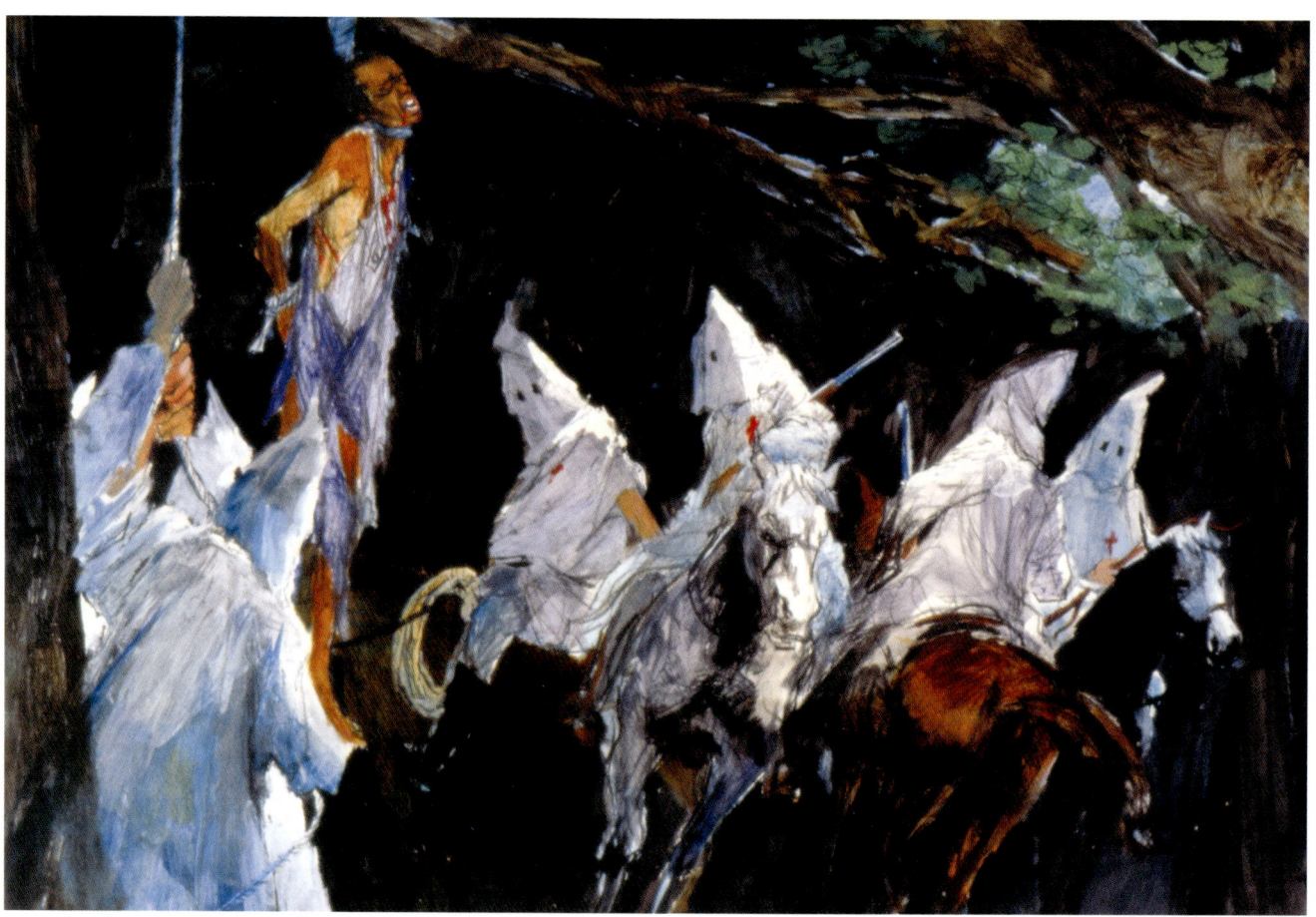

59. *Ku Klux Klan Lynching*

Mrs. Hamer's words rang in my ear, and the images of the doughty woman were all around me, eager to be given life on the page and on the screen. But to have that happen, we had to find one hundred thousand dollars to produce it. It was more money than our little company had ever raised for a project.

"Give me some time," I said to the Buckleys and June. "I'll find it." From my lips to God's ear, I thought. I hope he's listening.

We had mutually agreed that the film would be titled *Never Turn Back: The Life of Fannie Lou Hamer,* hoping it would reflect the resolution that had characterized her life. For us, *Never Turn Back* also became the touchstone of our fund-seeking mission. It was an endlessly challenging search that had to be pursued between freelance commissions to feed the family and Rediscovery deadlines that had to be met.

Early in 1978, long before any financing was in sight, we learned that black Tougaloo College and white Milsapps College in Jackson, Mississippi, were about to convene a conference of blacks and whites who had participated in the political and educational activities

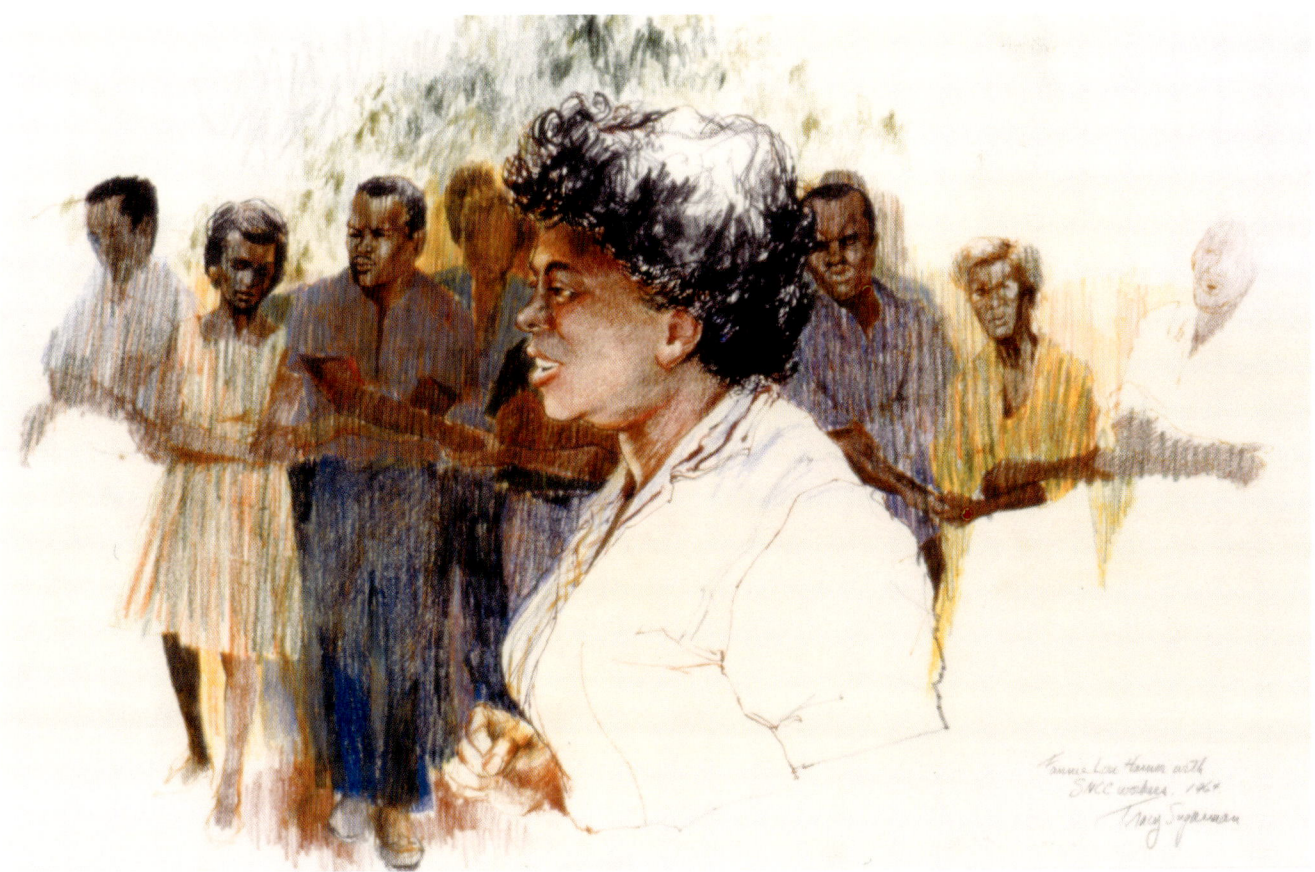

60. *Fannie Lou Hamer with Freedom Singers*

of the "long, hot summer" of 1964. The list of those who were coming was so comprehensive that we recognized that it was a once-in-a-lifetime opportunity to gather insights on Fannie Lou Hamer from those who knew her best. With one cameraman and a lighting man who could double as a soundman, June, Bill, and I breathlessly flew to Mississippi. It was a courageous bet on the future.

The footage we shot during those first frantic days was remarkable for the candor of the participants and for its inclusivity. These were the seminal men and women who had accompanied Mrs. Hamer through every battle in her long struggle, and memories were still green. By the time we returned to Connecticut we knew we had a trove of archival footage that was stunning. What we didn't have was the funding to translate what we had gleaned into a documentary film.

For the next five years, I would be setting up meetings with foundations, church organizations, black film consortiums, television networks, and potential patrons. Bill Buckley and I would screen some of the black history films we had produced, making our pitch for this significant biography of a heroine whom few outside of Mississippi knew. I can still remember how frustration and weariness would often tempt us to abandon the project, give up the endless letters, meetings, and phone calls. But Mrs. Hamer's mantra of "You got to keep on keepin' on" would sound in the night, and the next day we'd resume the search. And the next. And the next.

By early 1981, we had cobbled together enough resources to send June and me back to Mississippi to do the on-the-ground research for *Never Turn Back*. From the moment June and I arrived in the Delta, Charles McLaurin became an integral part of our Rediscovery team. My old friend who had led the two summer projects in Ruleville in the sixties, and had been the closest confidant of Fannie Lou Hamer, was an asset beyond price. His long experience in traversing the byways and back roads to avoid the vigilantes in the early years proved invaluable as he shepherded us around the Delta. Together, we started to scout the locations for the Rediscovery crews that would soon follow. But even more important was Charles's well-earned reputation for courage and integrity. McLaurin became Rediscovery's ambassador to the young and old in the black community. He was trusted, so we were trusted.

The researching, shooting, and editing of *Never Turn Back* was in every way a labor of love. When it was released as a one-hour documentary film in 1982, it was repeatedly telecast on 140 PBS stations across the nation, and was critically acclaimed. It won gold-medal honors in film festivals in the United States and in Europe, and was acquired by the Library of Congress, universities, schools, churches, and community-action groups. To our joy, we were able to see how Mrs. Hamer's legacy was being enhanced by our labors.

In our judgment, *Never Turn Back* was the high-water achievement of Rediscovery Productions. We took pride in many film projects that were to follow. But nothing would ever approach the feeling of satisfaction each one of us felt in bringing Mrs. Hamer to life for millions of Americans who might never have known her.

21

The Navy

There are places in my personal landscape that linger and somehow create a sense of circularity in my life. I pass them on my journey, and although they often disappear from view for long periods of time, when they suddenly reappear, I'm not really surprised. *I know that place. I've been there.* The U.S. Navy is one of those touchstones for me. What is always surprising when I once more close the circle is discovering that the place hasn't changed that much, but I have.

I first met the navy as a very young twenty-two year old, not knowing starboard from port, bow from stern, or whom I was to salute. And for the years I served as an officer, rising only to the rank of lieutenant (jg), I was low on the totem pole in officialdom. My essential focus was in ensuring that the enlisted men and noncommissioned officers in my charge were safe and protected. My vision was rarely directed upward. As far as most of the navy was concerned, I was one of those junior officers who flew under the radar. It was fine with me, and like most of the U.S. Naval Reserve, I was simply counting my days till I could get back and start the rest of my life. My life in the navy was spent on a variety of amphibious vessels. I never did set foot on an aircraft carrier, a battleship, a cruiser, a destroyer, or a submarine. I knew my job and performed it well enough to not embarrass myself or the men who served under me.

More than a quarter of a century after I saluted the ensign and the officer of the deck for the last time, and marched off to the life of an artist and family man, the navy hove into view again. The country was embroiled in the Vietnam War, and out on some of the navy ships in the war zone, bad blood between white sailors and black sailors was spilling into riots and racial confrontations. Admiral Elmo Zumwalt, who was in charge of the Pacific theater of operations, pronounced the racial altercations totally unacceptable and inaugurated a crash course for all hands in racial understanding. For a service that until 1956 had been completely segregated, the educational challenge was daunting. It was one thing to have a pronouncement on racial comity from the admiral, but quite another to have it implemented down through the ranks. Like many other traditional institutions, the navy tended to rigidly preserve turf and custom through the action or inaction of its middle management. Often, the decision of a chief petty officer to open a door or keep it closed could trump the orders from far above. In the meantime, all kinds of damaging relations could be creating fires. In the ocean off Vietnam, it was literally happening.

It was at this point, as the navy was reaching out for tools that could be useful in stimulating interracial discussion and understanding, that Washington discovered our Rediscovery series of films on black history and the black experience. They were rushed into service in every ship, every station, and every submarine in the Pacific area. It was the ultimate satisfaction of simultaneously doing good and doing well. The navy was delighted with our documentaries, and we were gratified that the sales served to reinvigorate the credit rating of Rediscovery Productions.

Two years later, we received a call from the Navy Department in Washington. They wished to confer with the man who had written the scripts for the black history films. I hurried to Washington and found myself in conference with navy captains and rear admirals, men whose sleeves and chests were emblazoned with records of distinguished service earned over many decades. They knew a great deal about aircraft carriers, battleships, cruisers, destroyers, and submarines. What they did not know was how to expedite the necessary educational programs that might keep racial problems on their ships and at their bases tamped down and manageable.

"You seem to have a very clear way of speaking about these difficult issues in your films," said the admiral at the head of the conference table. "The officers who run our ships and bases are good professionals. But they're ship steerers and base administrators. They're not social workers or chaplains or history teachers." He paused, and his gaze moved slowly around the table. "As these gentlemen can tell you, the directives they receive on all social issues—racism, alcoholism, drugs, rehabilitation—come in language that is so full of bureaucratic bullshit that they don't know what is expected of them or where to go if they need help. We need to correct that."

The navy captain wearing silver wings on his jacket who was sitting opposite me had been listening attentively. When the admiral paused, he spoke up, addressing his remarks directly to me. "These aren't 'feel-good' programs, Mr. Sugarman. The navy has major investments in its personnel, and it is vital that it protect those investments. It costs more than $150,000 to train one of my pilots. We can't afford to lose him to alcohol abuse or drugs. If he's got a problem, we want to fix it, and we want to get him back in the air. He deserves to know that we can get him help, and to believe that we know where to go to do it. We think that you can help us do that."

The officers around the table were quiet, probably wondering, as was I, what in the world I was equipped to do to help. I finally spoke up. "What can I do to help, admiral? You must know that I haven't been part of the navy for a very long time, and I feel out of my depth just being here."

He was tilted back in his chair, reading a file that he placed carefully on the table. He raised his head and looked over his glasses. His eyes were humorous. "It is a long time since you left," he said. "Never had any idea about a career here?"

"No, sir. I wanted to be a picture drawer, not a ship steerer."

He picked up the paper once more. "Short navy career," he mused. "You were amphibious on D-day, hydrographic officer for Utah Beach, shipped out on LSTs, and left in '45 as a lieutenant (jg)." He raised his eyes to mine. "Nothing in the dossier that I can see where you fouled up. Did you foul up, Sugarman?"

"You'd have to ask my skippers, admiral. No, sir, I don't think so."

He grinned. "I imagine your skippers are probably not ship steerers now, and I wouldn't know where to find them." He shoved the dossier aside. "You write good scripts, and I think we'll go with that. They're in language our people can understand. What we'd like from you is to have you take the mountain of literature that we've been feeding out in these important areas of human relations and translate them into directives that our ship steerers can understand. What we want is a simple 'navy handbook' that we can send to every ship and every station in the navy." He stood up, and the rest of the table rose with him. "We're done here, gentlemen."

For a full year, I worked on that assignment. It was a colossal job of first getting to understand the problems of each discipline, and then making the material accessible through conversational language. By year's end, the handbook was completed, and I returned full-time to the work of Rediscovery.

It was not long before the navy beckoned again. As before, it was the churning of American society as it dealt with issues such as racism and sexism that impelled the navy to invite Rediscovery Productions aboard. For nearly fifty years the armed forces had been at the cutting edge in pushing for a meritocracy for their men and women. Many arbitrary obstacles of race and gender had been removed, allowing performance alone to guarantee advancement. Their success had set the standard in dealing creatively with minority issues for countless institutions and corporations in American life.

In the aftermath of the war in Vietnam, the navy was challenged by the need to have talented women in its ranks reenlist. Most traditional of all the services, the navy had been loath to open some doors to advancement that had always been accessible only to men. Experienced and demonstrably competent women fliers, for example, were barred from duty in combat zones. It was a glass ceiling that cut off any chance for advancement for the women. As a consequence, many women were leaving to return to civilian life. By 1980, the navy determined that new attitudes and new gender-neutral standards had to be inculcated if it was to succeed in stemming the gender brain drain. Rediscovery's track record in these areas was well known, and we were once more summoned to Washington.

Our meetings with the navy brass were heartening. They were sensitive to the need for adult and candid discussions that were neither patronizing nor misleading. There were navy men and women who had to learn of the parameters of the problem, and to gauge the sensibilities of those who were feeling marginalized. The result of our long discussions made me proud of my old service. We were assured that spokesmen and spokeswomen from various theaters of operations would be brought to the campus at Annapolis to be interviewed and filmed by us. Rediscovery should structure the documentary in the best way it could that would convey the navy's desire for honest dialogue and resolution.

Knowing that experienced noncommissioned officers, enlisted personnel, and commissioned officers were being flown in from the four corners of the globe for our film shoot, we were very aware that the discussions should be as unfettered as possible. My function as writer, we decided, would be as an expediter, one who would, we hoped, insert into the spontaneous discussions the most provocative questions. We agreed that there would be no rigid script, and that the talk should be the relaxed bantering of a bull session among friends.

Happily, the sunny, cheerful greensward of Annapolis that Saturday morning made an inviting backdrop. By the time our participants had meandered down the sylvan alleys and past the statue of Tecumseh to our meeting place at the base of Bancroft Hall, Bill Buckley had our cameras set to roll.

I welcomed the travelers and explained that we desired them to behave informally, and to speak from the heart. "Ignore the camera," I urged, "and be yourselves. It's important to a lot of people in the navy to know how differently good, experienced personnel like you can see the same problem. Just arrange yourselves here on the steps or against the wall, and we'll get started."

Tentative and watchful at the beginning, I tried to oil the conversation and focused on a chief petty officer with ribbons that spelled out long years in the submarines. "You ready, chief, to bring women aboard your sub?"

His eyes flew open, startled by my question. "For what reason, sir? That's what we go ashore for!"

I joined the laughter and then pursued the thought. "I wasn't thinking about liberty, chief. But the navy's training a lot of women, some of them engineering majors, who can handle a lot of duties on a nuclear sub like yours. You ready for that?"

He scratched his chin and pondered the question. "I buy the idea that we gotta find more talented people in all the ranks. I even told my old lady that it was a hell of a good idea, and that really spooked her, I think. But, Jesus, not in submarines! We're away, locked together for months sometimes. That would be crazy. Even if I understood it, my old lady would go berserk!"

The laughter warmed the group, but a black woman lieutenant with wings on her uniform who had graduated from the academy spoke out when the hilarity stopped. "Subs may be a very special exception given the logistics of berthing and confinement for long periods of time. But what the hell is a logical reason for keeping people like me who have passed every flying exam and been commended for testing new aircraft restricted from doing my duty like every other flyer and kept out of harm's way? It's not only insulting; it's a Neanderthal way of thinking which is driving a lot of us out of serving the country which trained us!"

A lieutenant commander who had been flown in from a naval base on Okinawa addressed the lieutenant. "Our directives have been pretty damn clear about discrimination in race. I don't understand what justification command can possibly have to your getting an assignment. We have seven black officers in important positions at our base, and they're doing a credible job. One of them is likely to make commander in the spring."

"And how many of those black officers are women pilots or navigators flying support for our guys in 'Nam?"

The lieutenant commander frowned. "None. Our base is in a war zone, lieutenant."

"That's right. My point exactly. 'Nam is in a war zone, so I am suddenly considered too fragile to do what I've been trained to do? Not because I'm black. Not because I can't cut the mustard." Her voice grew strident. "But because I'm a woman?"

A boatswain ferried in from duty with destroyer escorts in the Caribbean joined the conversation. "But what if you got shot down over Hanoi? An American woman? What would you do? What would the navy do?"

Her eyes held his. "I'd expect you to come look for me just as you would for this lieutenant commander. Not a minute earlier and not a minute later."

Relaxed and amiable, the session went wonderfully well. My questions seemed to stimulate decided opinions, and the talk was spirited and provocative. There was a community of interest in making the navy better, but clearly there were strong views on how best to accomplish that goal. The differences were, however, not bitter, and, by the end of the session, there were new perceptions being explored by some of the most partisan speakers. Our ride back to Connecticut was a cheerful one, because we felt confident that we had the makings for an informative and effective teaching tool.

On our return to Washington with the finished documentary six weeks later, the navy brass trooped into the screening room. Before the lights were extinguished, I reported that the personnel they had flown in had performed well and that we were grateful for their honesty and candor. Bill killed the lights, and the screen revealed the Annapolis campus bathed in sunlight. As the camera moved in on the racially diverse group of navy men and women assembled at the base of Bancroft Hall, one began to hear the conversations that had been lovingly edited by Bill Buckley.

Not two minutes into the film, a voice said angrily, "Stop the film." The projector stopped its whirring, and the lights came back on. A commander had materialized in the back of the hall and was striding in fury to the front of the room. "No," he barked, "we can't show that."

I rose from my seat, absolutely stunned by this reception. "I don't understand what you just said, sir. Why can't you show that? We haven't even gotten to the discussion about promotion, or gender, or discrimination. What is objectionable? What can be objectionable in this footage?"

He glared at me. "Don't you people know anything about the navy?" His voice was incredulous. I stared at the three striper, angry at his condescension and totally at sea about what was occurring. Very deliberately, laying out each word as you would to a slow child, he said, "You have some officers standing, while there are some sailors and petty officers seated. And you have that happening here—at Annapolis! You are going to have to reshoot this whole film."

If the situation were not so horrific, I think Buckley and I would have dissolved into laughter. But it was horrific, and we did have to reshoot the film. Other personnel were flown to Washington from around the world. The shooting was done again, and the taxpayers paid for the production again. The second shooting had to be carefully arranged, and the spontaneity of the first was grievously lost.

The navy got its necessary training tool to help prepare its personnel for a dramatically new culture of racial and gender equality. But the scenario of our Annapolis adventure demonstrated yet one more time how the dead hand of tradition can throttle change. It was the last time we answered the phone when the navy called.

22

Rikers Island

The call from the *New York Times* was intriguing. The new art director of the op-ed section introduced himself and said he had an offer I couldn't refuse.

I had to laugh. "Why would I refuse?" I asked. "Outside of *PM*, it's my favorite newspaper."

"Well, for one thing, you may not get paid."

"You do have a way of engaging my attention. Is there a chance that I might get paid?"

"There's no way of knowing beforehand. Are you still there?"

"Hanging on every word. And?"

"Well, what I'm offering is the chance for you to go draw something you always wanted to draw, but never did."

"And?"

"And if we ever run an article in the op-ed section which is relevant, we would use your drawing to illustrate it. And then you'd get paid."

"You're really calling from the *New York Times*? Or are you shilling for *You Bet Your Life*?"

He chuckled. "No, this is serious. Are you interested?"

"And I choose what I want to draw? And the *Times* gets me there?"

"Right on both counts."

"Okay. I want to go to jail. I want to draw Rikers Island."

There was a pause, and then he said, "Why do you want to draw Rikers Island?"

"Because I'll likely never get to see Attica, and Rikers Island is in New York City."

The reference to Attica seemed to resonate. Much of America was still trying to estimate the impact of that riotous bloodbath, and much was being written about the state of our penology. Barely three years had passed since the Attica rebellion when thirteen hundred prisoners had held forty prison guards hostage for seven days, demanding reforms in living conditions, showers, education, and vocational training. In what was later described as the bloodiest one-day encounter between Americans since the Civil War, Governor Rockefeller ordered the National Guard and state police to retake the prison.

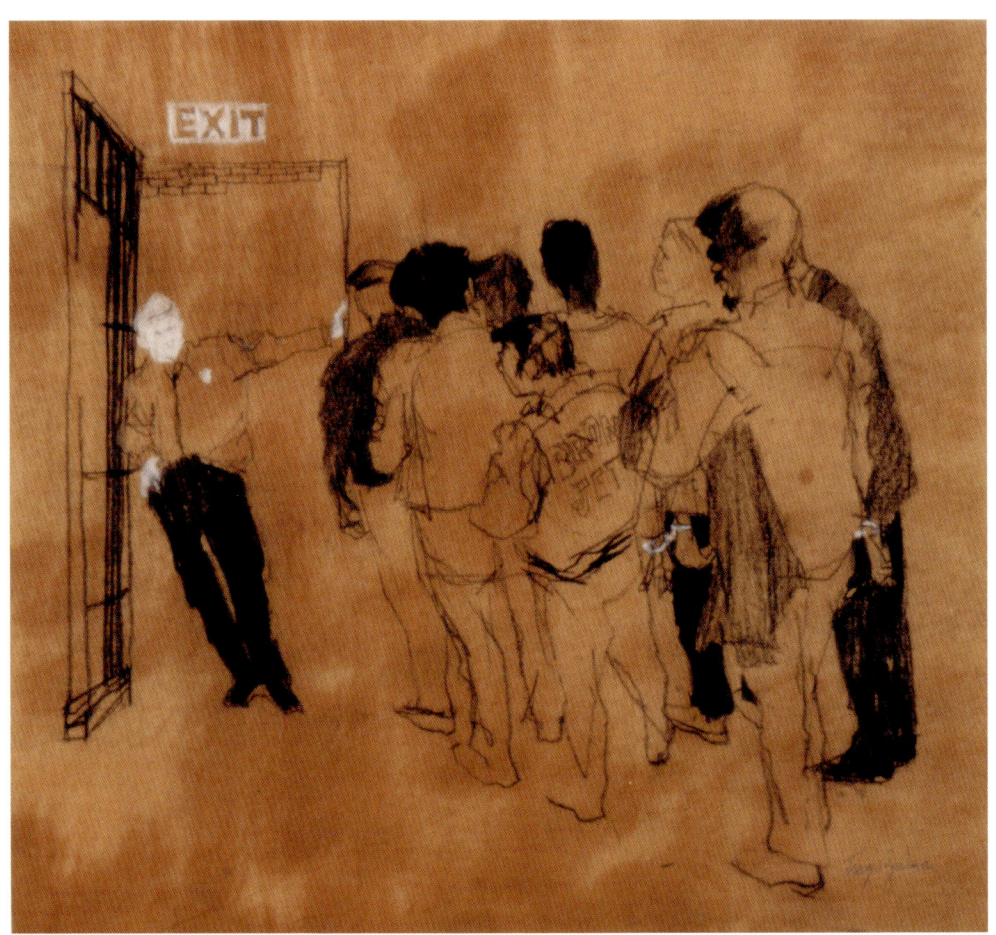

61. *New Arrivals*

The violence of the assault killed forty-three people, including ten of the hostages. The medical examiner's reports following the bloody aftermath contradicted the statements of prison officials who had contended that hostages had died from having their throats slashed by their captors. They died, rather, from the deadly fire of the assaulting party. The whole incident was so outrageous and racist in nature that as a reportorial artist, I wanted to get behind prison walls to help me understand a little of what incarceration felt like and looked like.

"Come in on Tuesday." The voice on the other end was sober, and the banter was over. "I'll have the papers for you."

If I was a suspect and had been denied bail, I could get to Rikers Island. Or if I couldn't post bail, I could get to Rikers Island. Or if I was just waiting for an empty bed in an upstate prison, I could get to Rikers Island. Otherwise, I couldn't get to Rikers Island, unless I had the papers provided by the *New York Times*. And that's how I got to Rikers Island.

It's larger than Attica, larger than Sing Sing. It is the largest jail facility in the United States, half the size of Central Park, the home to fifteen thousand prisoners, and no one I

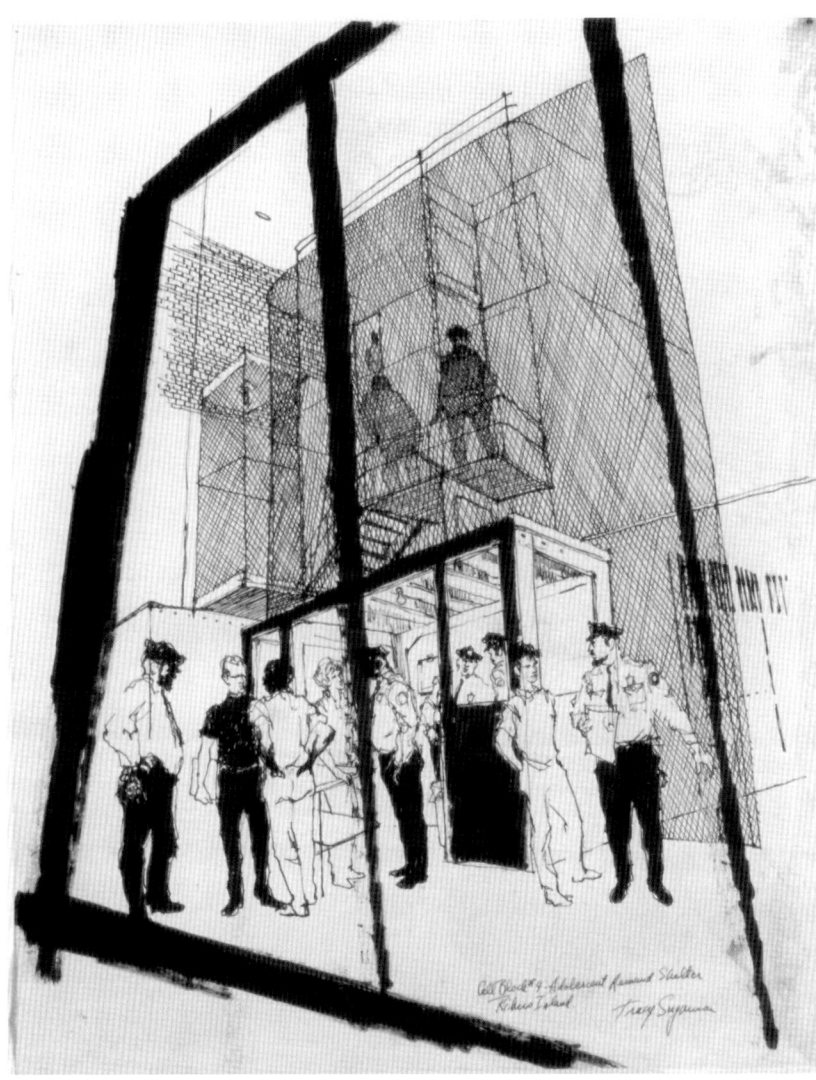

62. Adolescent Unit

had ever met had seen it. Two-thirds of the inmates are pretrial detainees who have been charged with, but not convicted of, a crime. Its essential use is to house temporary inmates or those serving one year or less. The daytime population including jailers, employees, and visitors can be as large as twenty thousand. It's on an island just off the tip of the Bronx, reached since 1966 by a forty-two hundred–foot-long bridge. Before that time, it could be approached only by ferry.

Now I was having my papers checked by a vigilant security and passed through into a world I had never really imagined.

Rikers is often called the Rock or Land of Darkness. Certainly, it was for me a week of grays, of blacks, of despair. To one who had worked in the civil rights movement to help empower black Americans who had been cheated of their full citizenship, Rikers appeared

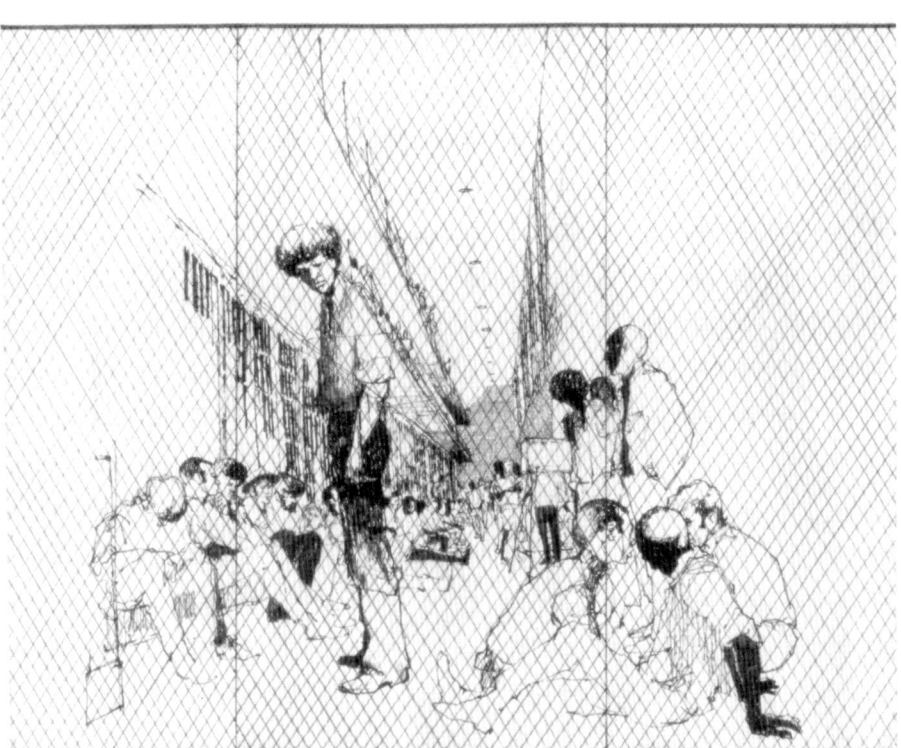

63. *Holding Pen*

to be a staggering monument to failure. Nearly all of the inmates were men of color, part of a breathtaking number of black prisoners throughout the nation that today numbers nearly one and a half million. It is a shameful number, higher than in any other Western society or even South Africa when it was totally an apartheid state. Our inability as a nation to courageously address the root causes of crime and poverty is dramatically on display here, a suffocating indictment of whom we believe ourselves to be.

Each evening as I cleared the high walls heading for home, I would open the windows wide and let the briny air off the East River wash over me, trying to shake the desolate feelings of waste and sadness I had enclosed in my sketchbooks. What an irony, I thought. On this very site in the Civil War, black regiments were trained to fight to achieve freedom. If I go to hell, I thought, it's going to be a lot like Rikers Island.

Every day a seemingly endless series of police vans would wheel into the receiving area, spilling out the new inmates who would queue up to be admitted. Most of them were young, and most of them were black or Hispanic. There was a sullen, resigned look in the droop of the shoulders, and many of the dark faces were impassive. Some gazed languidly around, nodding to themselves as they examined the buildings. *Yeah, I remember that.* A sprinkling of young whites moved forward with the group, eyes nervously checking out the scene. They stood silent, wearing the tough mask of "Don't mess with me." The corrections officers were the colors of the prisoners, but long past the litheness of the youngsters who shuffled past them. Heavy-bellied, stolid men, they were somberly watchful, speaking only to each other as they moved down the line, removing the manacles worn by the prisoners on the trip from New York.

Once in the belly of the beast I was able to be a voyeur, straining to see through wire fencing the lives lived in cages by men who were younger than my son and older than my father. And all around was the cascade of raw noise that encased the holding pens, the corridors, every corner of the metal box that was Rikers. TV sets set to blaring, endless rap and acid rock ricocheted off the walls and ceilings as the inmates sat or slouched on the bare floor of the holding pens. There was no escape from the crucifying noise. Heads inclined toward each other so conversation could be possible. And it would be that way every hour of every day, noise as implacable as the hours that hung like a shroud as men waited and waited and waited. Any attempts by the Rikers authorities to educate or rehabilitate were hardly in evidence. Moving just outside the steel-mesh screens were the heavy-footed, unarmed corrections officers, keeping vigil. And later the lights would dim, a raucous clang would ride over the rap and the rock, and the inmates would shuffle down the echoing corridor to the dining hall.

It was a week of unremitting sterility, unmarked by a single civilizing reminder of gentleness, beauty, or aspiration. If prison was meant only to dehumanize and punish the inmates, then Rikers Island was being successful. If jail time were to be used for education, rehabilitation, or recalibrating the future for those individuals who had known only failure on the mean streets, then Rikers Island was failing miserably.

On my last day a huge rip was torn in the suffocating gray envelope. Word raced through the prison: "James Brown! Today! In the rec hall. LIVE, man!" When I reached the cavernous hall, every seat was filled, and the place was pulsing. I moved swiftly to a corner of the stage and opened my sketchbook. Carefully spaced throughout the auditorium were the corrections officers, watching for any mayhem that might erupt. As I sketched the gray multitude, the guards seemed to rise like solitary islands, and my thoughts returned unwittingly to the carnage at Attica.

When the volatile, charismatic singer came tumbling out on the stage, his swift feet beating a tattoo as he seized the microphone and shouted, "YES!" the joyful roar of "YES!" from the audience transformed the ugly choreography of the prison that had reduced men to numbers. Fearful faces that had been carefully arranged as macho for survival were now alive. A group of effeminate blacks whom I had seen clutching each other for protection in the naked dormitory was now radiantly responding to the liberating music. Whites, blacks, and tans bobbed exultantly to the beat. An electric, human current moved from the antic figure on the stage to light up the hall. It was showtime! It was the man! It was JAMES BROWN!

23

The *Columbia*

It was the one day in my life when I could almost be Buck Rogers or Flash Gordon. Closer, anyway, than I had ever dreamed I might be. Buck and Flash, my heroes from childhood, were alive in my heart as I pulled into the Kennedy Space Center in the dead of night. And tomorrow I was to see the *Columbia*. I would be right there, so close I could throw a pebble and reach it!

For me, it was to be my one day in Wonderland. Summoned by NASA to help document the burgeoning space program, my assignment was to make drawings and paintings of the rollout of the space shuttle *Columbia* before its maiden voyage when it would roar its farewell to earth, tear loose from gravity, and soar into the vast blue of the Florida sky that arced over the Kennedy Space Center.

I rose before dawn, unable to sleep, with an excitement that led me out into the chill darkness that shrouded the still-sleeping space center. All I could see was an immense black shape that nearly blotted out the slowly melding grays and pinks in the East that promised a clear day. I was not alone. Shivering with me were journalists, photographers, and artists from all over the world, each eager to witness this new marvel of the space age. Murmuring quietly in the dark while sipping their coffee, they craned their heads, seeking to fathom the immensity of the building that was now emerging from the sheltering night. There was a hush as the sun tipped over the horizon, touching the very top of the vertical assembly building, then slowly drifting down across a vast facade unlike any I had ever seen, anointing it with light.

There seemed to be no point of reference in the flat terrain of South Florida to assist you in sizing up this building. It is one of the largest buildings in the entire world. Built originally for assembly of the Apollo Saturn vehicles, it was later modified to support the space shuttle operations that demand huge space. It stretches toward the sky for 525 feet, more than 200 feet taller than the Statue of Liberty! *Wilma! Buck! Dr. Huer! Its four doors on the high bays of the building are 456 feet high!*

Throughout that incredible day as I sketched and painted the extraordinary building, the *Columbia*, and the crawler-transporter that would move the colossus to the

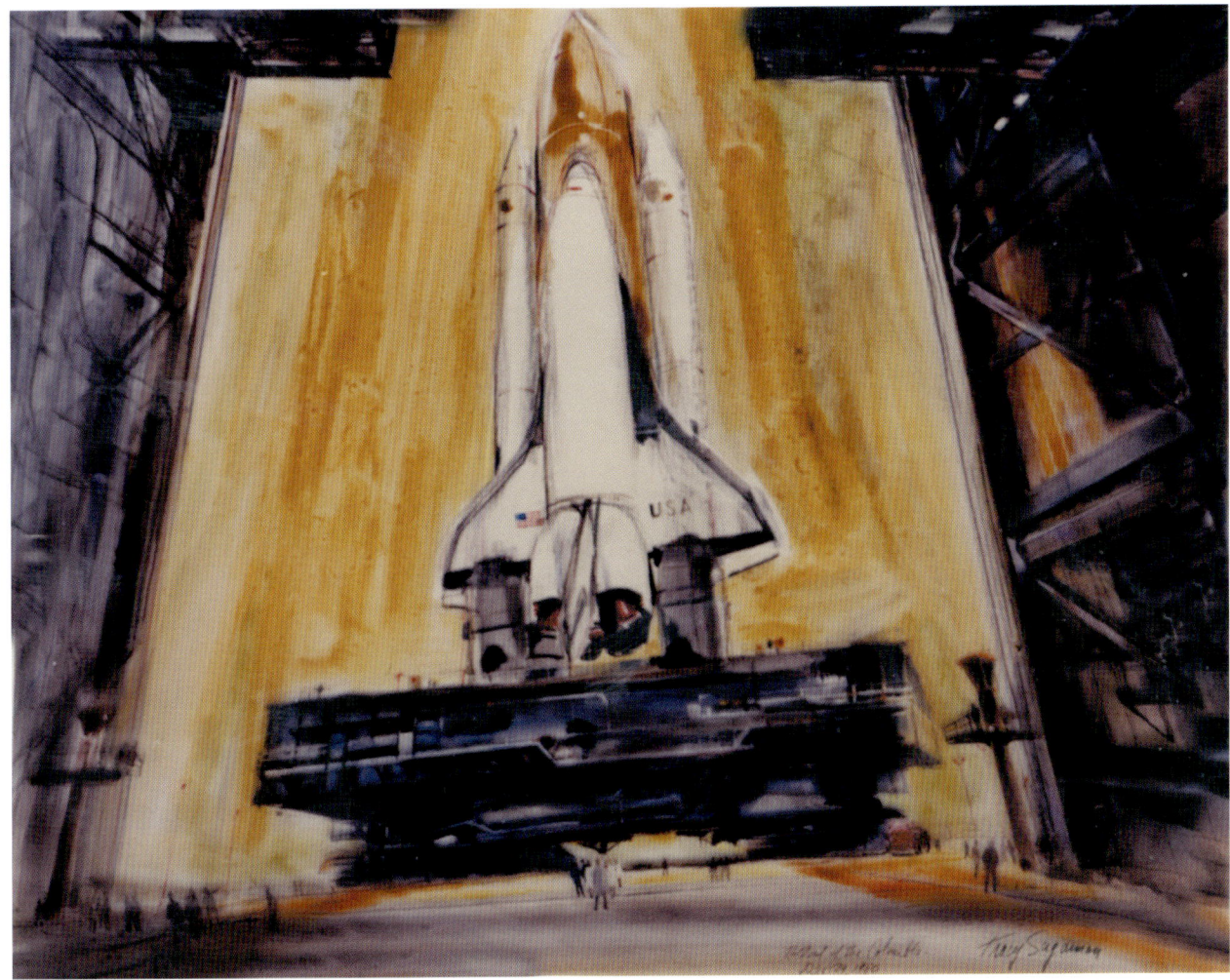

64. *The Columbia Space Shuttle*

launchpad, my mind was racing back and forth, pointing out the amazing details to my childhood friends.

Within the cavernous bays of the vertical assembly building integrated solid rocket-booster segments were hoisted onto a mobile launcher platform and mated together to form two complete solid rocket boosters. They were the explosive components that would hurl the *Columbia* from earth's grasp. The external tank that would be blown away once the launch was successful was attached to the boosters that were already in place. The stately orbiter (the *Columbia*) was then towed over from the orbiter processing facility and raised to a vertical position. It was then lowered like a giant's toy onto the mobile launcher platform and then joined to the solid rocket boosters. When the assembly was completed, the crawler-transporter entered the high bay, picked up the platform and the assembled shuttle vehicle, and started the voyage to the launchpad.

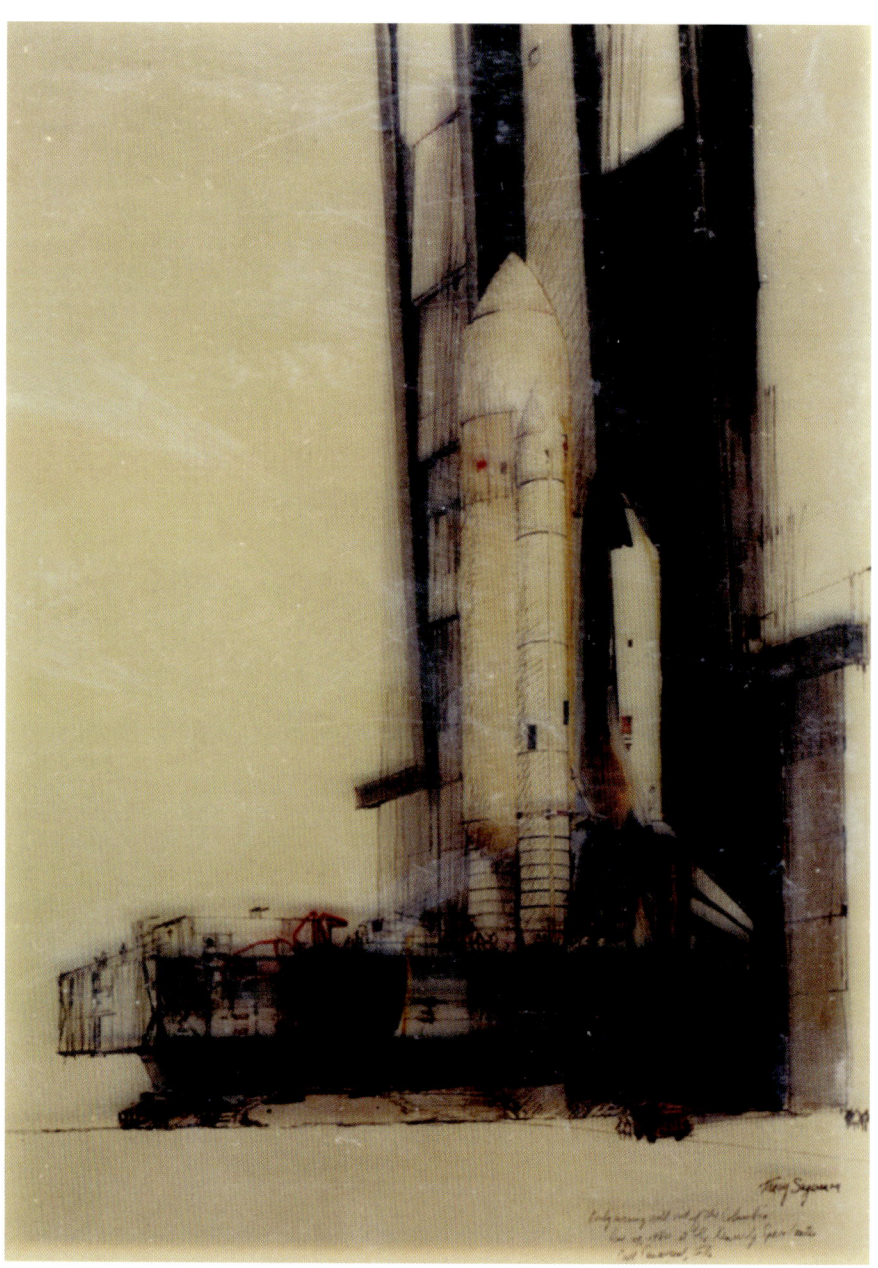

65. *Leaving the Vertical Assembly Building for the Launch*

An incongruous memory made me smile as I watched this ponderous choreography unfold. I was lying on my stomach in my parents' living room, building a rocket ship with my brother Bob's Tinkertoys. From the vantage point of the rug, my rocket appeared to be immensely tall. It tilted dangerously, supported by the heft of the old hassock from my father's easy chair. But from where I was looking, my rocket seemed almost to reach the top of the table that held our 1932 Philco radio.

But today's rocket, as it moved almost imperceptibly into the light, simply staggered my imagination. I have never felt so Lilliputian. The cave of the vertical assembly building rose high above my head. I strained to see the top, as it seemed to soar up and up, disappearing finally into darkness. One of the engineers in the predawn darkness had told me that the particular configurations of the building could produce its own weather, that there could be rain within the structure even when it was clear and sunny outside. Eyes popping now as I witnessed the rollout, I was prepared to believe him. I wedged myself into a corner near the cavernous doors, trying to capture on paper the sense of scale that was simply daunting. Filling the gigantic opening of the vertical assembly building, the Herculean vehicle appeared surreal, an immense silver tower astride the great doors. The *Columbia* itself was 122 feet long with a wingspan of 78 feet, one-half the size of a 747 airliner. Only in the imaginings of a ten year old lost in the grand voids of space in a Buck Rogers comic strip could such a creature even exist. *Buck! Wilma! Dr. Huer! Will you look at that!*

At the majestic rate of one mile per hour, the great ship moved through the cavernous space of the vertical assembly building and into the blinding light of the Florida morning. In my painting I included the bright-red fire engine, the largest fire engine I have ever seen, that crept alongside the crawler-transporter. It appears as a tiny toy, perhaps the only clue to the immensity of what I was observing.

The Mercury program and the Apollo program were now history. The glorious knights of "the right stuff" were already part of our national pride and memory. Now here was a vehicle for the future work of building celestial ladders to the stars. Here was *Columbia*, the first of the space shuttles that would make countless forays to the firmament through the end of the century and beyond.

Who could have foretold on that breathless day that the magnificent vehicle imperiously moving toward the launchpad could ever perish? Who could know that one day this man-made miracle that would be thrust toward the heavens in a Promethean burst of fire could be turned to ash as it sought to return to its earthly home?

24

Backing into the Future

The scudding clouds had shredded in the winter wind, trailing wisps over Long Island Sound. Now the February sun glanced off the water, filling my studio with an unexpected brightness. I leaned back in my chair, squinting at my watercolor, unsure what was needed in the new light. I heard June move down the corridor to my studio and stop at the door. She leaned against the doorpost. "You taking a break? Is this a good time to talk?"

I grinned at my wife, still asking after fifty years of my working at home. "Hell, yes. Come on in. I'm drowning in light."

She crossed to my chair and examined the painting on the drawing board. "Looks good," she said. "Still fresh. Don't beat it to death." She pulled up a chair and held up The New York Times. "I just read in the paper that this June will be the fiftieth anniversary of D-Day. Can you believe that?"

I stared at her. "Fiftieth anniversary? No, I can't."

"Well," she smiled, "it must be so. It says so right here in The New York Times." She stood up and looked me up and down. "You must be very old. And I must also be very old. C'est la vie . . . c'est la guerre."

I looked out at the placid expanse of the Sound. At the very edge of the horizon I could see the smudged outline of the Long Island shoreline. "Fifty years since Utah Beach? Jesus!"

June had paused at the door. "It really is. Let's see, we were barely out of college, younger than our granddaughter is right now!"

We both laughed, then I said, "Snoon, what the hell ever happened to the sketchbooks I sent you? All those drawings and watercolor pads?"

"They're in the cellar," she said. "They've been in every cellar of every house we've had. Packed with all your Navy letters. The last time we looked at them was when you came home in 1945."

I stared at her. I had no idea she had saved those long-ago sketches. I got up quickly from the board. "You really remember where the D-Day drawings are? I'd like to see them."

June laughed. "Are you that brave? You were very young, honey."

"I'm not that brave. Just curious. Fifty years?"

"Follow me," she said.

The brown paper parcels were right there in the cellar when we went to find them. Patiently waiting inside the wrapping were seventy-seven drawings and watercolors of my part of World War II, along with the letters I'd written to my new bride. Over a span of eighteen months, those fragile bits of paper had crossed the Atlantic Ocean while packs of German U-boats were ravaging the Allied shipping lanes. Upon receiving them, June would scan the drawings and letters avidly, seeking clues as to where I was and how I was.

For fifty years, the art and the three hundred letters had been out of sight and out of mind. I knew that the hundreds of letters June had sent me during the war had never made it back. Like most servicemen and women, I simply had no place to store the precious pieces from home. But June had managed to save everything I sent her. And when I tore open the brittle wrappings in 1994, I found my own Baedeker to a time when June and I were both twenty-one, and the war was the only world we knew (author's introduction to *My War: A Love Story in Letters and Drawings*).

The trip to our cellar was the very beginning of an odyssey that only a Merlin could have imagined. It was a journey that I could never have conjured for myself. And it was to lead me thousands of miles from home. What is extraordinary is that it began in Washington, D.C., in 1994, and ended in Washington, D.C., in 2003.

When I opened the long-forgotten trove of war drawings, I was overwhelmed with memories that came flooding back, unbidden. World War II had not been a part of my life for half a century. Yet here were friends I had cherished, men I had shared everything with, places and beaches and shattered towns I had known too well. I felt totally adrift, alone in a past I had thought was quite dead.

June remained silent, then gently murmured, "Fifty years, Sug. A long time, honey."

I nodded, riffling through the pages. "These sketches are so full of memories, Snoon, I have no idea how good they are. All I know is that I can remember doing every one of these, and I can remember every damn place I was when I did them."

It was not till a sculptor friend, Stanley Bleifeld, who had done a series of distinguished works for the navy, saw my collection and responded with enthusiasm that I began to see the work as work, not memory. He looked at me and shook his head. "Not many people were sitting around doing this." He smiled. "It's good, and it's very special. The navy's got to know about it."

Stanley's visit was followed by a call from the Navy Memorial in Washington. The curator, Jim Nemer, a retired commander, invited me down so the memorial could view the portfolio. When he and his colleagues had examined the work, they requested that I allow them to exhibit it as a celebration of the fiftieth anniversary of D-day. It was the moment when my lonely cellar treasure began to have a life of its own.

I decided to keep the show as personal a statement as possible. "No frames. Jim. Just mattes. And on the mattes I'll use excerpts from my letters to June that accompanied the drawings." Nemer was in happy agreement, and the show was mounted.

The exhibit that had been scheduled for a week was extended to four months. To celebrate the D-day anniversary, *The MacNeil/Lehrer Report* devoted a portion of their newscast to coverage of the show and an interview with me. My whole family was moved by the response to the event and the telecast. What was astonishing was that so many strangers could share something so personal to us. When the four months were over, I went to collect the art. Jim Nemer helped me pack up.

"What are you going to do with this collection, Tracy?"

I laughed. "Put it back in the cellar. Thanks to you, I've had more than my fifteen minutes of fame."

My friend turned serious. "You ought to think hard about it. So many people have asked us where they can see your drawings or read your letters, and I haven't been able to answer them." He cocked his head and faced me. "Maybe you should think about making a book of the art and letters."

"Hey, commander, I'm a working stiff. It's a sweet idea, but I've got deadlines and even some clients." I studied his concerned face. "I appreciate the thought, Jim. But it's time for me to move on. Hey, who knows? If I ever retire, maybe I'll do what you suggested."

Retirement was not something I ever contemplated, and the idea of a book remained only the vaguest of notions until the sudden death of June in 1998. The shocking end of a loving partnership that had lasted more than fifty-seven years was devastating. Children, grandchildren, and old friends rallied in support, but it was the saddest and most arid period of my entire life. The grief I felt was so profound and the rupture in my creative life so disorienting that the joy I had always felt in work seemed forever gone. And *gone*, itself, became a haunting word, constantly being redefined in the sterile emptiness of my life that I had so long savored and shared with June.

Old and familiar work habits slowly mapped the way back to the writing desk and the drawing board. The life I had fashioned over half a century of meetings with clients, research, sketches, and paintings gradually reasserted itself, filling the long hours in a house that was unfamiliar in its silence. What was missing was the pleasure of sharing the excitement of a new commission with my wife, discussing the approach to a project, meeting the challenge of a deadline, and doing work I could proudly display to my partner. The family joke had long been that if Dad could get past Mom's loving but tough appraisal of his work, he had no fear about encountering any art director or client. June's knowing eye, her taste, and her level of expectation for what I could accomplish had raised the bar for me since I met my first deadline in 1945. I missed that excitement, and I missed her.

In January, three months after she had left, I revisited the brown parcels of drawings and letters that had enshrined those first hard years when we were last separated. It was an emotional reunion, yet I found myself eager to reexplore the pain and joy of our first years together, and to find some guidance in how to manage separation one more time. I wanted to recover what we had learned more than fifty years in the past. What I could never have anticipated was that the excitement of that rediscovery would have an urgency I could not resist. For the next ten months, as I wrote *My War: A Love Story in Letters and Drawings*, I rode the roller coaster we had known so intimately during the war when we were very young.

When *My War* was published, I had the amazing experience of a national tour sponsored by my publisher, Random House. Over two weeks, and in ten cities across the country, I was able to meet with readers, be interviewed by the media, and discuss the origins of the book in depth. At several lectures, such as the joint assembly of English and history majors at the University of California–Los Angeles, I was able to display the war drawings, putting them in a personal context. The drawings seemed to make an almost tactile connection for many of the viewers, lending reality to a vanished time.

The interest in the letters and the drawings transcended the magic-carpet tour. In the following years, several were included in compendiums published about artists and writers in World War II. What I was totally unprepared for was the unbroken stream of letters and e-mails that have arrived since publication in 2000. That my very personal communications to my wife could touch such tender and vulnerable spots in so many strangers has been breathtaking and often moving. "Nobody ever asked me about my war, not my wife, not my kids, not my grandchildren. Let me tell you about my war." For whatever reason, so many of the letters echo to that theme, and I am humbled by their willingness to share their long-pent-up feelings with me. I have tried to answer each of my comrades who have reached out, often in pain, for a sympathetic ear. But I am saddened to see the loneliness and isolation that so many experience in their lives.

What was to be the most astounding climax of the odyssey of the brown parcels from our cellar was an event I will cherish forever. In 2003, the U.S. Library of Congress did me the great honor of acquiring all my letters, paintings, and drawings from World War II to become part of the permanent archives of the United States. Sharing that memorable event with my new wife, my children, my grandchildren, and my friends was a gift I shall always treasure. And for June it was the memorial she so well deserved.

25

Norwalk Hospital

The first time I heard there was a Norwalk Hospital, I was told that we weren't going to have our baby there. It wasn't the best introduction, but it didn't seem very important. Truth was, I didn't even know about Norwalk, Connecticut, let alone the Norwalk Hospital.

June had come back to our Bronx apartment from the obstetrician's office in Manhattan. She had shaken the snow off her coat, looking weary and chilled. The walk from the subway on icy pavements had been trying, carefully picking her way across through the slush and the Fordham Road traffic, very aware of the baby she was carrying in her seventh month.

"Dick's not back from Rockwood School yet?" She glanced at her watch and settled into a corner of the couch with a happy groan. "The school bus won't be here for another half hour. It feels like three in the morning instead of three in the afternoon." She grinned up at me. "It better be a very nice baby." She kicked off her shoes. "Is there any coffee left?"

"Be hot in a minute. So where are we having our baby when we move to the wilds of Connecticut? Did Dr. Gausse have a clue?"

"All he said was, 'You will not have your baby at the Norwalk Hospital.' He's very Texan, Sug, very Gary Cooper, very good-looking. Not overly talkative, though. So I said, 'Then where will we go?' And he said, 'Yale–New Haven.' And I said, 'But that's a half hour away, and Norwalk Hospital is five minutes away, and what if my water breaks?' And he said, 'You will not have your baby at the Norwalk Hospital.'"

So we had our baby, a very nice and beautiful baby girl, a half hour away in New Haven, and decided to call her Laurie on the way up the Post Road to the hospital. I wasn't to learn the truth about Norwalk Hospital until much later, and Dr. Gausse was dead wrong.

People who went to Yale think that everyone should have gone to Yale, and of course they're often wrong. Dr. Gausse from Gausse, Texas, went to Yale, and he could not imagine that a small community hospital could be seriously considered when one could choose Yale.

The truth that was revealed in our first years in Westport was that the whole region was being rapidly settled by excellently trained young doctors from every corner of the United States, all of whom wanted the joy of living in the suburbs, close to New York, and all of whom had "privileges" at Norwalk Hospital. And what had been a backwater facility (whose reputation had even reached Gausse, Texas) was swiftly being converted into a very good hospital. In the years ahead it was to become a medical center of distinction that would serve the needs of more than ten towns in southern Connecticut.

Our young family was blessed with good health, and we knew about Norwalk Hospital only anecdotally. Several of the young doctors who had arrived in our early years had become our friends, and their medical tales and hospital gossip were part of the conversational currency in our little town.

Watching the emergence of our local hospital into the mainstream was intriguing, and in 1979 I contacted the president and chief executive officer, Mr. Norman Brady, asking for a meeting. He was cool and pleasant on the phone, and politely inquired why I desired to meet him. I replied that I was an artist and thought I might be of service to the hospital.

"An artist?" There was the briefest of pauses. "I'd be happy to meet you. Can you come on Thursday morning about eleven? Barbara Klein, my assistant, will meet you in the lobby and bring you up."

A tall, pleasant woman came striding out from the elevator and made her way to the reception desk. She smiled and extended her hand. "Hello. You must be the artist. I'm Barbara Klein." She glanced out the front door where a succession of noisy construction trucks was jockeying for position. "Sorry about the mess outside. They've been breaking ground for the expansion. Did you find a place to park?"

I assured her that artists always find a place to park, and we made our way to the executive offices upstairs. When she tapped on the door, Norman Brady ushered us both inside.

"Welcome, Mr. Sugarman. I asked Barbara to go down and find the artist who was coming to see me." He turned and smiled at her. "Thank you, Barbara. Why don't you join us?" He guided us to two chairs and settled comfortably behind a very organized desk. Stocky, ruddy, with neatly combed white hair, Brady appeared to be a composed, authoritative, and quiet man. Most arresting was the challenging scrutiny of his bright-blue eyes.

"When I told Barbara an artist was coming to talk to me, she asked me why, and I told her I hadn't the faintest idea. The truth is, we don't get many artists up on this floor." He raised his hands, and a smile flickered across his face. "What can we do for you?"

"Thank you for making the time, Mr. Brady. But I think the question is really 'What can I do for you?' I'm a reportorial artist. I make drawings and paintings on-site. I've done it for magazines, and I've done it for corporations and a major law firm up in Hartford. I've done it in war in the navy and in peacetime with the civil rights movement in Mississippi." I looked at Barbara Klein and Norman Brady, both of whom were attentive but clearly uncertain where this conversation was leading. "It's what I do."

Brady shifted slightly in his chair and leaned forward, his elbows on his desk. His eyes narrowed but never left my face. "And what exactly brings you here?" he asked quietly.

"I'm intrigued by your hospital. As a neighbor over in Westport, I've watched you start to spread out across the top of your hill, and the little community hospital I found here twenty years ago is dwarfed by what's taking place, inside and outside. My doctor friends tell me that this is mostly good news. They say that the level of delivery of services is better than it ever was."

The president leaned back in his chair and nodded. "They're correct. But you said 'mostly good news.' That would seem to suggest that there is also news that is bad news."

"My information is only anecdotal, Mr. Brady. My only on-site observation here has been watching my daughter recover from a tonsillectomy. What I've heard from my doctor friends is that there has been a cost paid for the expansion that has to do with people, not money. The old collegiality has been stretched thin with new personnel, new labs, even new departments. A lot of the staff doesn't really know what other departments are doing, or whom those people are that they pass in the corridors and see in the cafeteria. And from my neighbors, I often hear that 'the hospital has gotten so damn big that we don't know it anymore.'"

Brady waited patiently, his brows furrowed. When I halted, he turned to Barbara. "That sound at all familiar to you?" His gaze returned to me. "Those are legitimate grievances, Mr. Sugarman, and they're not easily addressed during a time of great expansion. What is it that you think you can help with?"

"I'd like to make a reportorial folio of drawings which will mirror the kaleidoscopic life of the Norwalk Hospital over an entire year. Those sketches will reflect the drama, competence, compassion, and technical sophistication of this modern institution." I paused, embarrassed by the pompousness of my words. "That sounds a little overblown. But the truth is, I know I can do that for you."

The room was still. I glanced at Barbara Klein, who seemed to be taking notes in a leather folio.

Norman Brady said, "Please continue."

"I would be as unobtrusive as possible. I'd do the drawings 'in the wings,' and I'd want them to be spontaneous and candid. In department after department I'd show the men and women who guide Norwalk's daily life. The purpose of the reportage would be to show the community within the hospital, and the greater community it serves outside the hospital, the vital, human institution this really is."

Brady looked thoughtful and interested. "Wouldn't it be more effective to take photographs? We have a staff photographer."

"That would have to be your decision, Mr. Brady," I replied. "I can only tell you that *Fortune* magazine, the *Saturday Evening Post, Esquire* magazine, CBS Television, IBM, and the *New York Times,* all of whom have access to some of the best photographers in the world, have commissioned me to make drawings rather than use photography on certain stories. They have felt that an artist can bring a unique and very personal interpretation to particular subjects. A photograph shows everything you want and includes a lot of things you don't want. An artist can select and focus on what is particularly human or important to tell the story. I think I could do that for Norwalk Hospital."

Norman Brady rose from his desk and extended his hand. "Thank you for coming. You're really proposing that you be our Boswell. That's an interesting thing to think about." Smiling, he ushered Barbara Klein and me to the door. "We'll talk about it." He grinned. "Perhaps we'll get together after we have explored whether or not we need a Boswell."

As the door closed behind us, Barbara Klein broke into a huge smile. "The way I remember it, Boswell only had to pay attention to one doctor, Dr. Johnson. If Mr. Brady brings you aboard, you're going to have to watch out for a whole bunch of doctors, Mr. Sugarman."

"Mr. Sugarman is my father. I'm Tracy."

She laughed. "And I'm Barbara. You'll be hearing from us." As we reached the elevator, she said. "You're going to like it here, Tracy."

Within a fortnight, I was summoned to consult with Barbara, where we began a remarkable professional relationship that was to continue to grow for the next twenty years. Together, we fashioned a strategy that would introduce me to every corner of that medical world. With the skilled assistance of Doris Benton, a talented graphic designer with whom I had worked for years, we launched a bimonthly journal, *Inside Norwalk Hospital,* which was circulated to every part of the hospital and sent to friends of the hospital in the outlying towns.

Begun as a series of drawings, the project swiftly expanded to include my lay observations of what I was beholding in the labs, examining rooms, operating rooms, and the multiple services that kept the hospital fed, cleaned, and under rigorous operating readiness. A week at a time, I would make the sketches in a department, write my "Boswell" journal, and pass the material to Benton for production. Each issue included a boxed summary of the

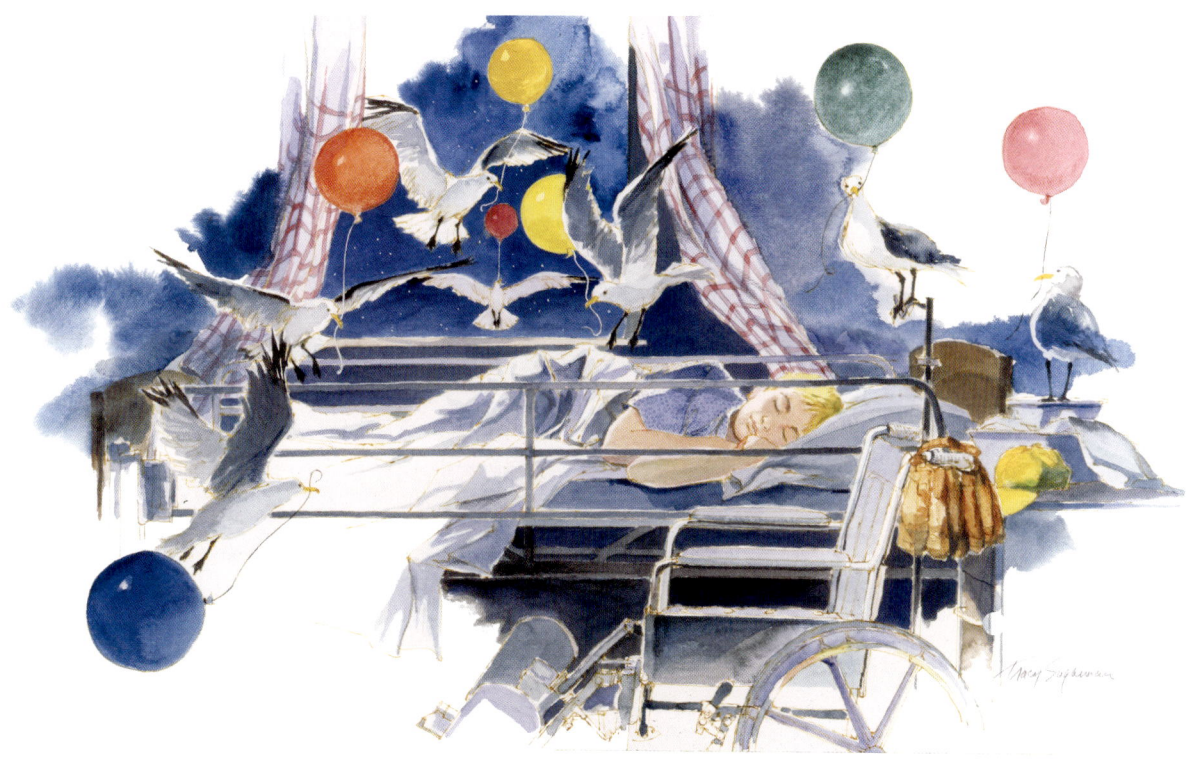

66. *The Seagulls Rescue Charley* (Norwalk Hospital mural)

hours, personnel, and costs of the department observed. *Inside Norwalk Hospital* became a familiar, valuable, and welcomed part of life there, and the drawings would reappear with pride on the walls of the various locations observed and reported upon.

Mr. Brady, who was a proud owner of our reportorial initiative, was very pleased. He was happy to have me address him as "Norman," I was "our artist," and Norwalk Hospital became the most important venue for my drawings, writing, paintings, and, finally, for my very first mural.

When asked to create a mural for the virginal walls of the new Pediatric Unit of eighteen beds, I was filled with anticipation and excitement. It was a mural opportunity that had occurred only once before in my life, a disastrous affair during my senior year at Syracuse University, as I was waiting to be called up by the U.S. Naval Reserve during World War II.

That first mural, *Syracuse Industry Goes to War,* was to be my senior project. Reflecting the grimness of the times, I painted it in black and white. It was vaguely Diego Rivera in style since I had recently visited Rockefeller Center and had viewed Rivera's mural. It had made an enormous impression on me. Until that date, I confess, I had never viewed a mural. My mural, like his, was a rather heroic picture. Mine was somewhat less critical of the capitalist system, however, and quite laudatory of the industrial weight of my

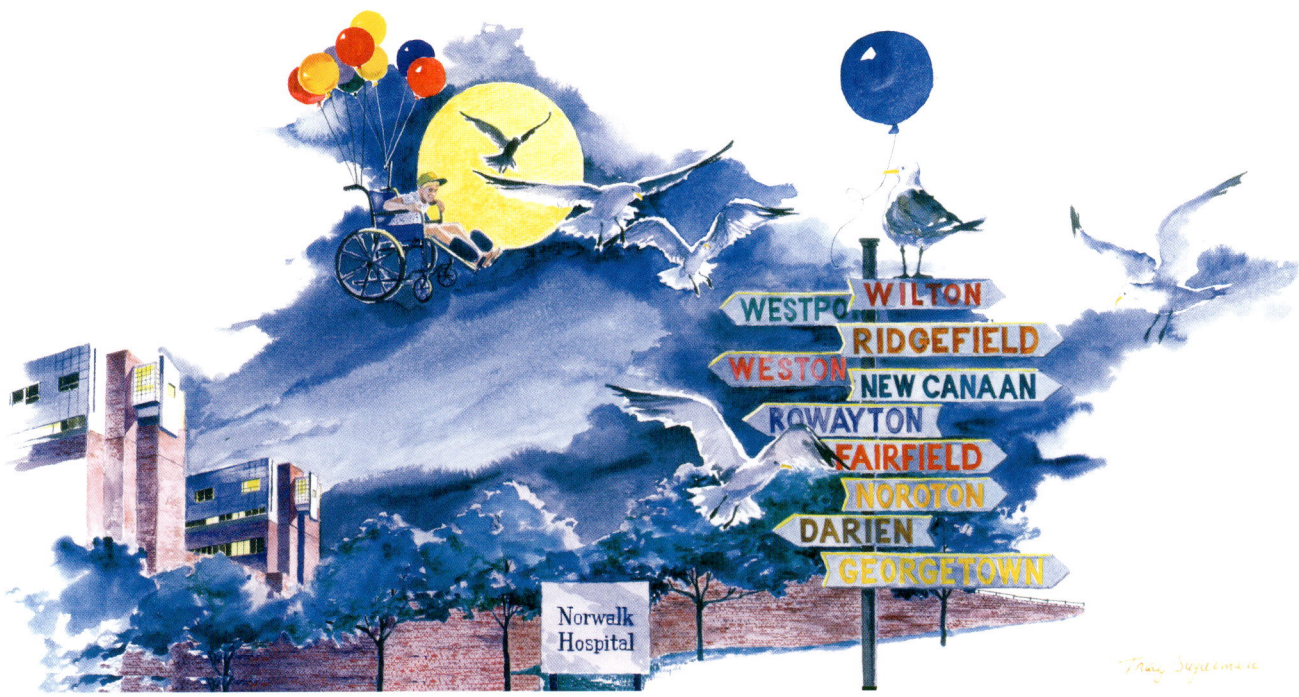

67. *Night Flight*

hometown industry. My whole illustration class had been an involuntary witness to the gestation period of my grand work that not only took up my whole senior year but also took up a hell of a lot of our limited studio space. We were all relieved when it was finally given birth.

And then a great thing happened. The owner of a downtown, second-tier women's department store bought my mural as a patriotic act "for the war effort," and he paid me the princely sum of one hundred dollars. In 1943 beer at the college hangout cost a dime. Giddy with the idea that I would never again have to work, I led my long-suffering classmates first to our campus pub, where I was a modest but generous host, and then down to the center of town to view the great work in the windows of the Jay-Cobb department store.

And it was then that I lost my innocence and recognized, as had my mentor, Rivera, that the world of commerce had agendas of its own. Lurking somewhere in the background behind a wall of girdles, bras, fur coats, dressing gowns, panties, slips, and sportswear for the woman who rode, and the woman who swam, and the woman who golfed was *Syracuse Industry Goes to War*. Marge Wende, my good buddy, squeezed my hand, and we were all silent. The fact that I survived that trauma and lived to paint my next mural, forty years later at Norwalk Hospital, is testimony to the love and loyalty of good friends.

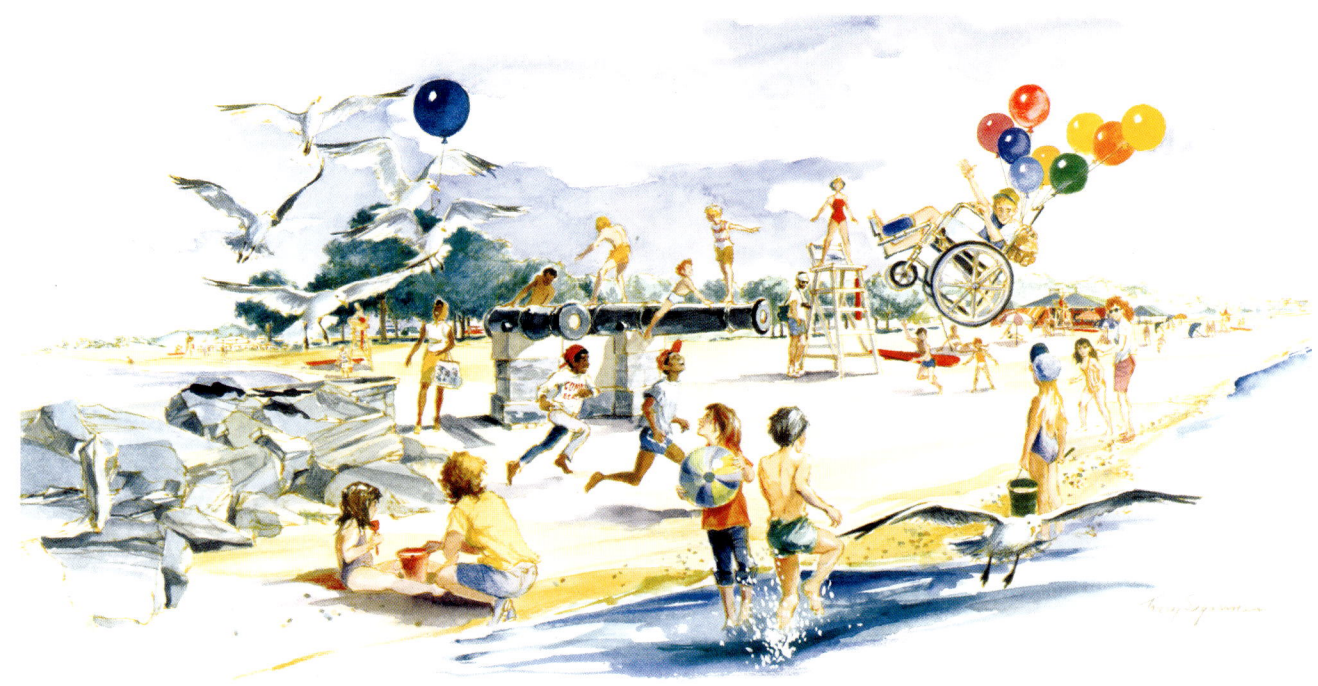

68. *Approaching the Cannons at Westport*

When I approached this new opportunity at Norwalk Hospital unfettered by Jay-Cobb's commercial restraints and bad old humiliating memories, I couldn't wait to get at the walls. But, said the vice president in charge of hospital walls, one can't paint a mural on hospital walls because hospital walls have to be repainted very often, a requirement of good hygiene. Momentarily stunned, I nevertheless resolved to find a way to paint a wall mural without the wall. And in finding it, I discovered a wonderful new digitized world that I first could explore with my trusting hospital. The result was *Sky Wheels.*

An article in the *New York Times* describing this new technique of reproduction led me to the small New York office and the warm attention of Mark Steinberg, graphics director of Big Apple Color and Graphics. Ridiculously young, bright, confident, and optimistic about the new digital world he was exploring, he counseled me that there were indeed new ways to skin the cat. Since the digital process employed no photography, he assured me, my digitized paintings would never suffer the fate of so many photographic prints that often wither into pale shades of yellow, blue, or pink. My digitized mural would remain true to its original paintings and be archival. By the time I left Manhattan to begin my end of the creative process, I felt assured that with Mark's technical magic, I could paint a wall mural without the wall. And we succeeded beyond my most extravagant imagining.

The challenge was the eighteen bedrooms being constructed for the young patients,

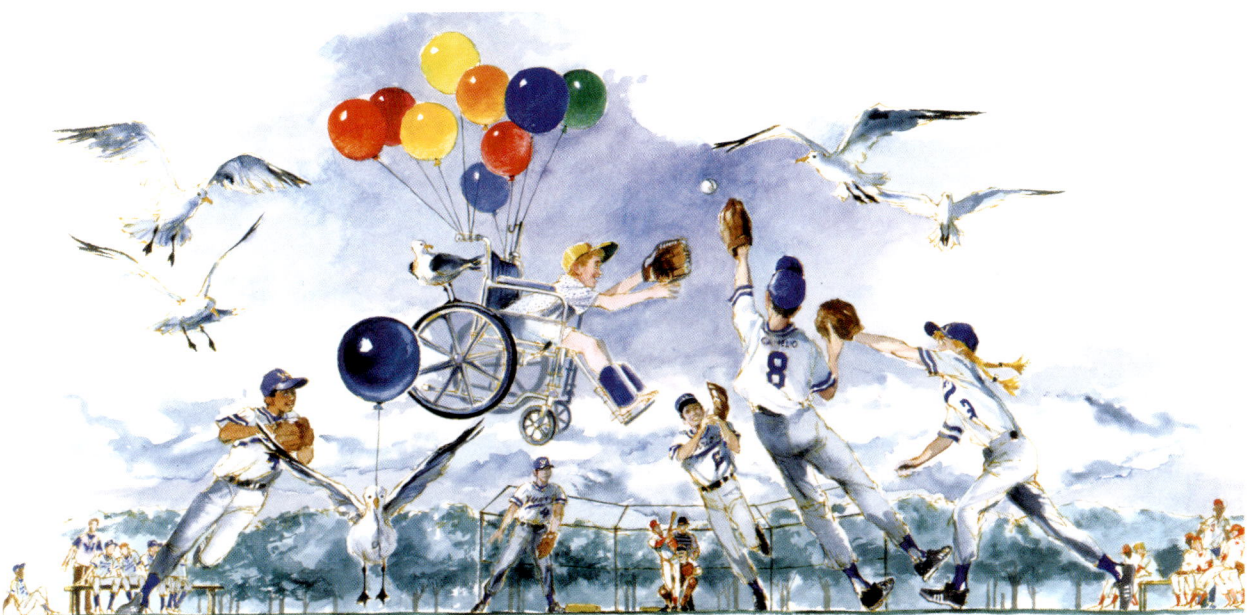

69. *Roving Shortstop in Wilton*

and the long, lonely corridors that connected them. The answer was in designing a colorful theme that could knit the parts together, establishing an environment that would be a happy one for the kids, the patients, and the nurses, as well as for the worried parents who walked the halls.

I wrote the outline for a story about Charley, a boy in a wheelchair in the Norwalk Hospital, and sketched an opening panel for a mural.

Every summer, Sandy the seagull and her seagull friends would meet in the sky high above the Norwalk Oyster Festival. They liked to watch all the exciting things down below. There were always shows for the kids, and every kind of food you could imagine! Great tall ships would anchor in the harbor, and enormous balloons, as tall as houses, would slowly be filled with hot air for the race across Long Island Sound. Sandy and her friends loved to race with them. One night, as the gulls soared over the festival, Sandy saw a tiny red balloon slip from the hand of one of the kids on the ground. She watched as it rose higher and higher, and ended up bobbing in the night sky with other balloons that had slipped from the crowds below. It was right then that Sandy had an awesome idea. "Help me catch those balloons," she called to her friends, "and follow me!" She seized a dark-blue balloon and sped away to the Norwalk Hospital high on the hill. She wanted to see her friend Charley. When the balloons borne by the seagulls are attached to Charley's wheelchair, he flies off with his seagull friends. In the adventures that occur in each of the towns that the hospital

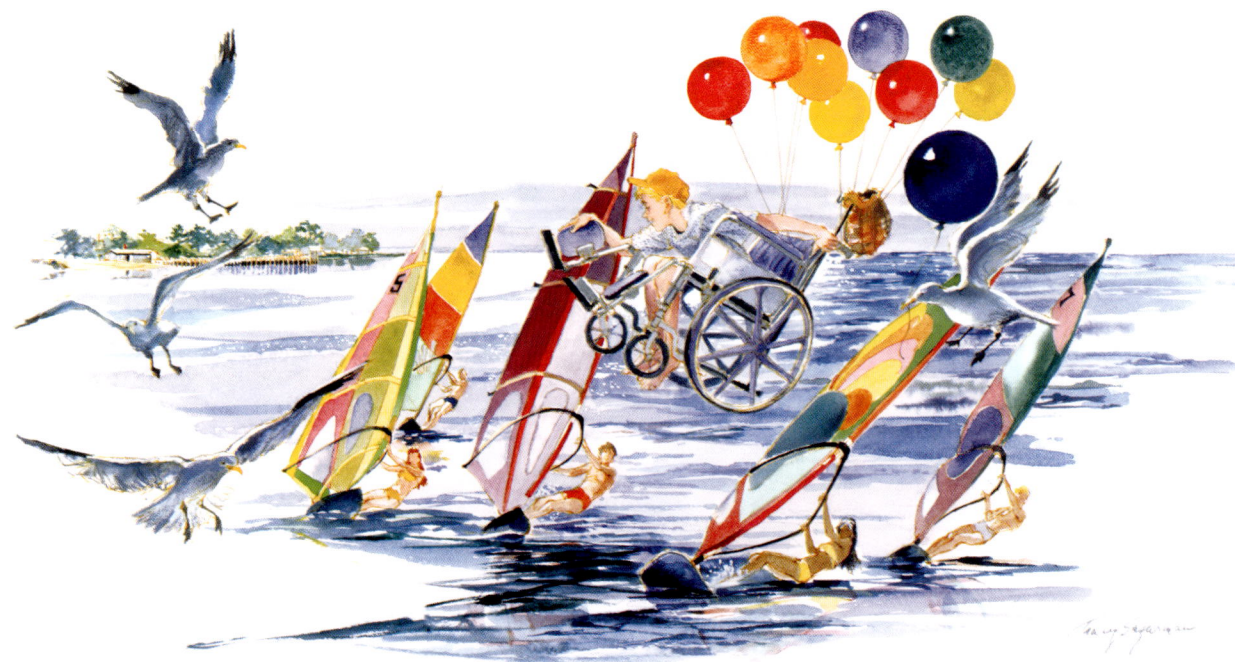

70. *Racing the Wind in Darien Harbor*

serves, he performs actively while still in his wheelchair. Charley plays baseball in Wilton, windsurfs in Darien, feeds the ducks in New Canaan, visits the beaches in Westport, goes fishing in Fairfield, does all the things that a kid might want to do if he did not have to be confined to a wheelchair.

I was only concerned that such a fantastic journey might be discouraging for the children who do not have a magic vehicle like Sky Wheels. But a meeting with the pediatric staff reassured me that the kids would delight in such a fantasy. With their imprimatur, I started to write and illustrate my story. The result was a series of eighteen small watercolors that could tell our fable, one panel in each of the bedrooms. When the paintings had been approved by the Pediatric Department, I took the watercolors to Mark Steinberg in New York.

A chrome transparency was made from each painting, and in the days that followed the color information from each chrome was fed into a computer, then programmed to deliver exact re-creations by a digital printer. Each watercolor, fourteen by twenty inches, gave birth to a digitized panel of three feet by five feet. Printed on watercolor paper, the panels were glued to backing boards, framed, and hung by hooks that allowed easy removal from the hospital walls. Accompanying each panel that now bring life, light, and color to the corridors, we placed a description of that specific adventure in Charley's story.

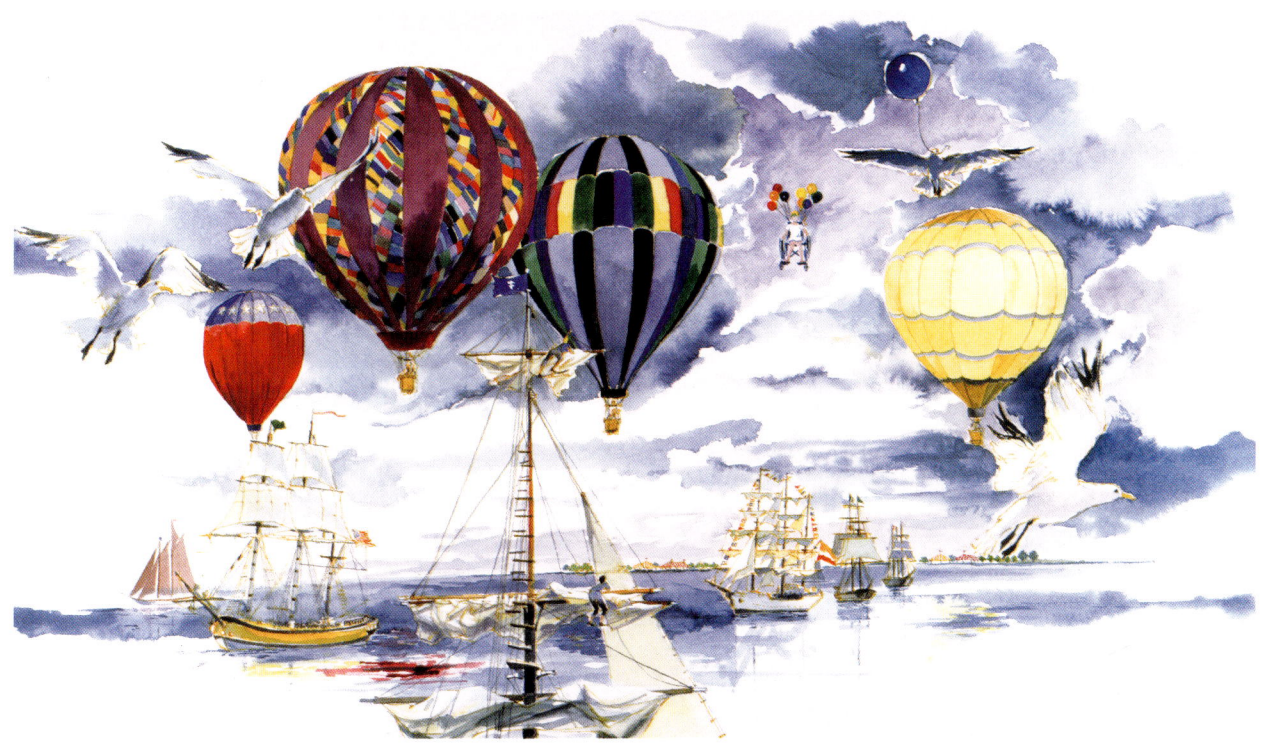

71. *Taller Than the Tallest Ships*

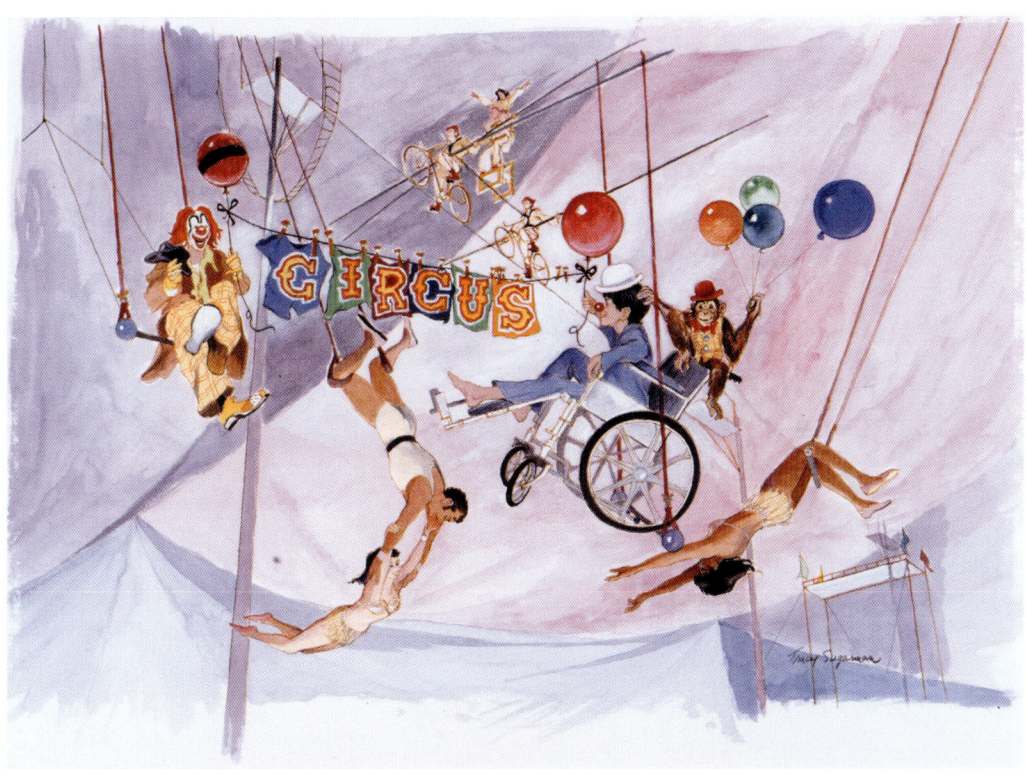

72. *Charley Flies*
in the Circus (Elmhurst
Hospital mural)

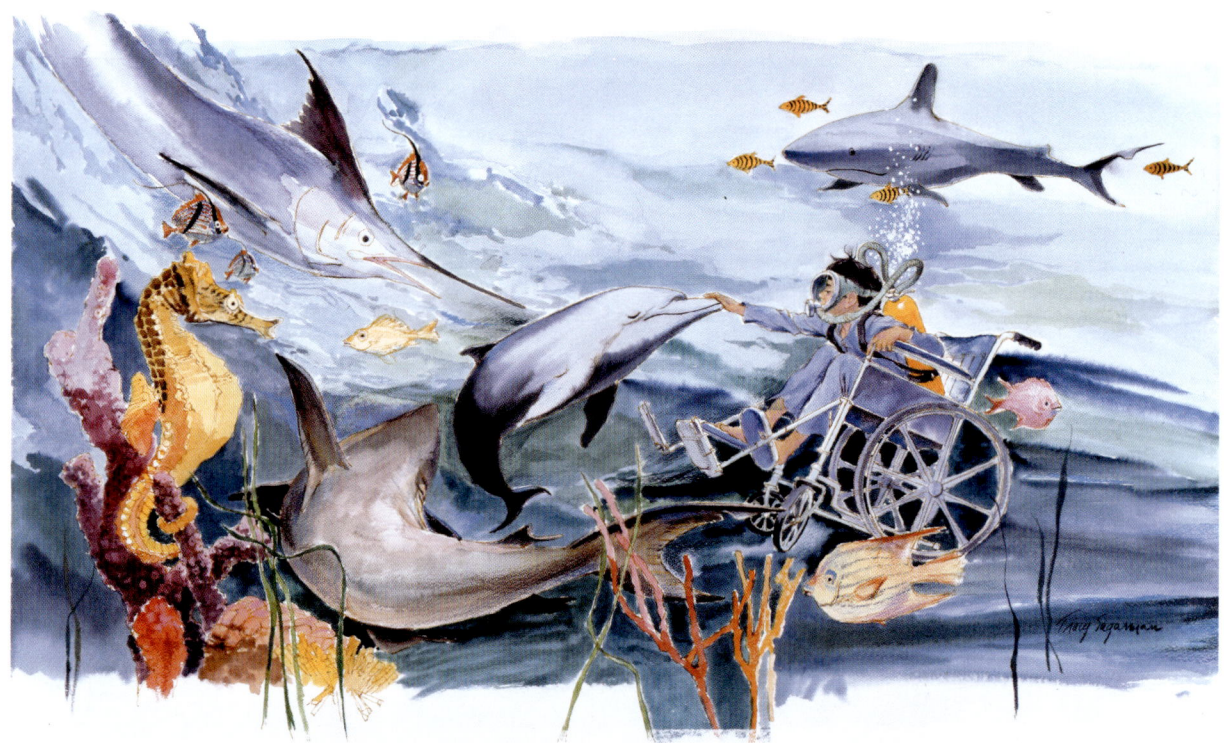

73. *Charley Explores the Ocean* (Elmhurst Hospital mural)

In the intervening years, I have revisited *Sky Wheels* many times. It has been a pleasure each time, for I've watched the faces of so many kids as they proudly display "my picture" to their visiting parents and families. When they move down the colorful corridors, reading together about Charley's awesome journey, it is a feeling of connection that an artist rarely is allowed to experience. It has been a joy to see how my words and pictures have helped to transform a place that too often has been frightening or grim for the youngsters.

I have enjoyed making other murals, each with its own story line or theme, for the Sound and Shore Hospital Pediatric Unit in New Rochelle, New York, and for the Pediatric Unit at the Elmhurst Hospital in New York City. Each hospital commission has enabled me to bring some fantasy and imaginative journeying to kids for whom hospitals are the very last place they wish to be.

The wonderful world of digitalization has made that possible. I am forever grateful for the skill of young wizards like Mark Steinberg and his talented colleagues. What would Michelangelo have given to have access to it when he contemplated the daunting geography of the Sistine Chapel ceiling?

26

Collecting Cathedrals

I often find myself remembering Martin Tafel, and I invariably smile. White haired, with merry blue eyes that challenged you from behind his glasses, he was a small dynamo of energy and enthusiasm, Moving swiftly, his voice resonating with the cadence of the Seventh Avenue garment district from which he had migrated, he radiated a love of learning that simply transported his middle-school students. At an age when most teachers were beginning to dream of retirement, Tafel left his successful garment business and threw himself into the world of teaching, a place he had long dreamed of. His science laboratory was an exciting place to observe, and the good-natured interplay between teacher and students was as special as was the fact that Tafel was the oldest teacher in the entire Westport school system. Having reached seventy, the mandatory age for retirement, Marty had sued the State of Connecticut on the grounds of age discrimination. When he won, it established the precedent that a teacher could be denied his position only for failure to perform his or her duties. Westport kids were the beneficiaries of the judicial challenge, and a beloved role model was created whose vitality contradicted the stereotypes of ageism.

It was during the filming of *Old Is*, a documentary film I had written about aging for Rediscovery Productions, that I came to know Tafel well and to recognize the singularity of his youthful enthusiasm. He appeared to be perfect for our film, a wonderful example of a person who recognizes no barriers of years. With a seemingly insatiable intellectual curiosity and a delightful sense of fun, Tafel made an indelible contribution to our documentary.

At the end of a long and demanding shoot where Bill Buckley had to choreograph several camera moves between Tafel and his students, I approached the still cheerful teacher. "You never seem to run out of gas," I said. "What's your secret, Marty?"

He laughed. "There's no secret. It's never really exhausting doing what you love to do. Besides which, I just came back from my annual trip abroad. And that sets me up for the whole year."

"Did you lie on a beach or just chase the girls who love Americans with white hair?"

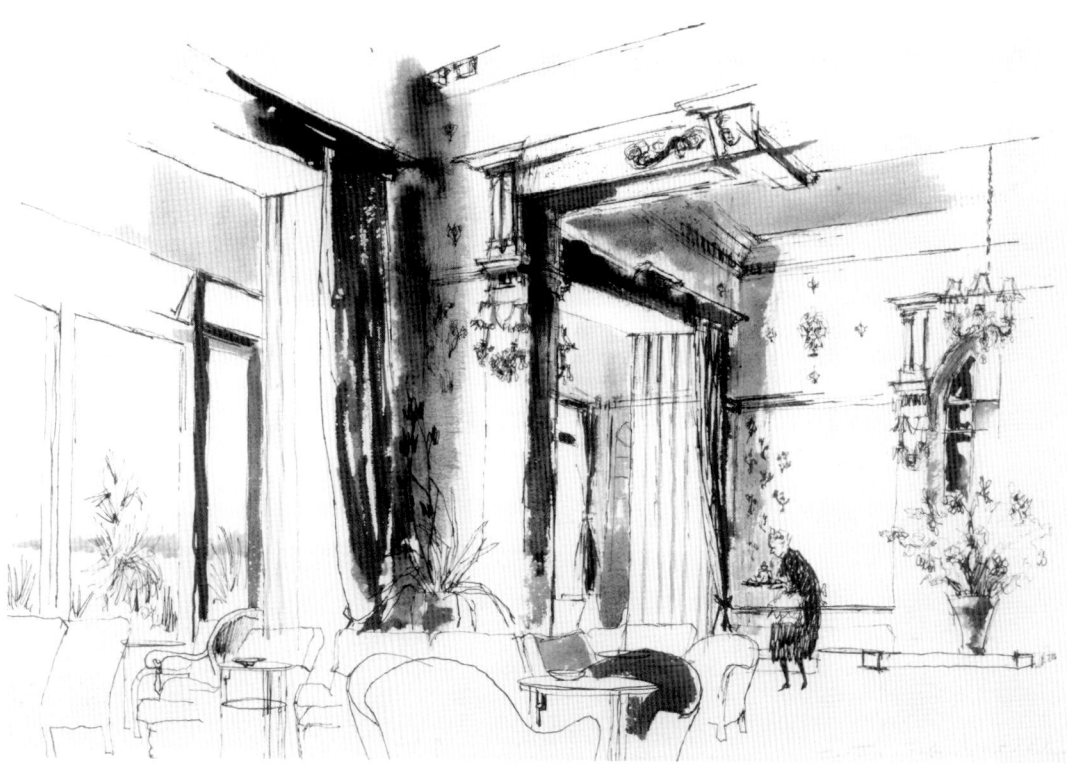

74. *Teatime in Bournemouth, England*

"Two good ideas, but I didn't have time for that. I was too busy collecting my cathedrals." He grinned at my puzzlement. "Been collecting them for years, Tracy."

"Tough getting them through customs?"

"No," he smiled, "I leave them for the next guy who's smart enough to go visit them. But I have spent the most glorious hours of my life in those cathedrals. And there are so many more I'm longing to see."

I watched the lined face of the elderly teacher relax as his eyes seemed to focus on a distant, happy place. "I think I know what you're talking about, Marty. When we took our two kids on their first trip to Europe, we went to see the cathedral at Chartres. And I still remember my ten-year-old son, standing rooted in the middle of the sanctuary, gazing up at the rose window, and asking, "You mean man made this?"

"And isn't it extraordinary," said Tafel in a hushed voice, "that he did."

Over these many years I've seen a lot of cathedrals, synagogues, mosques, and simple churches, each someone's heartfelt acknowledgment of longing and connection to something beyond his reach. Like Marty, I've left them there "for the next guy." But what I've brought back with me is the nourishment of the soul that comes from great conviction and often great art. The unique gifts of every culture are there to be savored. My walls bear testimony to the pleasures I've found in centuries-old inns and taverns and castles in Britain; in thatched cottages and horse shows in Ireland; in port towns and village squares and glo-

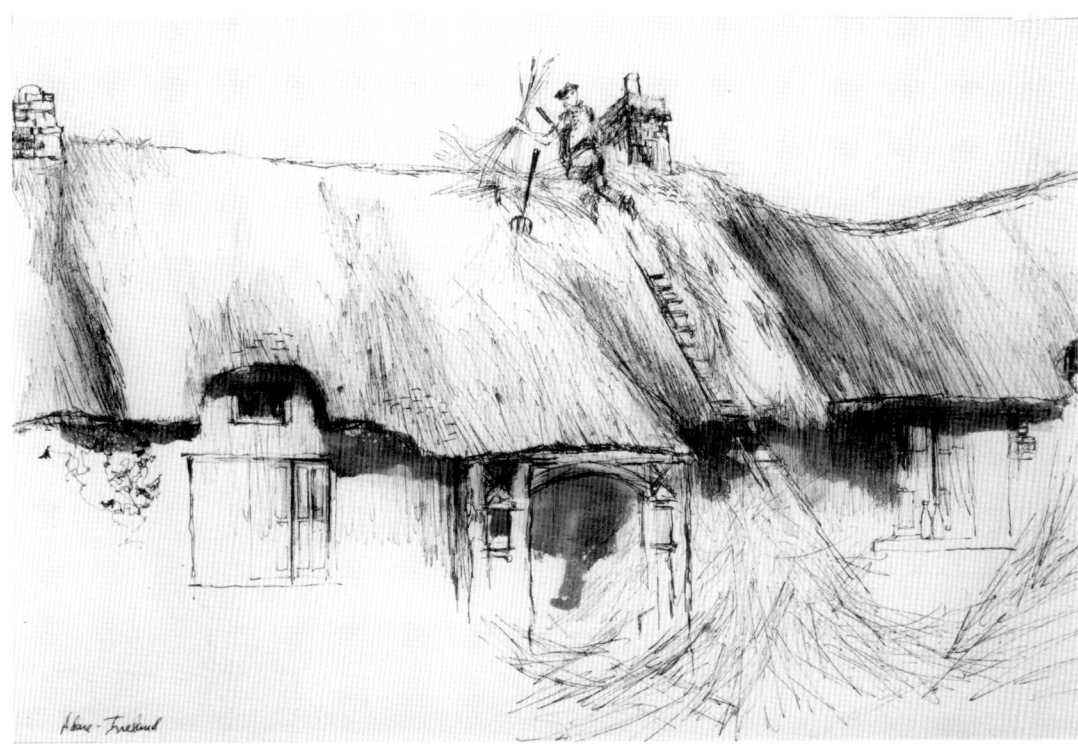

75. *Roof Repair in Adare, Ireland*

rious boulevards in France; in hill-town churches, piazzas, and glorious vistas in Italy. They ensure shared memories that bring smiles and comfort when the "now" seems less lovely than the "then." At those moments, I think of Marty Tafel.

A sweetly remembered story from my childhood is about the boy who wanders westward, out into the world, seeking to find gold. After many travails and frustrating adventures, he heads eastward for home. It is late in the afternoon, and when he scans the horizon he sees gold glistening in the distance. He hurries to capture it, and when he breathlessly arrives he finds the gold is the radiant reflection of the setting sun, and it is shining in the windows of his own home. For this reportorial artist, the fable seems appropriately apt. Reportorial assignments from magazines such as *Fortune* and *Gentlemen's Quarterly* and corporations like Western Electric, AT&T, and IBM have sent me to many of the farthest corners of my own country. Exploring and drawing the grand variety of the American heartland have been unending adventures for me, and I have come to know and cherish the disparate faces of America.

But in 1990, I began an investigation in depth of my most native turf, the towns and cities of Connecticut. Over the past dozen years I have painted more than fifty watercolors, drawing on the particular architectural treasures, churches, and monuments from more than fifteen communities that have too often been overlooked or unrecognized in these historically rich New England communities.

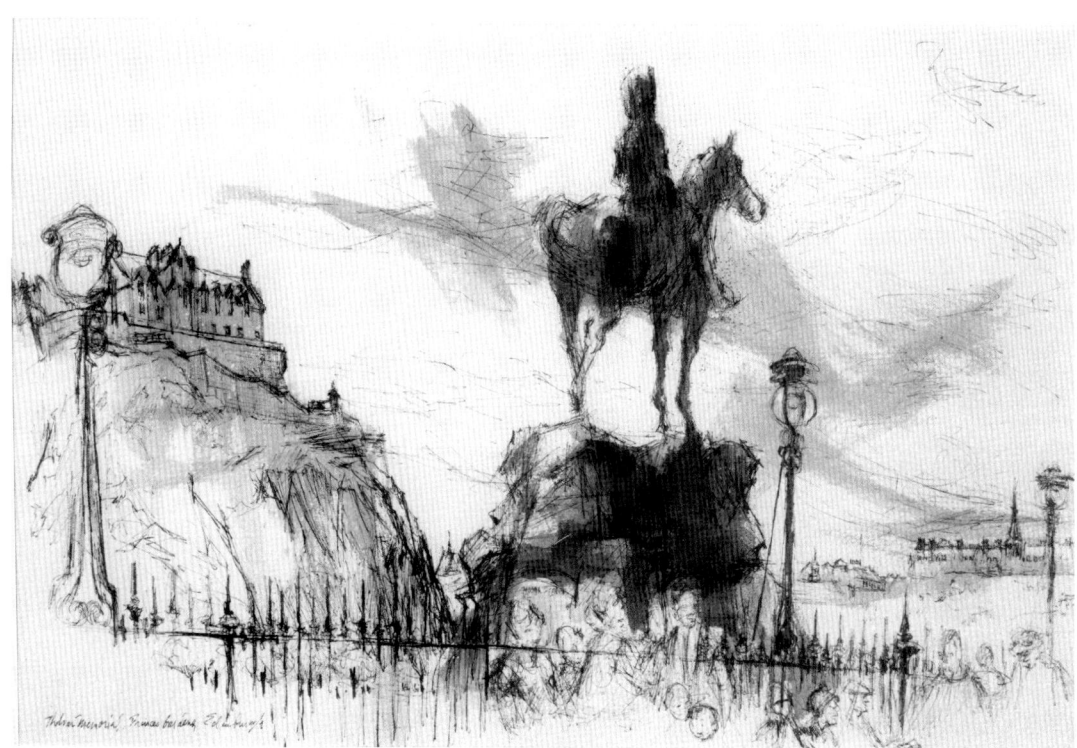

76. *The Royal Mile in Edinburgh, Scotland*

As a stranger who is exploring a new place, I come eager to see. There are no preconceptions of what might be there to choose. Nothing is commonplace to me, for unlike the local citizens, I have not walked past this corner, this statue, this town green a thousand times. What is forever gratifying to me is to have someone who has spent a lifetime in Waterbury or Norwalk or Danbury look at one of my paintings of their town and say, "How could I not have noticed this? You've made me see this for the very first time."

Some towns have reproduced folios of the paintings as posters, raising vital funds for redevelopment and community outreach. Some have used the paintings to decorate the local town hall, church social rooms, library, restaurants, and taverns. Still others have hung them in the schools, bringing a prideful attention to school students when they have seen their community celebrated by an artist, and the scenes they have loved appear on their classroom walls. Perhaps the white churches, the mossy grave sites, the green vistas, the explosive glory of the New England autumn, the striking snowscapes that are our own Currier and Ives reality serve as my own Marty Tafel cathedrals. My quest continues to be a labor of love, perhaps my own homage to the corner of America I love most dearly.

27

The Kindness of Strangers

One of the more interesting things one encounters when he is sitting somewhere in public making his art is the public itself. I first became self-consciously aware of this naked examination of what I was doing, and evaluations of how I was doing it, on my first ship, awaiting D-day in 1944. Lost in my own pondering and decision making while sketching the activities aboard ship, I looked up to see I was surrounded by several silent sailors, some of whom were under my charge as their officer. (*The guy who's looking out for me is an artist?*) It was a little unnerving at the beginning, but an experience that repeated itself so often that I learned to be comfortable with the role, and found it revelatory to me about the men who were observing my reportorial efforts. In a letter home to June in the week preceding the invasion, I wrote,

> Invariably when I sketch, a bunch of enlisted men gather around to watch. I've been delighted to find things in some of them I either never knew or had forgotten. Many of them are really and honestly interested and excited by drawing and color. Some of them sit near me and don't say a word . . . just watch. They're just curious to watch pictures being born, but they're always there. It's funny. The tough language falls away, the laughter is quieter . . . and they're just kids again. I don't really mind at all. The effect of the war on these 17 and 18 year olds makes them a jangly, discordant, and raucous gang. The veneer is pretty tough, but then you catch a glance, a word, a silence, and you remember it's only a veneer. They're just kids.

My early initiation into the navy has stood me in good stead. For reasons I can only speculate about, simply performing the act of re-creating the scene before you seems to have almost magical powers of protection. During the most confrontational crises I bore witness to in the civil rights struggle in the South, simply sitting there and drawing the scene seemed to depressurize tensions. Curiosity would often win over hostility, as armed, uptight deputies would cluster around my work. On one memorable morning when a

fearful caravan of blacks was courageously walking up the courthouse steps to try to register to vote in Indianola, an act that had often provoked a violent response by the authorities, equally frightened armed deputies were nervously patrolling the scene. As I sat in the
middle of the lawn making my drawing, the sheriff sauntered from the courthouse and
planted himself behind me. His obvious pleasure as an observer was demonstrated when
he asked me, loud enough for all to hear, if he could get a copy of the drawing. From that
moment on, the morning tension was defused, and the line of black Americans seeking
the right to vote moved unimpeded into the registrar's office.

A much more ritualized scenario that I have come to expect is when the spectator has
watched me long enough to feel comfortable with intruding with a question or comment.
"You doing that for fun?" "You get paid to do that?" "I was good in art in high school, but
I never did anything with it," or the most common one, "My cousin" (my aunt, my brother-
in-law, my nine-year-old daughter) "is a real good artist." Invariably, the comments are the
chatty stuff of friends, and I've welcomed the conversations. For a few moments, an opportunity to actually talk with an artist has been presented. The quality of what I might
be doing is never as important to them as the exotic happening of having "a real artist" on
their block.

The most hilarious such episode occurred as I was sitting in a chill December wind
near the New Haven green, desperate to finish my painting before the light faded or I froze
to death. I was alone on the deserted green but for a vagrant who, perhaps, had no warm
place to go. Silently, he hovered over my shoulder for a long while as I worked. But then he
started to trot over to the church, examine it, and trot back. He would regain his position
behind my shoulder, panting, as he once more would examine my picture. Darkness was
creeping in, but I became fascinated by this demented choreography of my uninvited companion, but daring not to laugh for fear of offending him. His looking, trotting, examining,
panting, looking, trotting, examining, panting went on until, with a chilled hand and a
frozen jaw from suppressed laughter, I started to pack up my painting.

The man stared at me and then asked, "Are you painting that church?"

In the dusk, a light snow began to fall, and I looked at my companion of the afternoon,
hunched against the cold. "I thought so," I said.

That silent or halting dialogue between the artist and his audience has been one
of the most heartening and revealing aspects of my reportorial life. Invariably, people
have been kind, and I cannot ever recall derogatory words or behavior by people who
have witnessed me working. On the contrary, I have often been the recipient of great
generosity, particularly from those individuals whom I would have thought had the least
to share. I gratefully recall the Hispanic family in Laredo, Texas, who left their pathetic
shanty when they observed me making drawings in the brutal midday sun, and hurried

out to relieve my parched throat with fresh fruit and cold drinks. It was the kind of act of spontaneous humanity that was often repeated when I was working with poor whites in the abandoned coal towns of Appalachia and with long-exploited and -abused blacks in the Mississippi Delta. A life lived with people is humbling. And often it is beautiful.

28

The Music I See

I wish I had drawn the grand upright wind-up Victrola in our spare room in Syracuse. Its mahogany presence from my earliest memories had lorded over the jumbles of Lincoln Logs and Lionel train tracks that my two brothers and I never seemed to gather up when we were done. But one day when I was out of the house, I returned to find that our suddenly widowed grandmother, Sarah, had taken over the spare room, and our play area was no more. Afterward, the Victrola, my wonderful friend on dismal snowy afternoons, disappeared as well, and I haven't a photo or even a sketch of it. But I'll bet I could draw it for you. I wonder whatever happened to those Red Seal and Black Seal Victrola records of Flagstaff, Galli-Curcci, Caruso, and Lily Pons that first introduced me to opera, or the scratchy 78s of "The Student Prince," "Roberta," and "Show Boat" that made my parents tear up with happy memories, and made me believe that musical theater was something wonderful I should know.

My mother could play the piano well enough to lead the singing around the piano on special occasions. She was the only one in the family who could knowledgeably open any of the yellow sheaves of Schirmer that filled the piano seat. My father couldn't read music like my mother but was nevertheless a master of improvisation. Smiling, his usual cigar hunkered down in the corner of his mouth, blue smoke hovering over the piano, he would play with the chords, creating facsimiles of any tune that we challenged him with.

Looking back, I think of those times as watching my father sketch. It pleases me to think that's so because nowhere in my family history is there evidence that any other artist ever bore our name. My brothers and I were never graced with any musical gifts. Our talents were oral, literary, or graphic. (Marvin could sell ice cubes to the Eskimos, Robert could sculpt and write, and I made a living as an artist.) Yet music has continued to touch my life in numerous ways through my art.

It is not accidental that I have drawn jazz musicians such as Louie Armstrong and Dizzy Gillespie at their recording sessions in New York, the fine Boston Symphony Orchestra at its Tanglewood Festival rehearsals, concert divas like the great Jessye Norman, and world-renowned conductors such as Leonard Bernstein, Seiji Ozawa, and Leonard

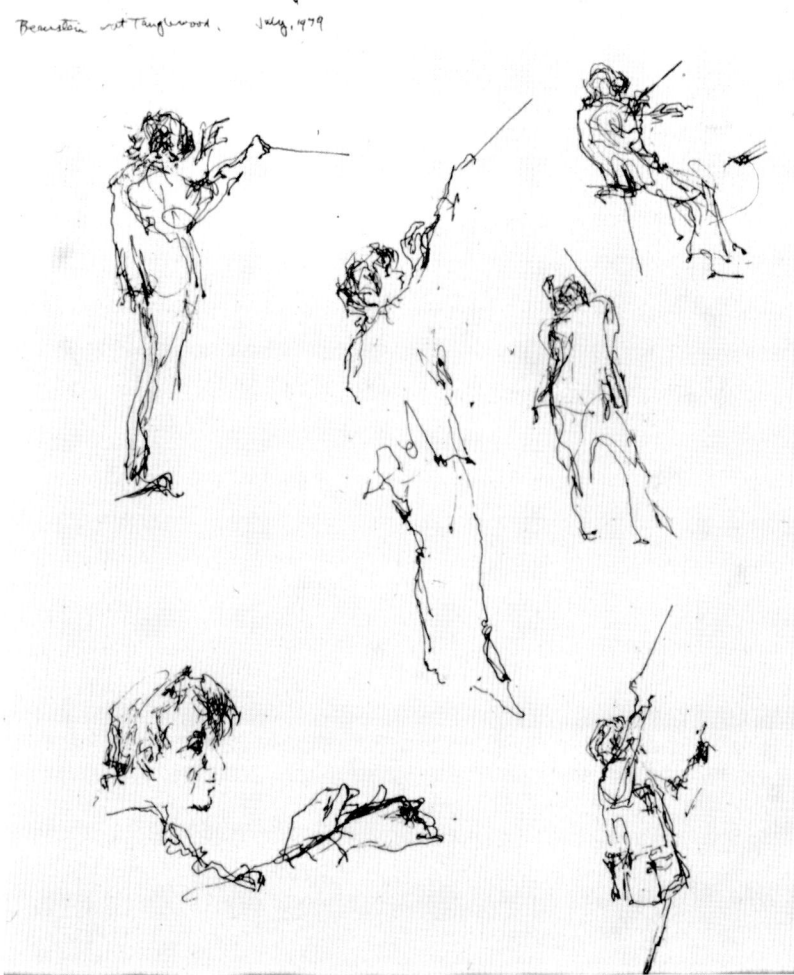

Bernstein at Tanglewood. July, 1979

77. Leonard Bernstein at Tanglewood

77. *Leonard Bernstein at Tanglewood*

Slatkin. Their world of music has offered irresistible challenges to capture them in line and color.

But music has moved with me like a loving companion wherever I have gone in my wandering. Of all the drawings I made during the civil rights struggle in Mississippi, none were more heartfelt and precious to me than those of our black and white volunteers singing together, and of Fannie Lou Hamer lifting the church roof in the Delta with her joyous rendering of "Go Tell It on the Mountain."

It was while on a liberty from my ship in wartime London that music made two days forever memorable. Soon after checking in at my hotel on my brief holiday, I spotted a notice that distinguished pianist Dame Myra Hess was giving her daily concert at the Albert Hall. So on that raw and rainy London day, hungry for the sound of music other than "Doing the Lambeth Walk" and "The White Cliffs of Dover," I made my way through bombed-out rubble to the Albert.

At the end of that day, I wrote my wife about that concert. "At 2:30 I was at Royal Albert Hall (a tremendous, ugly, Madison Square Garden sort of place, and cold), for the Beethoven concert. The concert was probably the real highlight of the leave. It was that good. Myra Hess, the soloist, was excellent and the concertos were played with a humor and delicacy that was really something special."

My review of Dame Myra's performance was purposefully slim, having nothing to do with the excellence of her music. When I arrived at the very chilly barn of a hall, I was struck by the sight of the great Victorian glass ceiling that arched across the vast room. Once Dame Myra began her Beethoven, the crowd of service people and Londoners grew silently attentive. Suddenly, a German V-2 rocket landed only a few blocks away. The roar shook the hall violently, and every head but Dame Myra's looked apprehensively skyward to the ceiling. The glass shuddered and wobbled, but the doughty pianist played on. To my observation, not a single person left the hall. The ceiling remained intact, and to great applause, Dame Myra Hess finished her concert. This was not the kind of communication you sent home to your concerned wife during the war. Only when I returned to the States did I fill out my sketchy review of that concert.

On the following day I saw my first ballet. It was staged by a touring Monte Carlo Company that may or may not have been at all good. Suffice to say, for me they were marvelous. Perhaps it had been the total lack of cultural riches in my diet for all those months overseas, but the work unfolding on that bare English stage simply transported me. It was a feast of color, of music, and of movement that spoke to the artist in me in a language I had never heard before. I resolved that dance would be something I wanted to share with my wife when I returned home.

While I had been overseas, June had witnessed the arrival of George Balanchine in the United States, and had become an enthusiastic ballet-goer as dance was first taking root in the New York cultural soil. Dance became a natural part of our theater life as ballet companies proliferated. The New York City Ballet, Ballet Theater, the Alvin Ailey Dance Company, the Harlem Dance Company—all were eagerly sought out, each having a particular character. Dancers' names were as familiar to us as the names of favorite actors. Oddly, given my enthusiasm for the medium, it took half a century after that first ballet exposure in London before I made my first attempt to capture dance in my work.

Perhaps I had sensed how challenging it would be to try to pin those fragile butterflies of movement to a watercolor sheet. The sheer swiftness and thrust and change that were signatures of ballet seemed too daunting, demanding, rather, the trigger of a camera than the contemplation of a graphic artist. Even Degas seemed to content himself with quiet set pieces of dancers in repose rather than in flight. But trying to seize that world of exotic motion remained a nagging idea that would never quite go away.

When I was interviewed prior to an exhibit of my work in 1994, I was asked if there was anything I had always wanted to draw that I had not had the chance to do. I confessed that I had always wanted to draw dancers, and perhaps one day I would have the chance. That chance came on the very day my show opened. Harold Levine, the former chairman of the board of the Alvin Ailey Dance Company, who had read the press story, offered to open the doors of the Ailey company. "Go have fun! You'll find they're wonderful."

Levine's kind intervention was evident when I presented myself at the Ailey studios near Lincoln Center and was ushered in to meet Judith Jamison. Now the director and spiritual heir to Alvin Ailey's rich legacy, Jamison had long been the premier dancer for the troupe and one of the most charismatic modern dancers I had ever witnessed. Older now, but still very tall and regal in her bearing, she had moved beyond the willowy vision I recalled and evolved into a handsome and very confident woman who was clearly in command. She welcomed me, told me to feel free to sketch wherever I wished, and then excused herself, for classes were beginning and she wished to participate.

It was a remarkable day of discovery for me. On every floor of the building, classrooms full of youngsters from their early teens were moving rhythmically in step, doing dance exercises being called out by the demonstrating teachers. What was astonishing was the singleness of focus and the obvious determination to learn that permeated every venue. Nearly all of the boys and girls were children of color, though a small minority appeared to be white. At breaks between classes, there was the easy, noisy mingling in the halls that one found in any high school. But in the classes, there was silence but for the staccato commands of the teacher, the swish of dance slippers, and the occasional beat of music underlying a particular exercise. I slowly made my way to the advanced class of students, where I slipped into a corner and unwrapped my sketchbook. For the next hours, I was drawing furiously.

These young men and women were clearly more than accomplished students. They were rigorously exploring specific aspects of choreography, teaming up with an assurance born of many hours of shared discipline. As I scanned the room, I saw that Judith Jamison was sitting quietly among some students on a bench, her whole being attentive to what was happening on the floor. From time to time she would simply rise and step to the side of the dancers. When they would step back, Jamison would seemingly, without effort, demonstrate the complicated relationships of the choreography. The decades of years that separated this great dancer from the students would disappear, and she would show the way to the wide-eyed and appreciative youngsters with skill and grace. Then she would gesture for them to begin again and return quietly to the sidelines. By the end of the long day, my sketchbook was filled with images and partial images, and I felt as exhilarated and exhausted as any of the sweat-drenched dancers.

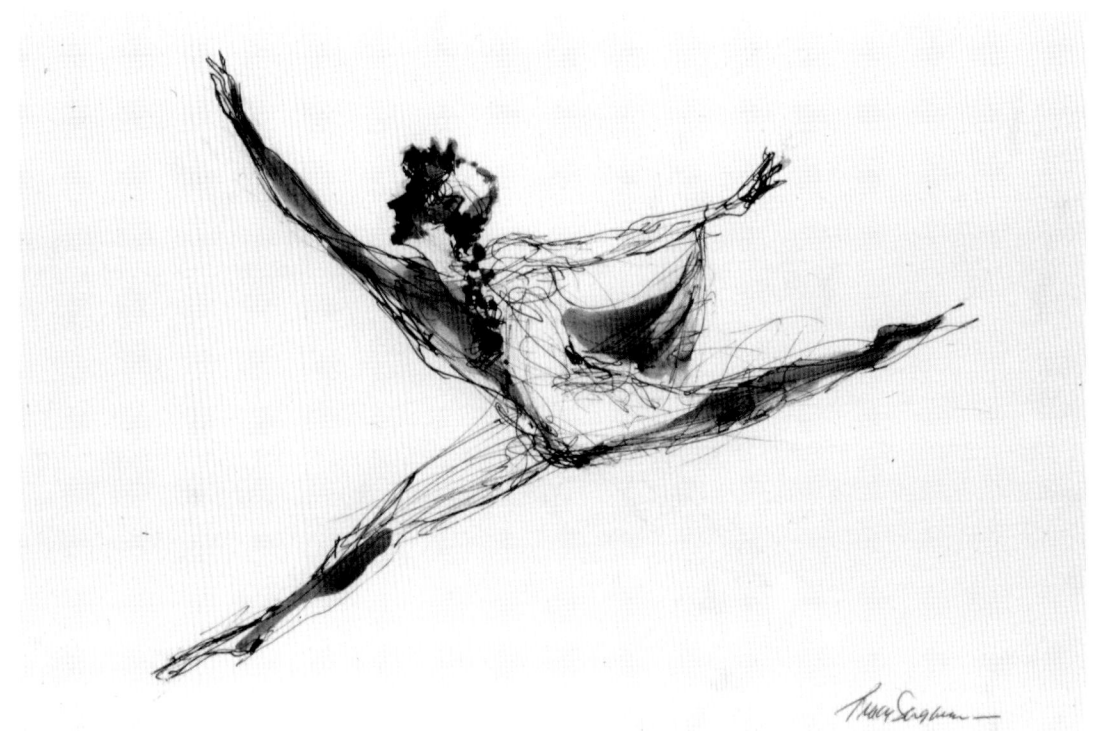

78. *Michael Byars as Puck in*
Midsummer Night's Dream

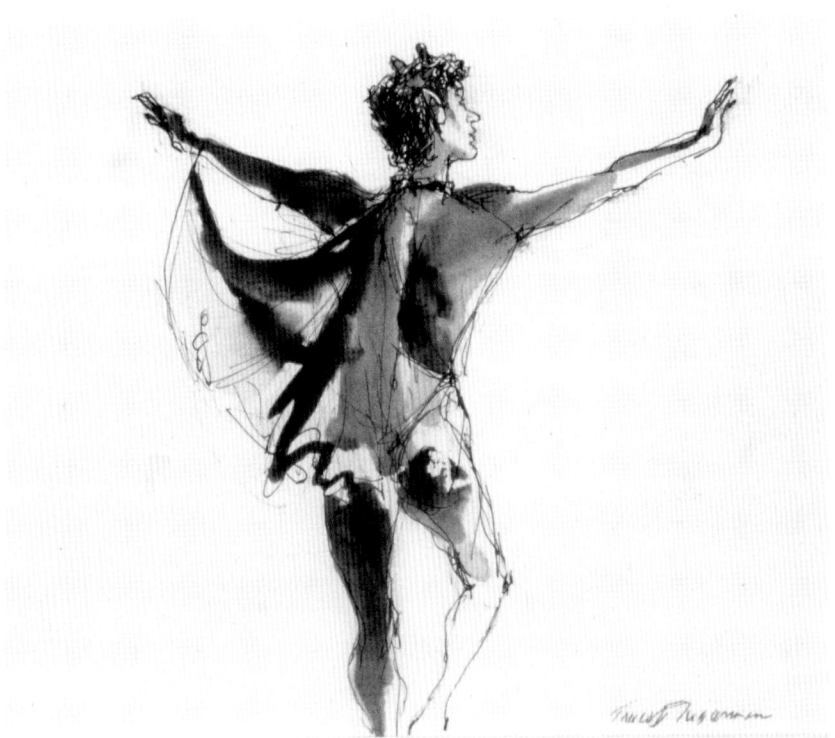

79.

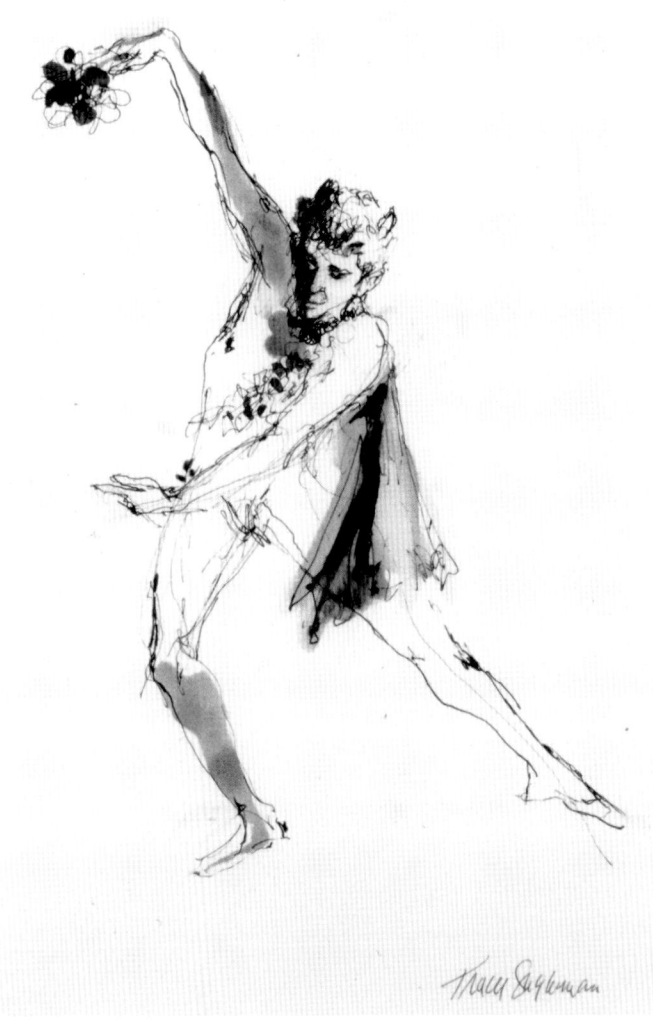

80.

Grateful for the opportunity Harold Levine had provided me, I gave him one of my Ailey sketches. And as so often happened, the Ailey sketch that had been done only for its own sake and for my own pleasure of discovery was seen by someone who then proposed a commercial project. The publisher of *Dance* magazine, Roslyne Stern, a friend of Harold Levine, asked me to illustrate an article the magazine was about to do on the character Puck in the ballet *A Midsummer Night's Dream*. So in the space of two weeks, I would now have the second chance to make drawings of dancers, a chance that had eluded me for almost sixty years!

What ensued must surely be a unique occurrence for any artist. *Dance* magazine presented me with a male ballet dancer who was dancing the role of Puck for the New York City Ballet, and I was to use him for my model on the following Saturday morning. He would appear in costume and would meet me at nine o'clock in a reserved rehearsal room in Lincoln Center. I was told by my client that the dancer's name was Michael Byars, he was a featured dancer, and he would have to leave by noon since he had to rest for the evening performance. As I drove from Connecticut that early morning, my head was spinning. I had never even met a dancer before, and now I was about to have a fine professional dance just for me. At the appointed hour, Michael Byars (a.k.a. Puck) opened the door and introduced himself. He, too, was a little perplexed about how to proceed, but appeared game to do what was necessary.

As I unpacked my pens and sketchpads, I said, "Michael, why don't you just turn on the

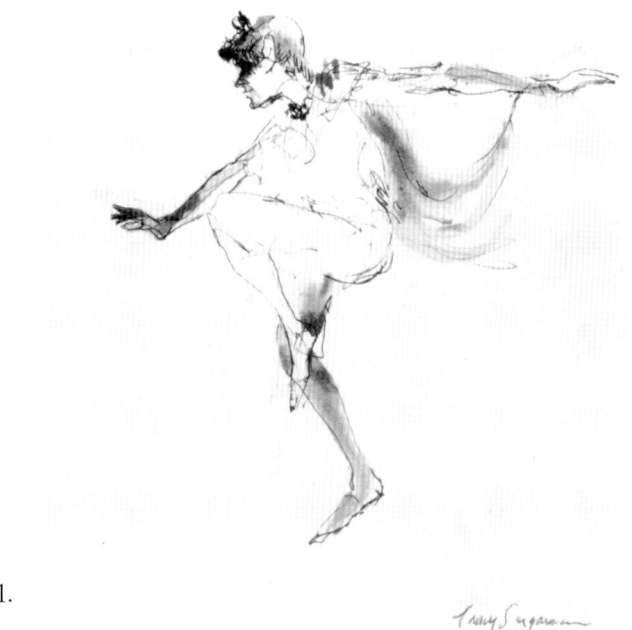

81.

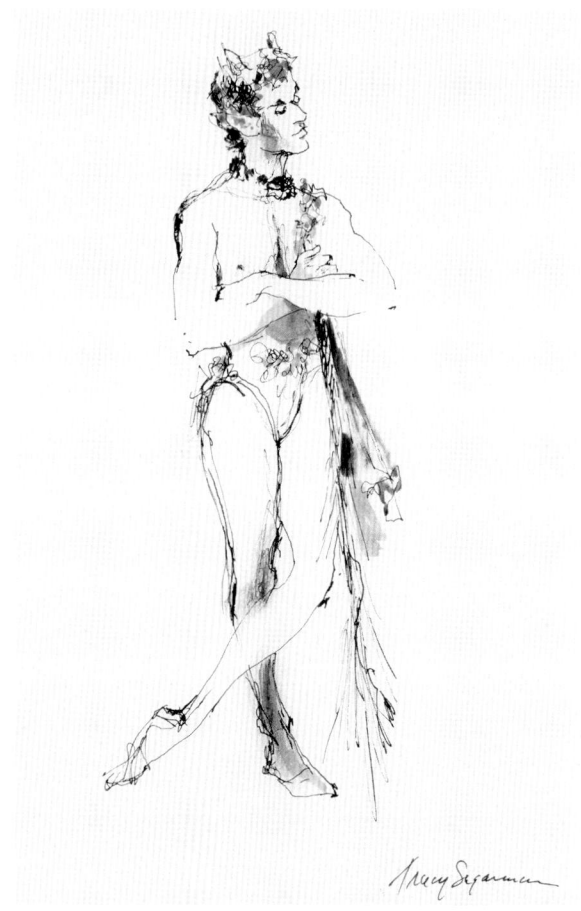

82.

Mendelssohn music, and we'll take it from there." When I turned back to face him, he looked flustered.

"Mendelssohn? I don't have any music, Tracy. Nobody mentioned music."

"But you dance to music, right?" I asked in panic.

He stared at me and then burst out laughing. "Well, of course I dance to music. But there's no music here." He spread his hands out. "There's just Puck."

"Jesus, Puck, can you dance without music?"

"You better hope I can," he grinned.

And for the next three hours Michael Byars danced, and I drew at a pace I never thought I could maintain. It was extraordinary. At noon he left to take the subway home so he could rest for the evening performance. And I wondered if I had the strength left to drive the fifty miles back to Connecticut.

One uses the instrument he can to make music. Michael Byars made music with an exquisitely trained body. I never really had a musical instrument of my own once the Victrola was taken away and Sarah moved into the spare room. My chords and clefs, stops and vibratos have had to be found in my pens and inks and tubes of paint. It's the way I've learned to see my music, the only way I can play.

29

The MacNeil/Lehrer Report

The appointment with producer Al Vechione was for 9:00 in the morning, and I had risen early to take the 7:05 train to New York. "On Thursdays everyone is here," he had said on the phone. "It's the day we lay out the *Report* for the next two weeks. Be here by 9:00, and I'll take you in to meet Robin." I was excited by the opportunity for access that had been arranged by the editors at the *Lamp,* the prestigious corporate magazine of Exxon, one of the two sponsors of *The MacNeil/Lehrer Report.* I was determined to get there in plenty of time. So when my cab was stuck in traffic, I bolted from the car, dodged my way to the sidewalk, and ended up running the last three long blocks west on Fifty-seventh Street to the offices of *The MacNeil/Lehrer Report.*

The receptionist took one look at my flushed, perspiring face as I gasped, "Vechione. I'm here to see Al Vechione," and said, "Please take a seat." She glanced at a schedule on her desk. "You must be Mr. Sugarman. Al ought to be here any minute. He's very punctual, and it's past 9:00. It's not at all like him. Can I get you some coffee?"

"Thank you. Just as soon as I catch my breath, it would be wonderful."

Moments later the door swung open, and a slender man with curly black hair and very dark eyes hurried in, glancing sideways at the wall clock. "Christ, Helen, I thought I'd never make it. What a tie-up all the way across from Fifth Avenue! My cab driver was going nuts, and so was I. Is everybody here?"

She smiled. "Now they are. Al, this is Mr. Sugarman. He's your nine o'clock appointment. From the *Lamp,*" she added helpfully.

He swung around and saw me for the first time. A smile spread across his lively face, and he extended his hand. "Hi. I apologize for the late start. But I see Helen has fixed you up with coffee. Come on into my office." He held open the door, then cocked his head, his eyes darting around the reception room. "Where's your camera bag?"

"I don't have a camera bag," I replied. "I have an old Leica in my briefcase, but I only use it as a backup when I have to."

Vechione leaned back against the door, his dark eyes searching my face. "A backup? A backup for what? Aren't you here to take pictures for the *Lamp?*"

"No. I'm here to *make* pictures for the *Lamp*." I had to laugh at his wide-eyed consternation. "I'm an artist, Mr. Vechione."

"It's Al. And you just draw pictures without using the camera?"

"Most of the time. Yes."

"But wouldn't it be safer if you used the camera, and then drew your pictures?"

"It might be, but it's not the way I like to work. I like to work without a net."

He grinned and gestured for me to enter. "Without a net!" He laughed, shaking his head. "Come meet Robin."

Robert MacNeil, Robin to his family and friends, was a television persona who for years had been our nightly companion, a man we reckoned to be a gentleman of intellect, humor, and quiet charm. So there was more than a little trepidation for me that morning, wondering how accurate we had been in our assessment, and whether the real MacNeil fitted the imagined last.

It was a needless concern. His warmth and generosity made my reportorial project a relaxed and delightful assignment. Being in his company was to witness a genuinely inquiring mind, and a spirit that invited candor and inspired confidence. There was a comfortable, measured, yet approachable quality to the man that made him the fine reporter he was. You felt he was really interested in knowing what you were about. He seemed intrigued by my nonphotograph reportorial mission and did everything he could to ease my way with his colleagues.

In 1976, the time of our first meeting, there was a very different format for the half-hour telecast than what later morphed into the one-hour telecasts of *The MacNeil/Lehrer Report,* the first of their kind in television. Still later, the program would evolve into *The News Hour with Jim Lehrer.* There were many ingredients that flavored that quietly revolutionary dish: the skill and bold intelligence of Al Vechione, the producer; the dedication of a staff of smart reporters and correspondents who happily and loyally worked below the radar, spurning the blandishments of more affluent network newsrooms; and, most of all, the chemistry of Jim Lehrer and Robin MacNeil.

Former marine Jim Lehrer, small-town and Texan, who had started out as a correspondent on the original *MacNeil Report* telecast, had soon become a friend and complementary personality to the more reserved MacNeil. Working from his studio close to the Capitol while Robin labored in the heart of Manhattan, the two mined rich veins of expertise that explored politics and foreign affairs, and, unlike most other television news shows, would sometimes include writers, artists, and scientists in the scope of their inquiries. When I first carried my sketchbook into the New York studio, *The MacNeil/ Lehrer Report* was already setting a high standard of television journalism, building an influential audience that responded to discussions of depth and nuance. And even at that early date, only three years into the program, Al Vechione, Robin, and Jim were

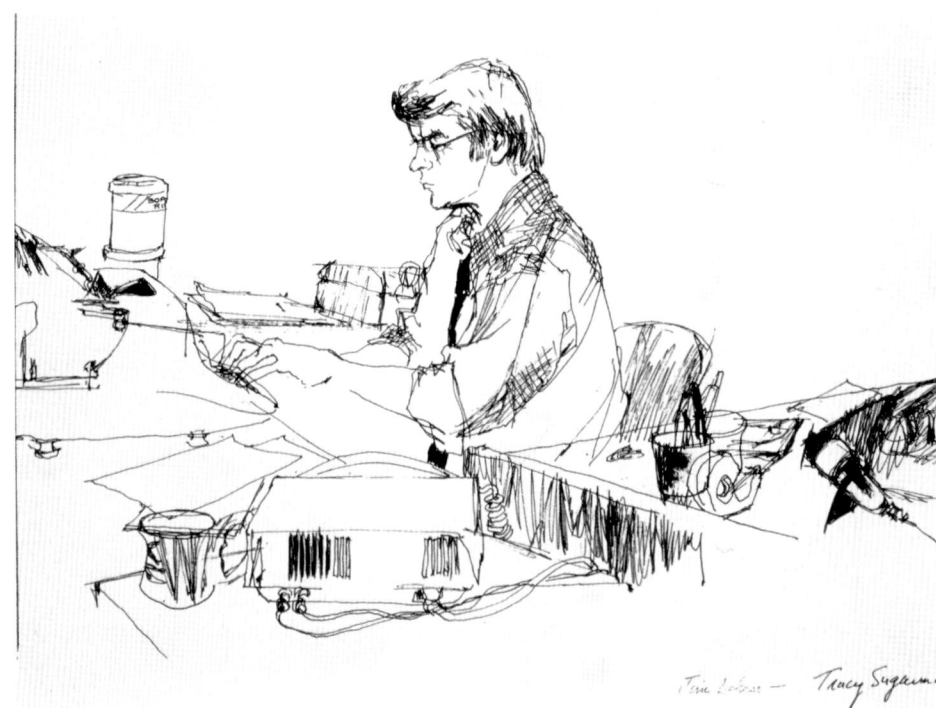

83. *Jim Lehrer in Washington*

seriously exploring the feasibility of expanding the format to an unheard-of one hour of "talking heads."

With MacNeil's stamp of approval, I was welcomed into the corners of the New York operation, compiling impressions of the bright, young reporters, technicians, writers, and correspondents who knit the telecast seamlessly with the broadcast of Jim Lehrer's people in Washington. For another week, I became equally familiar with the Washington operation, and my pile of drawings grew. An insightful story about *The MacNeil/Lehrer Report*, written by John Kobler, was the long featured article that appeared in the spring 1978 issue of the *Lamp*, and the nonphotographs of Tracy Sugarman illustrated the text. Al, Jim, and (now) Robin were very pleased with the folio of drawings, and they soon were acquired to grace the halls of *The MacNeil/Lehrer Report*.

In the fall of 1977, the nation marveled as Vice President Huburt Humphrey, fighting a gallant but losing battle with cancer, continued to pursue his public obligations in government, refusing to give in. Even bitter enemies of the man who had fought so valiantly in his Democratic Party and in the halls of government for civil rights were moved by the personal courage and unbreakable spirit he continued to display.

In October, Al Vechione called me and asked if I would come into New York to discuss an idea he was starting to develop. He envisioned a *MacNeil/Lehrer* memorial that would wed art and documentary film footage and would be a fitting celebration of a rich public life that was soon to end. I was deeply honored to be part of such a project, and immediately

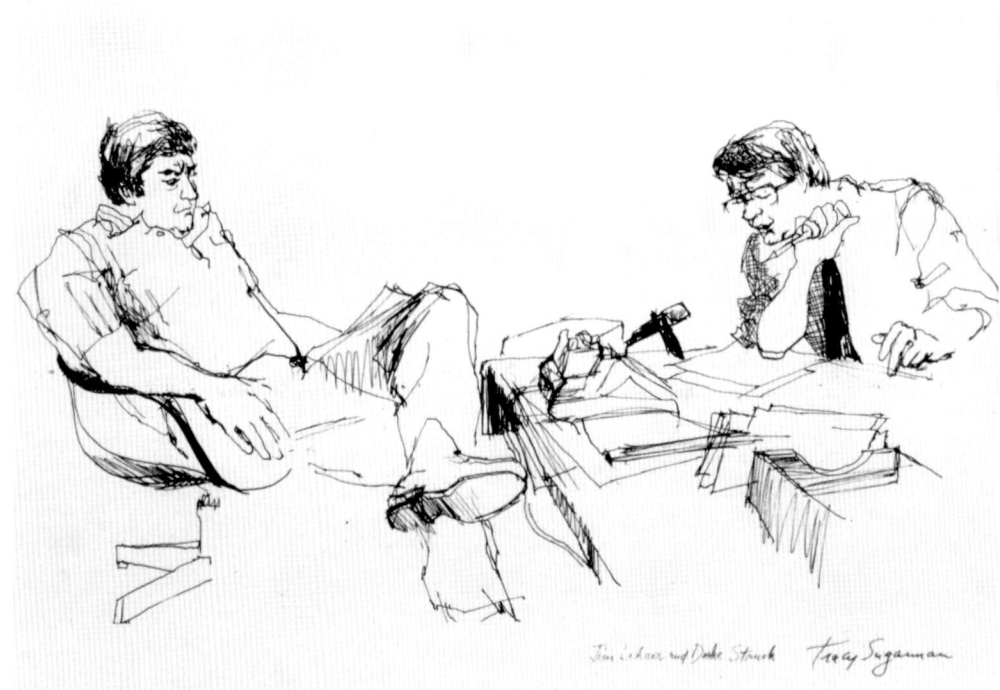

84. *Lehrer with Editor*

begin to research and draw an extensive series of depictions of the vice president's long and colorful career.

Rendered in black charcoal and white chalk on plain tan craft paper, I attempted to capture the populist informality of a quintessential American icon, a man from the heartland of the country who was both a politician and a statesman. When the news of his final surrender to death in January 1978 was announced, I could not help recalling the morning when I had accompanied those visitors from Europe to Humphrey's office, and saw again in my mind's eye the unfeigned joy of the man as he described the country he loved, the land they were about to discover. There were few in public life who so wore his heart on his sleeve for all to see.

It was with great pride that I viewed the fitting tribute that Vechione and his colleagues had fashioned. My drawings were used with sensitivity and discretion, adding an additional dimension to the storytelling. Whereas CBS, NBC, and ABC were racing madly to acknowledge the loss of this special man with jerry-built constructions of old film footage, PBS took to the air with a beautiful, artistic, and poignant memorial. Today, all of the original drawings from that memorial are on permanent display at the Hubert Humphrey Institute in Minneapolis.

My last intersection with *The MacNeil/Lehrer Report* occurred in 1994 when Al Vechione's talented successor, Les Crystal, invited me to meet him for breakfast and get acquainted. It was over coffee and scrambled eggs that he learned about my exhibit of D-day

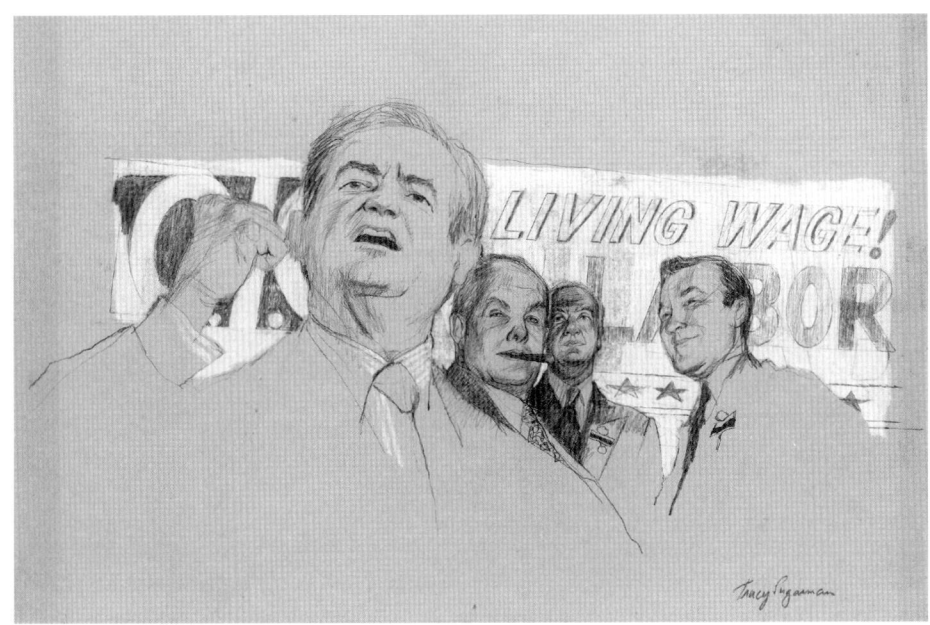

85. *Hubert Humphrey at AFL-CIO Convention*

drawings that was being mounted at the Navy Memorial to celebrate the upcoming fiftieth anniversary of the Normandy landings. Crystal's long news experience with major networks had made him a confident producer, and a man who recognized the potential of an occurrence that could be creatively shaped to his own ends. The fiftieth anniversary was a significant event, and Crystal recognized the special hook of an "I was there" artist who had recorded that vanished time. By the time the waitress had cleared the table, plans were afoot to shape my words and my drawings into a celebratory D-day segment for *The MacNeil/Lehrer Report.*

The only difficulty I could see was that the June 6 anniversay was only a few days away. That did not seem to deter Crystal. The very next day a film crew was dispatched from the Washington office to shoot selected drawings at the Navy Memorial. Another film crew was sent to my home in Connecticut where I was interviewed and asked to read from the war letters. And on June 6, I had the special pleasure of having Robin MacNeil introduce this special tribute to D-day.

The skill, finesse, and taste demonstrated in that Les Crystal swiftly conceived and executed production have been repeatedly demonstrated over the intervening years. Until 2006 he continued as the executive producer of *The News Hour with Jim Lehrer* that now operates from it headquarters in the nation's capital. Robin MacNeil has retired from the news business and become a successful full-time author and lecturer. Jim Lehrer continues to happily juggle two careers. While remaining the knowledgeable anchor of *The News Hour,* he continues to write and publish books that are critically and popularly acclaimed. And I am sort of a proud visiting alumnus who never really enrolled.

30

AFL-CIO

I wandered to the window, looking at the throng of traffic and people that seemed to make K Street the busiest scene in Washington, D.C. From Steve Coyle's seventh-floor corner office at the AFL-CIO Housing Investment Trust, you could see all the way to the park across the corner. Only a few blocks beyond the green swatch of park, out of sight but only a brisk walk away, was the national headquarters of the AFL-CIO, its building only a long stone's throw from the White House. How challenging it must be, I thought, to be this close to where so much power resides.

I had been ushered into Coyle's office and advised that "the CEO's meeting will soon be over. Make yourself comfortable." The office was large and comfortable, and the walls full of photographs of politicians and labor personalities, many of them seemingly intimate with Coyle. I was studying a framed cover of *Boston* magazine that had caught and held my eye. It displayed the magazine's "Boston Man of the Year," Stephen Coyle.

The door had opened noiselessly behind me, and I was startled to hear, "I'm really a lot better looking now than that picture. I've matured." Steve Coyle, a crooked grin on his face, slowly crossed the room, his bright, careful eyes taking my measure. "Glad to see you," he said. "Sorry that the meeting took so long. Come put your feet up." He settled comfortably on a short couch, nodding me to an accompanying armchair. Coyle was a man of middle height, ruddy coloring, with surprising gray hair that made his youthful face seem even younger. It was his searching, appraising gaze that indicated the very experienced executive who had skillfully guided the Housing Investment Trust through a turbulent time. But there was a sense of repressed Irish good humor about him that was reassuring. "Tell me about Mississippi and why you were there."

It was the kind of direct, unadorned beginning of a conversation I later came to anticipate, but at that moment I simply could manage only, "Thank you," and sat down.

The question was not a total surprise, for I had received a call from the AFL-CIO Housing Investment Trust making inquiries about *Stranger at the Gates*, asking if I was that Tracy Sugarman. I had responded that there surely was no other Tracy Sugarman. My mother's imaginative naming had made me unique. "Who wants to know?" I had asked.

"Our director, Mr. Steve Coyle. He remembers meeting you in '94 at the Navy Memorial when you had a show of your drawings from World War II to commemorate D-day."

And then I remembered and started to laugh. It was the night of the opening of the exhibit, and June and I were standing, watching the reactions of the visitors who were examining the drawings and watercolors. Two men standing directly behind us were comparing notes about the show. "Tracy Sugarman . . . Tracy Sugarman . . . Mississippi!" The man sounded pleased he had unearthed the elusive association. "Yeah, Mississippi! I'm sure he was the guy who went down in '64 and made all those drawings. I think I still have the book at the office someplace."

His companion had hesitated. "I don't know, Steve, look at the dates on these pictures . . . 1944 . . . 1945 . . . these drawings were made fifty years ago."

And the man called Steve said, "You're right. Fifty years . . . I wonder if the old guy is still alive?"

"He is," I said turning to see who had been speaking.

Steve Coyle cocked his head and raised his eyebrows. "You know that?"

"I'm damn sure. I'm him!" And June had chimed in, "It's true. The old guy is alive."

And now, years later, Steve Coyle was interested in talking to me and was inviting me to fly down to Washington.

His alert eyes never left my face as I sketched the reasons that had led me to Mississippi. "It was probably the most difficult, dangerous, and wonderful project I ever got into. Looking back, I feel my drawings did the job I had hoped they would do. They were used on television, by the USIA overseas, and in magazines and documentary films in this country. It was an important story to tell."

When I concluded, Coyle nodded, seeming to have arrived at some personal conclusion. "Did you ever hear of a *colonia?*" he asked, rising from the couch and walking over to his desk. I replied I had not. He selected a small pile of reports and returned to the couch with them, placing them on the small coffee table between us. "*Colonia* is a Spanish word for a neighborhood or a new community," he said. "It sounds benign. *Colonias* are not. The secretary of Housing and Urban Development [HUD], a guy this Housing Trust works closely with, describes them as 'third world shanty towns.' He says that if you set the worst public housing in America among the *colonias*, it would appear a mansion in the middle of misery." He paused, a deep frown altering the good humor of his face. "I've seen them, and that's how bad they are. They're a disgrace." His eyes held on mine. "I've seen your Mississippi drawings, and I found them very moving." He leaned forward, tapping the sheaf of papers that lay between us. "I want you to go to Texas and make drawings of what you find in the *colonias* in Laredo and El Paso. And I want Congress to see those drawings. Our collaboration with HUD is important, and we want to make sure that they continue to have the support in Congress for the kind of housing projects we're both contemplating in Texas and across the country. I think your drawings could help."

When he stood up, he handed me the sheaf of reports. "Read this stuff on the plane home. It will tell you what we're hoping to do to turn those *colonias* around. I want to get you to Laredo soon."

That's the way it started, and that's the way it's been for a decade. No fuss. No ceremony. The assignments from the trust come abruptly, are enormously engaging, and are frustrating as hell when it comes to time lines. I have come to understand that executives like Steve Coyle have agendas of their own, not always visible. You determine that fact through a coterie of people at the trust who love and respect Coyle and can translate for you. But if you think the project is challenging enough, and it usually is, then you swallow your frustration and climb aboard. What has never wavered is the appreciation and support I have always received from Coyle, my Irish Medici, and his remarkable team.

On that first flight home in 1983, I learned that the *colonias* were only the most poignant evidence of a much larger problem. The entire region of the Texas border not only has dehumanizing rural poverty but is also home to four of the five poorest cities in the United States. The lack of economic opportunity and affordable housing in those cities had created the *colonias* in the first place. *Newsweek* described these rural slums as "the worst America has to offer." When I read about Laredo and El Paso where I was about to go (eighty thousand Americans living in 310 *colonias*), I was stunned to learn that it was common to find two or three generations living together in an eight-by-ten-foot structure. As a result of these extremely unsanitary living conditions, many of the residents repeatedly suffered from infectious diseases and illnesses. Many of the *colonia* land contracts contained no obligation on the developer's part to provide water and sewer services.

By the time I had finished the instructive materials from Steve Coyle's desk, I realized I was about to revisit the dark side of American society. Like the racially exploited blacks in Mississippi and the victimized whites in Appalachia, I was about to meet the most recent victims of economic discrimination, the Hispanic Americans in the Rio Grande Valley.

Soon after I arrived in Laredo, I began the patient journey required to make one a sensitive observer rather than a voyeur. I became a familiar presence to the families, an unthreatening stranger with pens and drawing pads. They soon learned that I was happy

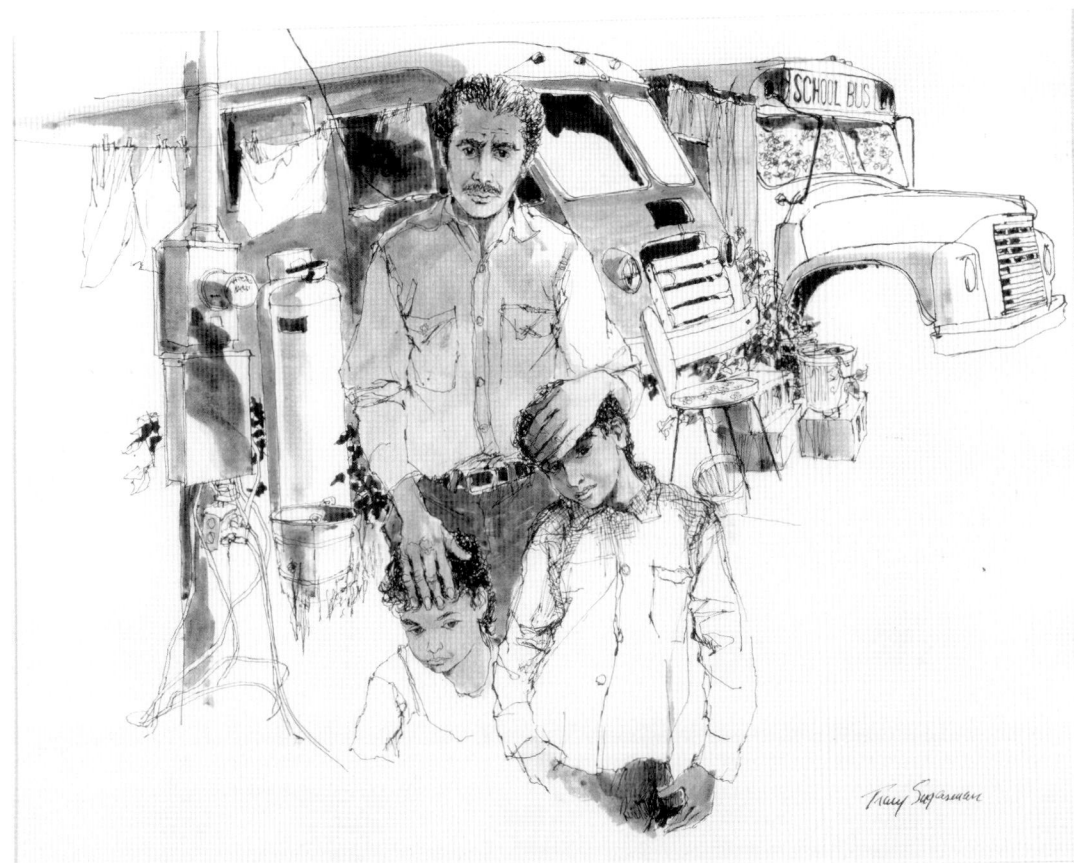

86. *Laredo, Texas,*
Colonia Family

to stop my drawing and chat with them, and that I was a gringo who had sympathy for the hard hand these young Hispanic families had to play.

What was heartbreakingly clear was that the residents felt such great pride in starting to put down roots in the American soil and were so eager to pursue home ownership that they accepted incredible conditions that required they go far afield just for potable water. From the arid pieces of turf where they lived, I watched them as they had to travel many miles just to reach a job, and place their children on school buses that had to travel long distances to schools that were often inadequate and overcrowded. And I often observed them spend what little money they had on building materials for their homes that were often little more than shacks.

In our conversations as I made my drawings for the trust, they would describe how unscrupulous developers were exploiting them through "contracts for deed." "A contract for deed," one explained, "is the only way we can finance a house here. But with a contract for deed, we cannot obtain title to our lots until all our mortgage payments have been made. Here in the valley, our wages are very low, and we are never sure how long our jobs will last.

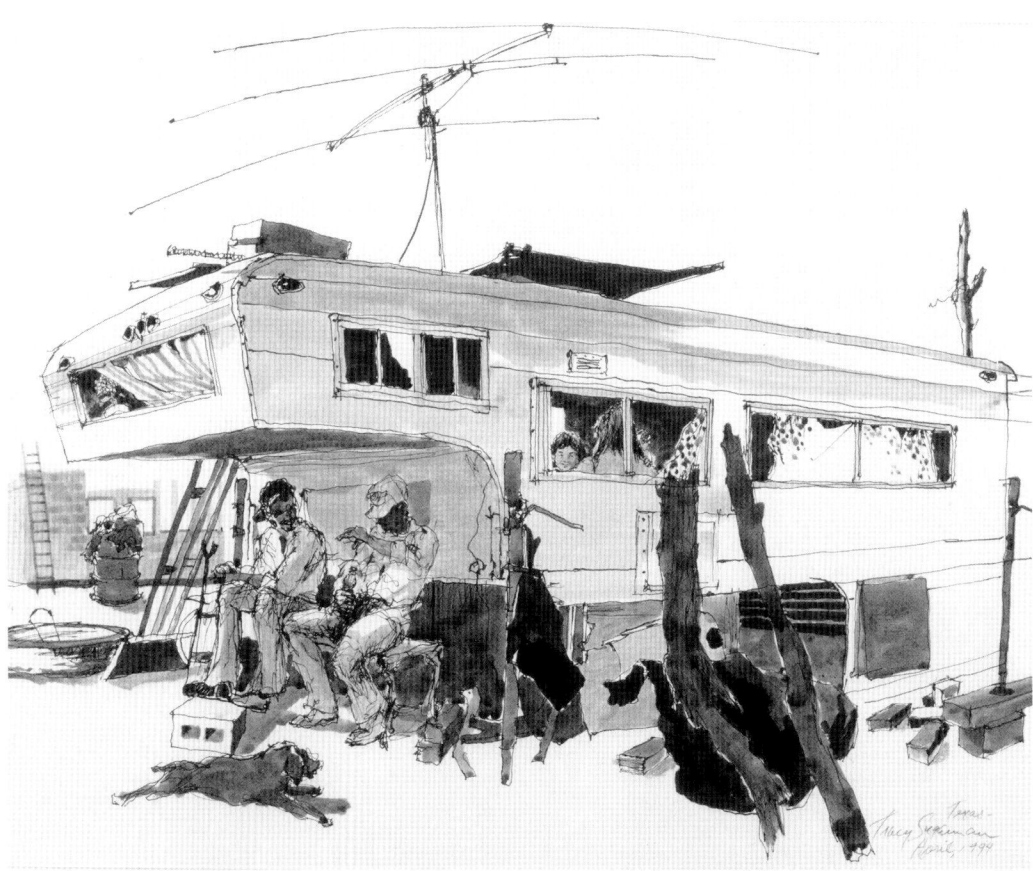

87. *El Paso, Texas,*
Colonia Family

If we miss a payment, we can lose our whole investment. Then the developer gets the land back and sells it to another family like ours."

I began to understand why the Housing Investment Trust was assembling the capital, expertise, and labor necessary to create healthy, sanitary, and affordable housing for these cheated American citizens. When I was about to leave after my weeks in Laredo and El Paso, I sent Steve Coyle these observations to accompany the drawings I had completed:

It's as if the Conestoga wagons had paused here, and the exhausted men and women had simply dumped the ragtag contents of the wagons on the cracked sienna earth. Perhaps they had spotted the river beyond the rise and thought, "Maybe this is a place where we can start again."

But there are no Conestoga wagons, only a crazy quilt of jerry-built dwellings and rusting hulks of pickup trucks. Each throws a knife-sharp shadow under an unforgiving sun. There is hardly a tree to offer shade or a green meadow to comfort the eye. All

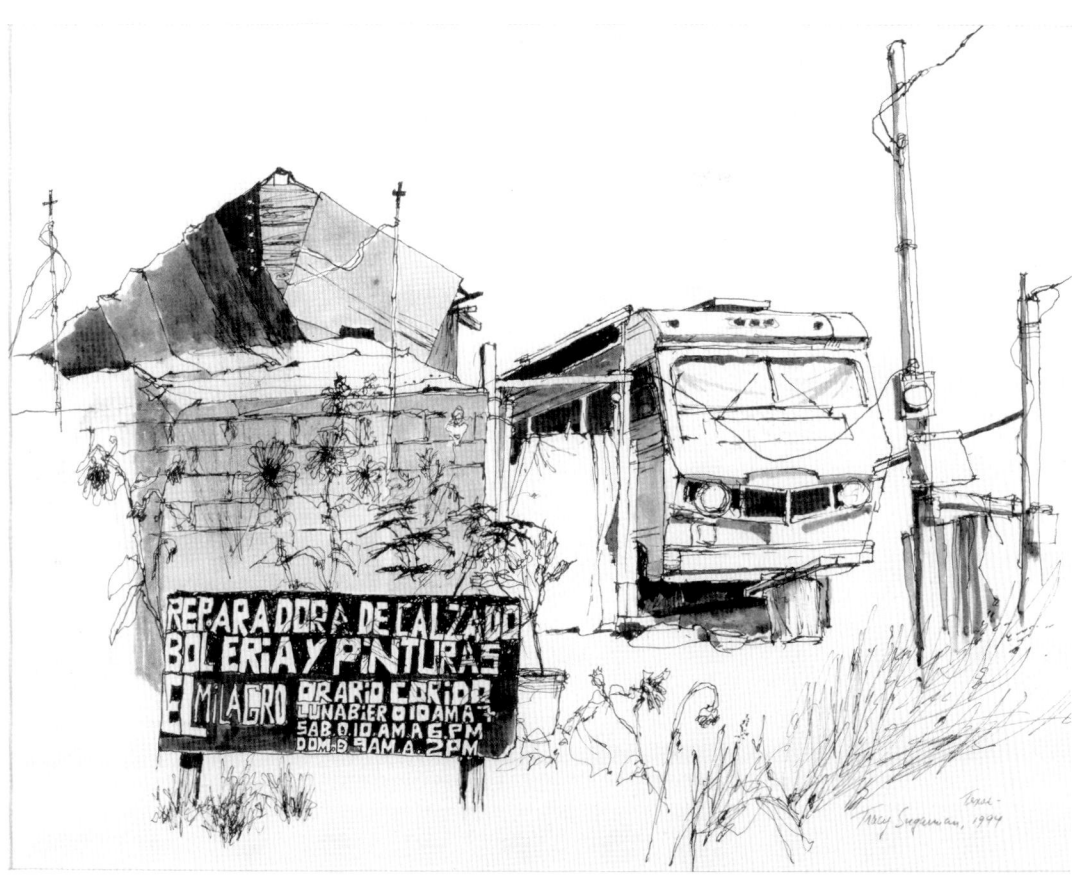

88. *Colonia Landscape*

that knits the haphazard structures into a semblance of neighborhood is a parched and crumbling clay road.

In the glare of noon the only movement is an old woman hanging wash behind a spattered trailer, and a tiny child who flaps her arms as she runs, giggling, after a chicken in the dusty yard. Everyone seems to have left this place for the fields beyond the distant highway or for the factories beyond the horizon. Two ancient, abandoned school buses sit on blocks, silent in the glare. Their windows are covered with scraps of burlap and bold, bright cotton remnants to give some privacy to the family of seven who lives here. Plastic buckets to tote water flank the flowered curtain that modestly hides the bus door.

To the east, behind the chicken-wire fence, salvaged lumber uprights rise from the packed adobe earth, waiting for a roof "if the money is enough this year." The whole family of migrant workers has left for the verdant North and the flowering orchards. Awaiting their return is the wreck of a trailer and an outhouse. Both will have to do for another season. Or the one after that.

Scraps of old lumber, stumps of trees, baling wire, cracked concrete blocks, dented pails, mending tools—all the rejects from life elsewhere are put to use here. They are lashed into nests, shelters from the bitter winds of January and the sweltering heat of August. "When you've got kids, like us, you got to do what you can do."

But even in the pinched, marginal life here, a stubborn insistence on being oneself brings surprising grace. Brightly painted adobe walls frame a yard, cleverly shaped to mimic a remembered place once loved. A carefully watered, fragile sapling is guarded by a truck tire. The green spike seems a bet on the future.

Across the way, brick walls that have been lovingly laid speak of a skilled hand and a meticulous eye. Above them a staircase is silhouetted against the fierce blue sky. It leads to nowhere yet. But there will be a room there.

At the end of the rutted road, a tiny spread has been transformed into a minifarm. Goats bleat and scamper behind a wire fence. A satellite dish throws an incongruous shadow on the scuffling chickens and barking dogs below. The dogs pace restlessly, guarding their barbed-wire turf. A carefully laid-out garden of vegetables fills every inch of open space behind the tar-paper shack, and new plants sprout in a dozen jelly jars and coffee cans. Beyond the pen of goats, a concrete foundation has been laid and a bed of flowers has been seeded. From here you can gaze down to the brown river that meanders below and to the sere Mexican hills beyond where cardboard shacks seem to stretch endlessly across the sandy landscape. Compared to the vibrant helter-skelter here, they seem forlorn and sad.

At the end of the afternoon, the county's bright-yellow school buses disgorge their flood of noisy kids. They race down the caked roads, kicking up tiny clouds of dust that follow in their wake as they enter the huts and trailers of the *colonia*. As the sun goes down, the men and women wearily return in their battered trucks and dusty cars. The noise of the *colonia* builds with calls and laughter and the impudent sound of salsa. They've come home to their kids, to their gardens, to their unfinished wall, to tomorrow.

In the past, as a reportorial artist, I've recorded the fatigue and quiet despair of abandoned Appalachian coal towns. The dreams died there when the company pulled up stakes, leaving the polluted streams and the raped hills. And I've watched with wonder the tentative stirrings of black liberation in the Mississippi Delta where dreams, for the first time in centuries, seemed possible. But here in these parched and exploited *colonias*, the American dream seems alive and real. It seems incredible, but it's so.

It's as if the Conestoga wagons had paused here.

31

The Children

Kids have always been in view, straight ahead, or at least in peripheral vision. I notice them. And when I don't see them, I find myself looking for them. Maybe it's because I enjoyed being a kid, something you can't tell a lot of people. *Are you kidding?* I can't remember the last time at a party when someone held forth about his happy childhood. If I ever did, I don't anymore. It's not only bad form, but even good friends don't believe you. So I simply hang back and watch the avid competition among those who had a really terrible childhood, who seem to be finally at the point of getting pleasure from that awful time. Or maybe it's because I liked having kids, liked them having kids, and liked watching them become interesting people. But it's really not just a family thing with me. Kids charm me, even other people's kids. And I've met them all over the world. When it was okay with them, I even drew a lot of them.

Sometimes, of course, where you meet them makes you see the whole landscape a little differently. It's not just a bombed-out neighborhood you're drawing. It's where these kids live. In February 1944, shortly after we landed at our first base in Plymouth, I wrote to June:

> I can't seem to drink in enough local color. How I wish I could record it all! The pink-kneed, pink-cheeked kids, smaller than kids at home, with lots of hair—mostly blond, it seems. Too many with pinched faces. They swarm around. "Penny, mister? Got some gum?" The minute you reach in your pocket—who can say no to kids—they multiply like rabbits and you find yourself leading a caravan of Oliver Twists down the street. After chow, I took my sketchpad and went hunting. I found two ragamuffin girls, age 7—Iris Rose Mary Oskin and Sandra Bond—at the expense of one penny to Oskin and a half-penny to Sandra. I had run out of pennies. The demand is terrific. When they asked me, "What are you takin' our picture for, Yank?" I told them I wanted to show my wife, way over in America, what pretty little girls they have in England. This pleased them, and they posed as graciously as the Queen herself.

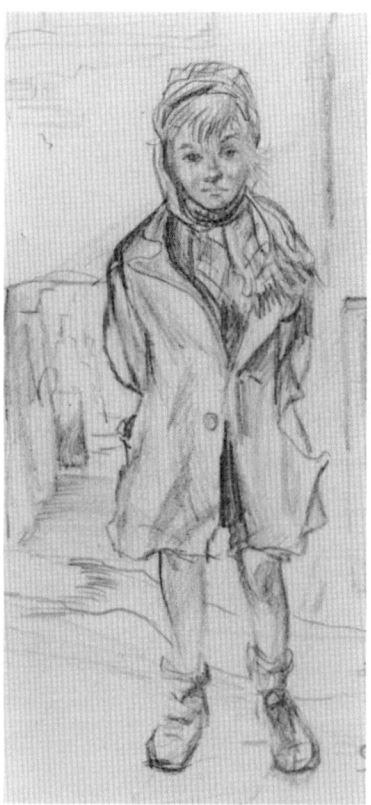 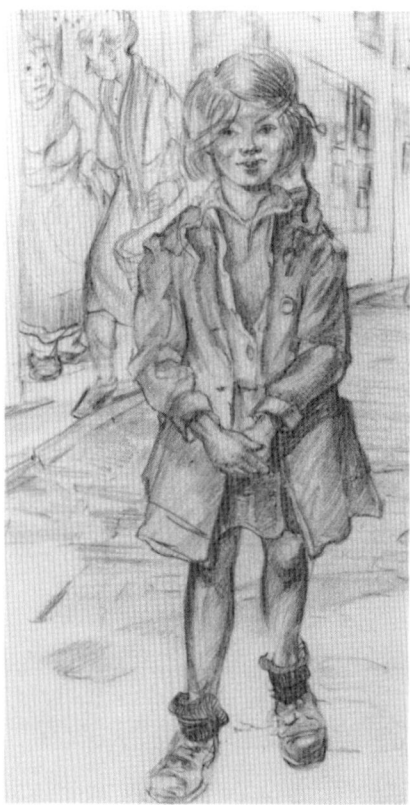

89. *Iris Rose Mary Oskin and Sandra Bond, Plymouth, England, 1944*

All these years later, more than four decades, and still the heavy, hot, and humid feel of the Mississippi Delta that murderous summer can rematerialize in a corner of my mind. Witnessing the daily grind of the voter registration drive, trying to convince the poorest black citizens of America to defy the sheriff, defy the white man who hired him on the plantation, defy the faceless night riders who torched the houses and razed his black church, to walk up the steps of the courthouse and demand the right to vote. Those memories are etched forever, and the faces of those nameless black and white heroes will always be a personal treasure.

Yet when I can summon to memory the sweet and indescribable beauty of the Freedom School classes in that wreck of an abandoned farmhouse that summer of '64, I can be moved to tears of pleasure. To watch young children, unfolding like petals in the warm Mississippi sun, starting the marvelous journey to learning, was a miracle that happened every day. I wrote in my Delta log:

> The excited talk of the enthusiastic teachers mingled with the suppressed excitement of the Negro children. One watched the young teachers, bending to the task, starting to probe, to move, to make curious. The youngest children were quickest to be fired. Their surprised laughter and exclamations showed contact was being made. The older boys and girls shyly smiled, frowned, or dropped their eyes. No white teacher had ever taught them, and the northern speech sounded hard and strange in their ears. And no teacher had ever reached out to them with such ardor and trust. It was new, but not uncomfortable. They watched from lowered lids, said little, and noticed everything. In the next room, a dozen four-through-seven year olds were discovering the delights of the new bookshelves. Heidi Dole, her smiling pretty face animated

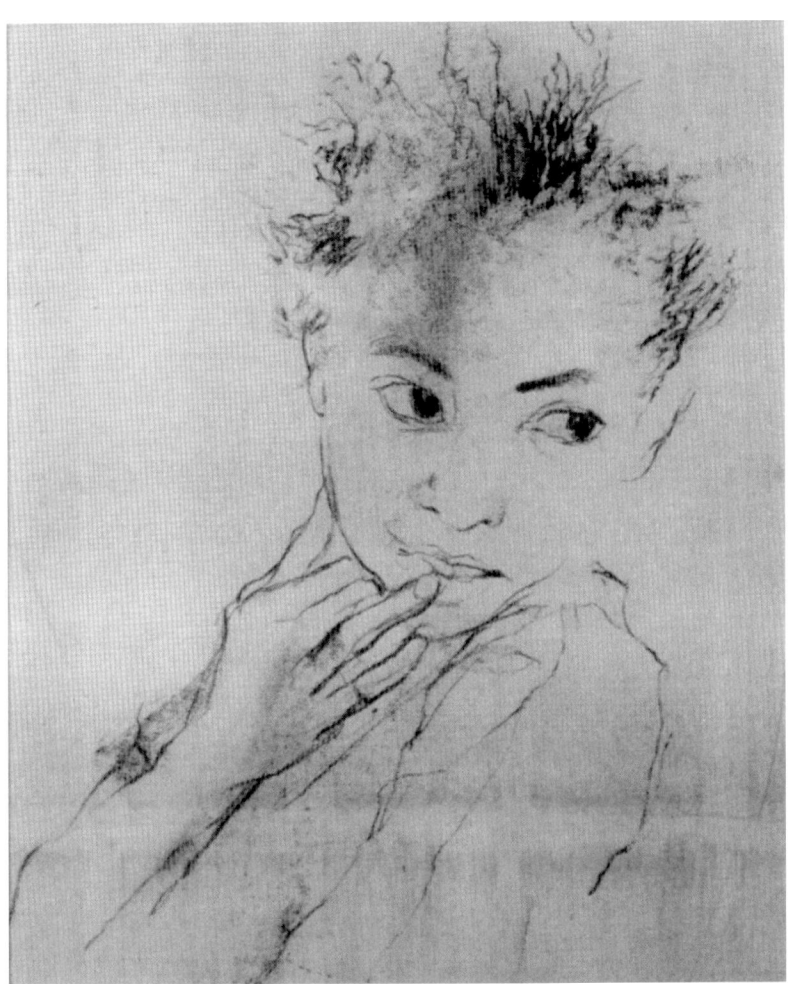

90. *First Day at the Freedom School,
Ruleville, Mississippi, 1964*

with pleasure, was handing books to the bright-eyed youngsters. They would curl up
on the floor and excitedly thumb through the volumes in search of pictures and color.
A world beyond the Delta began to unfold, and a wonderful silence fell in the room.
Heidi's gentle voice said, "These books are yours. We can find all sorts of things in
them. You can always come and use them here. And, if we take care of them, you
can even take some of them home to read. In your own homes." She tucked her feet
under her and picked up a book. "Why don't you all gather around, and we'll read
this one together."

I can find kids scattered through sixty years of my drawings, fragile, delicate, perish-
able kids. Whatever happened to that little girl who posed for me, staring wistfully, wondering perhaps if there really was a place other than her Fonde, a sterile main street that
boasted of a fuel pump, a grocery, and a post office? Or the blond eight-year-old boy in the

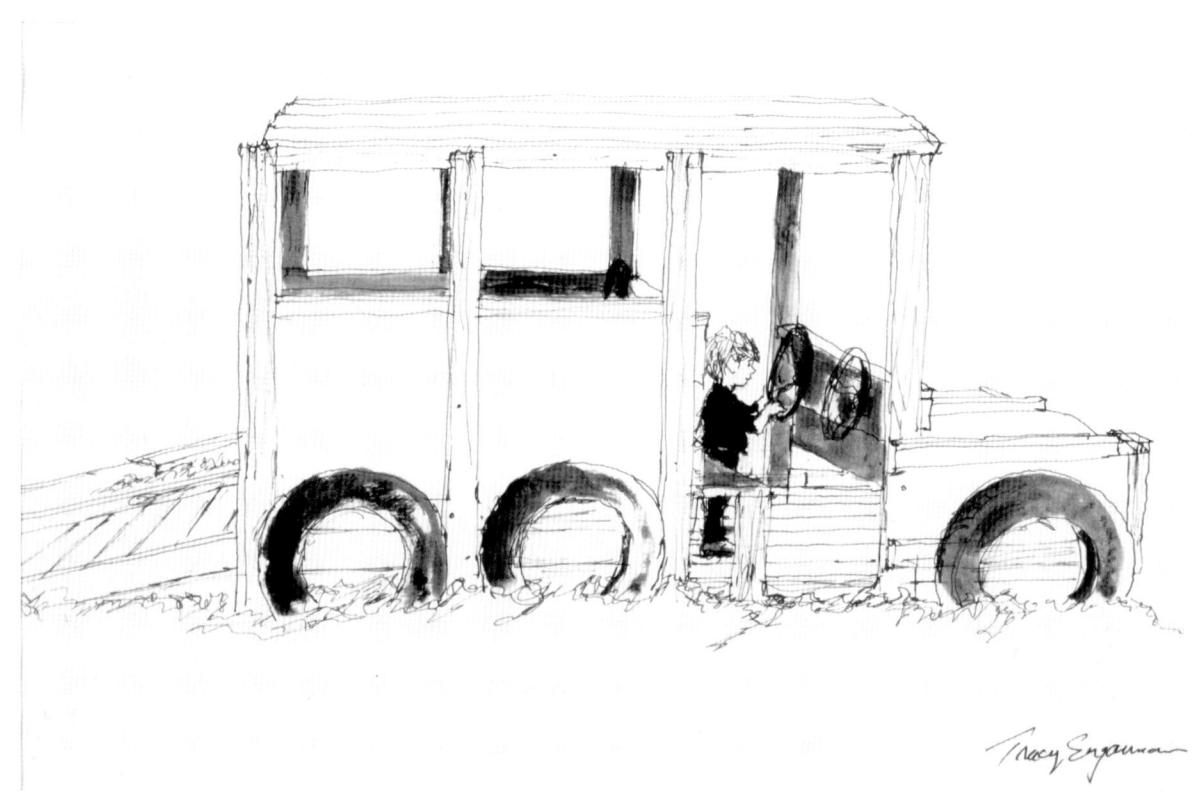

91. *Preschool Kids, Norwalk, Connecticut, 2004*

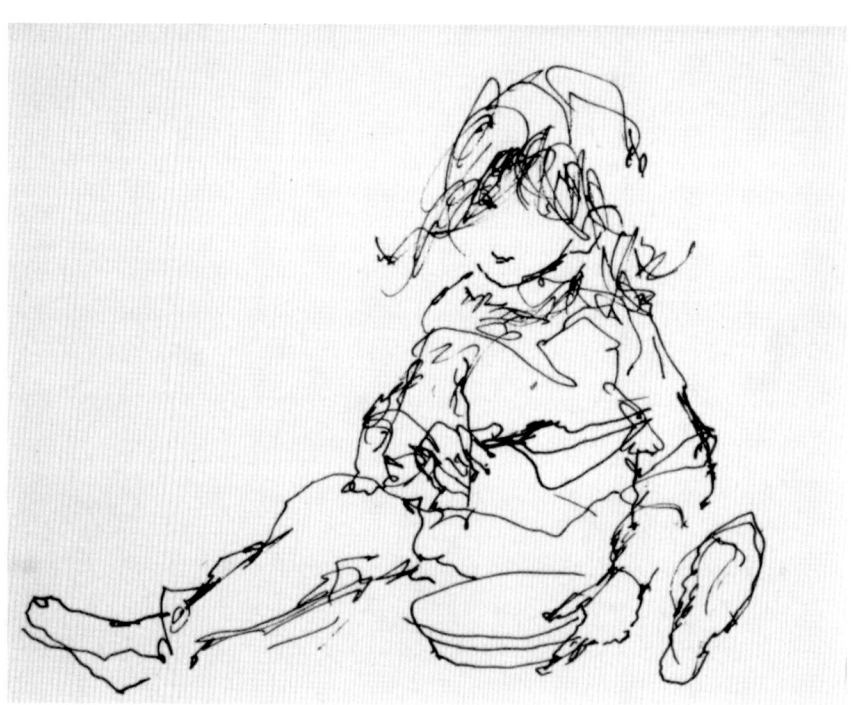

92.

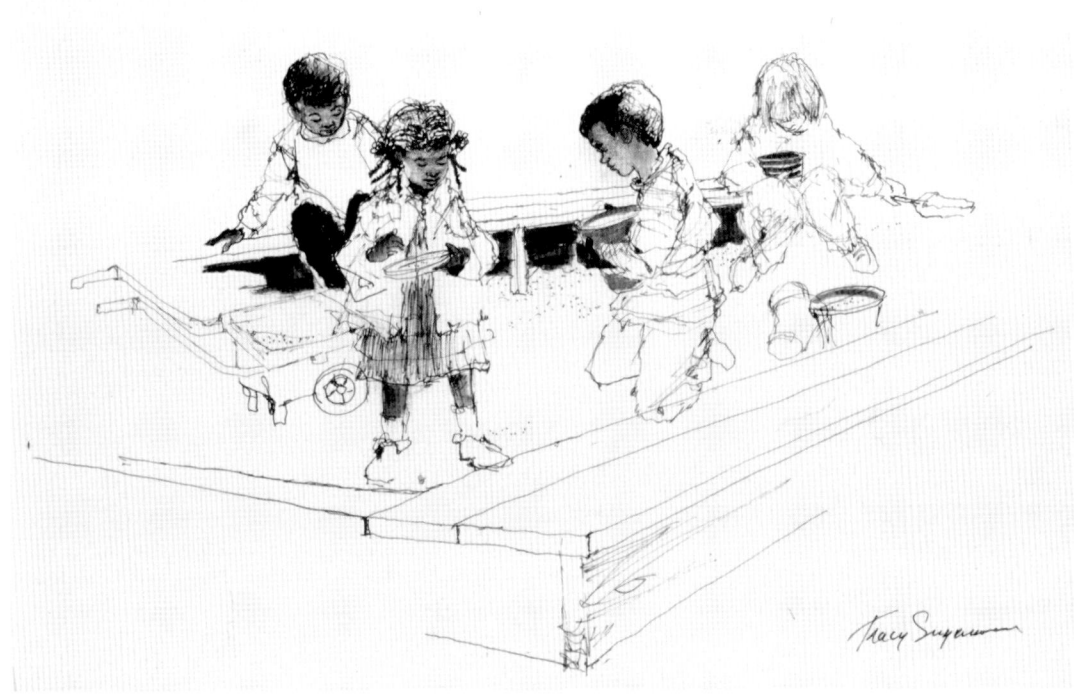

93.

too big, soiled T-shirt who stopped dead in his tracks when he saw me drawing, challenging me with gray, angry eyes. I had been drawing the rusted, dilapidated coal tipple and abandoned coal cars that seemed to say, "This is Fonde, Kentucky." Could he ever know that his image would complete my drawing? That it would leave that town and be seen by people thousands of miles away?

But kids just being kids, not symbols, continue to invite my time and move into my welcoming sketchbooks. I chose to spend a week with the preschool children of the Rubino Center in Norwalk, Connecticut. It is run by STAR, a nonprofit organization whose mission is to assist people with developmental delays and their families. At the Rubino Center, children who are developmentally challenged share sandboxes and easels and music with children who have been spared those difficulties.

The harmonious mix of happy children learning together under the guidance of dedicated young teachers is an enchanting and unique scene. The innocence of the young who have not yet been taught to fear is a touching reminder of our own frailties. It was hard to leave the Rubino Center.

32

End of the Beginning

June died
everything was the same
nothing was the same
everything was
nothing was
everything
was
nothing

It's extraordinary that your life can come apart in your hands. When she left me, I was holding her. But not tight enough. I didn't want her to go. I knew that then. What I didn't know was that I mourned, too, for the fifty-five years we had made our own. They disappeared for endless months, surfacing, half-remembered, when I'd struggle awake in my suddenly enormous bed. It was a bitter and lonely time.

What intrigues me now is to remember how I learned over these last years that the measured ordinariness of life doesn't really stop because you're weeping. It's not an easy lesson to learn. It's edged with guilt when you find that the weeping can stop. And after the shadowed, chilly life of being a widower, stepping into even a winter sun of social life with old friends seems self-indulgent and a little inappropriate. What continued was the work. The ordinariness of going to work. The muted pleasure of finishing the painting. You straightened the bed. You put up the coffee. You learned to make a pot roast. There wasn't much joy.

I think that being born and raised in Syracuse implants a seasonal metronome that beats in me now wherever I roam. I was nurtured where winters are tough, springs are fragile, summers are endless, and autumns are gorgeous warnings that winter is coming again. For a long winter of the soul, I hunkered down, almost not daring to hope that the ice would break and spring would light my life again. "The saddest word in the English language is *gone*," cautioned my friend Jerry. And he was right. But I was learning that there were other words. And maybe spring was coming after all.

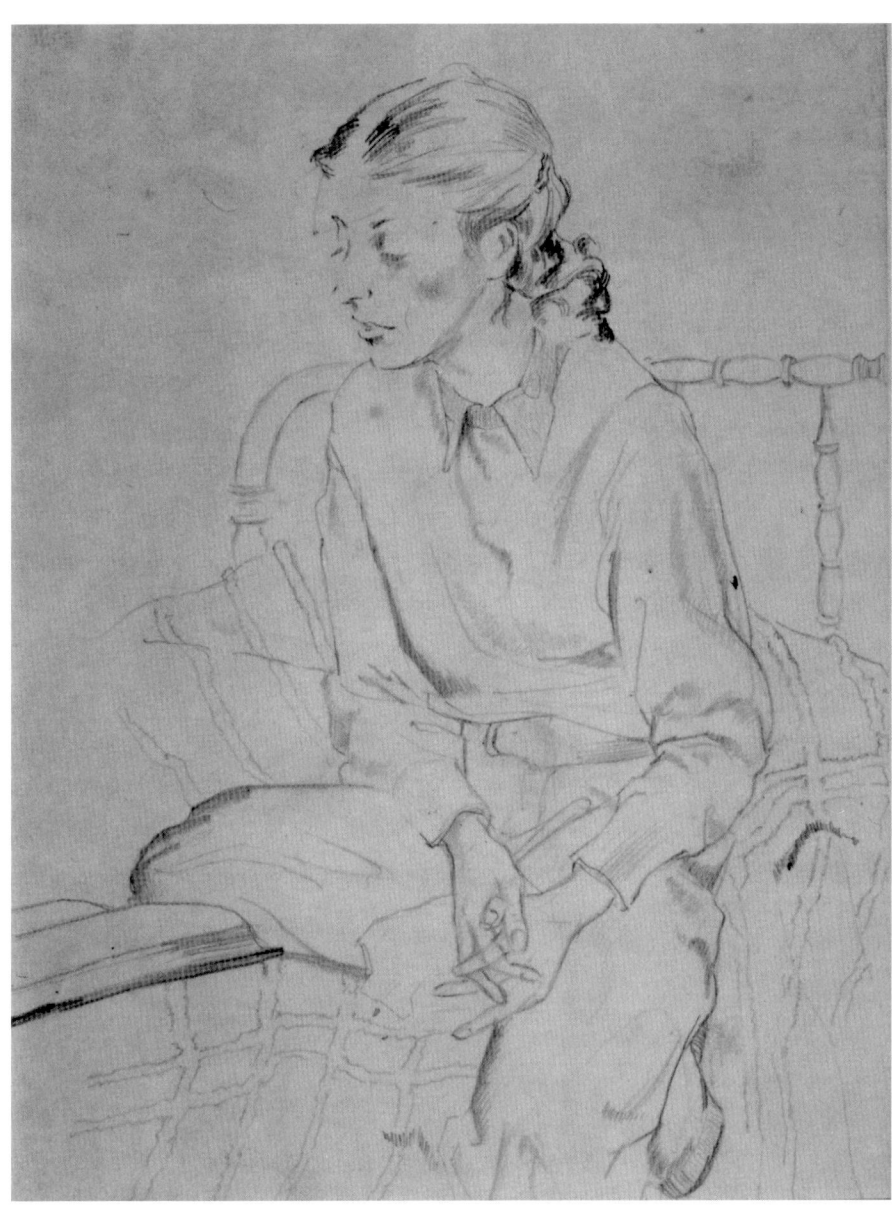

94. *June Sugarman,*
Nantucket, July 1945

At seventy-eight, I realized I was now a bachelor, something I had never had the chance to be when I was twenty-nine. By that time I had been married for eight years. So I surveyed the scene with a little trepidation. There were very attractive women, widows, divorcées, even restless wives. And in this part of the world they were often intelligent, worldly, well traveled, and politically sophisticated. And I was still vertical, still playing tennis, apparently a rarer specimen than I realized. Had I the interest, I really had a lot to choose from. They apparently had much slimmer pickings. It should have been a joyous romp. It wasn't.

And then there was Gloria, our beautiful friend for thirty years, whom June and I had cherished. Gloria Cole and her husband became our friends when they moved to Westport from Chicago in 1964. We knew their three children from a very early age, shared an active circle of friends and community activists, and even traveled with them on a winter holiday. We were saddened when their marriage of twenty years foundered. Taking responsibility for raising their children, Gloria remained in Westport, a close friend whom we admired greatly for her courage and independent spirit. To help provide the necessary economic support for her growing children, Gloria resumed her career as a journalist that had begun before her marriage. Once Michael, Loren, and Suzy had completed high school and gone on to higher education, she sold her house and took an apartment in Stamford. Her successful career as a theater critic, editor, and feature writer has continued without interruption for nearly two decades.

"Come on down and have some supper," she said on the phone. "I remember you like lamb."

Her deep chuckle made me smile. "Tracy Sugarman, right?"

An invitation to dinner with an old and interesting friend was really welcome. We had always enjoyed talking theater together, and Gloria delighted in her critic's prerogative of seeing everything new that was on the boards. I quickly said yes. The lamb shank was delicious, the talk was stimulating, and the evening a relaxed and delightful experience. When I left, I felt a warm and somewhat new level of friendship had been offered and accepted.

Over the following months our friendship grew. When she sent me the used computer she no longer needed, I started my halting and reluctant steps into a new realm. Before discovering I could use it for my writing if I just had the courage to abandon my yellow pads, I was captivated by the e-mail that could erase so many miles on I-95 as I scurried back and forth between Westport and Stamford. And on the e-mail, I found facets of wit and tenderness in Gloria I had only suspected. For someone as awkward and tentative as I am when confronted with a computer unless armed with a grandchild, I am frank in acknowledging that my used computer served as an audacious Lothario that helped transform a life-affirming friendship into a loving partnership. We gazed at this new landscape with surprise and the appreciation of two mature adults who were no longer sure they could navigate those waters again.

In November 2000, we married in the somewhat startled presence of our five children and ten grandchildren, my two brothers and their families, and a small gaggle of close relatives. It was on Gloria's seventy-third birthday, Veteran's Day, and three days shy of my seventy-ninth birthday.

If we appeared a little wan at the ceremony, it was only because we had just completed a national book tour to announce publication of *My War: A Love Story in Drawings and*

Letters. Besides, we were about to go off again, doing research together on my new book, *We Had Sneakers—They Had Guns*. We were in love and were awed only by the insistent pulse of the life force that didn't seem to have a clock or a calendar.

"Man proposes and God disposes," the farmers say, and God was not yet ready for me to go off on another venture. In February I went to the hospital and underwent a double bypass to relieve some nearly clogged arteries that might well have given me a heart attack or a stroke. Humbled and grateful for the medical skill that made me dodge a bullet, I tried to be patient as Gloria abetted my recovery with tender, loving care. At seventy-nine, recovery takes its own sweet time, and it was not until late September that we planned to fly off to investigate the new book I was itching to write.

We Had Sneakers—They Had Guns was to be a revisit to the men and women with whom I worked in Mississippi, and a measured reappraisal of what had been achieved by the sacrifice of so many, and what remained to be done to realize justice. It was an exciting opportunity to see old comrades, share memories, and introduce Gloria to the real people I had written about in *Stranger at the Gates*. Gloria was unhampered by old attitudes and conventional wisdom, so she brought a bright, intuitive, and sympathetic questioning to our research. Our trips to Washington and Mississippi were revelatory and great fun. And by year's end, the book was whipping into a coherent whole.

33

Drawing Conclusions

"The paper is putting us up at the Thayer Hotel. Right on campus at the Point!" Gloria was excited at the chance to see beautiful West Point. Her assignment was to write a travel piece on the Hudson Valley, and it would be a welcome opportunity for us to go off on a brief holiday.

Early the following morning, we rose to glorious sunshine. "Let's stop at the desk on the way to breakfast," I said. "I want to get directions to the Storm King Art Center. It's something you've got to see, and it looks like a perfect morning for it."

When we arrived in the lobby, we could hear the muffled sound of voices and a television set in the adjoining room, but the desk was strangely empty. After a few moments, I tapped softly on the bell, and a young woman hurried from the office, drying her tears as she came. She looked ashen and frightened.

Gloria quickly joined me at the desk and asked, "Are you all right?"

"Yes, thank you." The young woman took a deep breath. "I'm really all right. But something terrible has just happened. An airplane, a large jet, has just flown into the Trade Center in New York. You can see it on the television set across the lobby. I can't believe it was an accident." Her voice shook. "My husband is in the service, and I don't know what this means. What if it's not an accident?"

I took Gloria's hand, and we trotted into the television room as the second plane made a great arc and buried itself in the heart of the tower.

"No! My God, NO!"

Even as the tower, bright in the morning sun, shivered, sagged, and incredibly started to drift down into the roiling ocher clouds of steam and dust, black evil mushrooms of smoke stirred and wove into the noxious brew.

My eyes would not believe it. "NO! Stop! God, please STOP!"

And then there was only the merciful shroud of the surging, lifting smoke that shielded our eyes from a scene too terrible to behold. We stared at each other, unable to speak, unable to accept the obscene verdict of our eyes.

this is the way the world ends
this is the way the world ends
this is the way the world ends
not with a bang
but a whimper

No one in the crowded room had moved. We stood, transfixed, as the television repeated and repeated the hideous choreography of death.

In silence, we left the Thayer, engulfed in the calamity we had witnessed. Neither of us could escape the feeling of dread that permeated that morning, or the feeling that we were helpless to do anything about it. But Gloria's assignment was a reality that had to be faced. "I have the directions, Glor'. Let's start at Storm King."

Gloria nodded absently, still unable to relinquish the barbarous events we had stumbled upon. As we eased the car down the drive from the Thayer Hotel, one could see a sudden quickening of activity across the sprawling campus. Men were running, and a series of jeeps gunned their way up the grade as we left the West Point gate.

The Storm King Art Center was a place I had visited a number of times in years past, yet every time offered additional vistas and settings for the great sculptures that were on display. More than five hundred acres had been lovingly shaped for the creations of David Smith, Alexander Calder, Louise Nevelson, Isamu Noguchi, and Nam Juin Park. I had never seen so generous a gallery as nature provided for contemplating the heroic work of the best sculptors of our time.

Hand in hand, we climbed to the highest point to a grand sculpture by Henry Moore and gazed across a landscape that celebrated the excellence of the human spirit. It appeared that we were the only visitors that morning, somehow magically transported from the wickedness of the world. We hardly spoke. The sun was at its zenith, touching the September day with a grace note of warmth. The sky, the same sky we had seen besmirched with smoke on the morning's television, had never seemed more blue, nor nature more at peace.

When we climbed back into the car, Gloria said, "I'll never forget this morning. All of it." There were tears in her eyes. "The story can wait," she said. "Let's go home."

The red lights were flashing on the answering machines as we entered our studios, exhausted and dispirited, but glad to be back. Sounding troubled and subdued, the sober voices on the machines were the calls from our five children. I could visualize them, calling with their kids standing attentively near, not wishing to add to the tension that must have filled their homes while we were away. "You guys are okay? You weren't in the city? We weren't sure that you weren't in the city. You both go there a lot."

And then the calls from the grandchildren, a little tremulous, trying to sound quite grown up. "Gramps, what do you think? Did you watch?" And the breathy pause that followed. "Gramps, what do you really think?"

And I wasn't sure what I really thought. "I think it's very scary," I said. I knew only that much. They should know it's okay to be scared.

Late in the afternoon, I stepped out on our terrace to clear my head in the fading light of that endless September day. I stared at the last rosy smear of sky in the West. At this hour in the twilight, we would often watch the circling planes over the New York airports. They would appear like tiny fireflies, catching the last light on their wings. Tonight not a single dot moved in the sky. I shivered. The air was getting chill, and I went back inside. I wanted to talk to my kids.

Something strange, slightly sinister, seemed to have arrived on this pleasant beachhead. It was a disquieting intruder. And when I recognized it, I remembered when we had met during the war. Everyone who has gone into action learns its name, knows where it lives, and learns to coexist with it. It is fear. Now my innocent children and grandchildren were feeling its clammy breath and finding the beast living right here. And they didn't have a clue as to how to coexist with it.

I told them about the British I observed during the war, because they had taught me so much. "The Nazis were trying to scare the English to death," I said. "They were dropping lethal rockets onto neighborhoods in London, leveling homes and churches and schools. They believed they could terrorize the Brits by hitting them viciously and randomly. And if they were terrorized, they couldn't stand against them. They would give in to their fear and try to hide in a corner till the cruelty stopped. And the Nazis would win."

"What did the English do?" Abby asked in a small voice. "I'd just want to hide."

"They just kept on going to work, going to play, going to church, going to libraries and theaters and hospitals. And going to help people who were worse off than they were. It's the way they stayed sane and the way they stayed human. And as long as there are people who choose to use terror to beat you, it's the way we can stay human and sane, too."

How poignant it is that the most tragic attack on our country in our entire history should happen in the opening days of the new millennium. Even as we searched the future about to unfold, we were assaulted, robbing us of our innocence and our very American sense of invulnerability. Through our tears we counted our dead and missing, cut down like wheat by the hands of barbarians in airplanes. The buildings crumbled, and the civilized world shared our grief and loss. It was a moment when the whole human family had to transcend shock and outrage, and to seek to find a fitting human response to the unspeakable horror. And it was not to be found in our institutions or our political structures. It was not in our armies or emblazoned on our flags. It was in our people. It was as

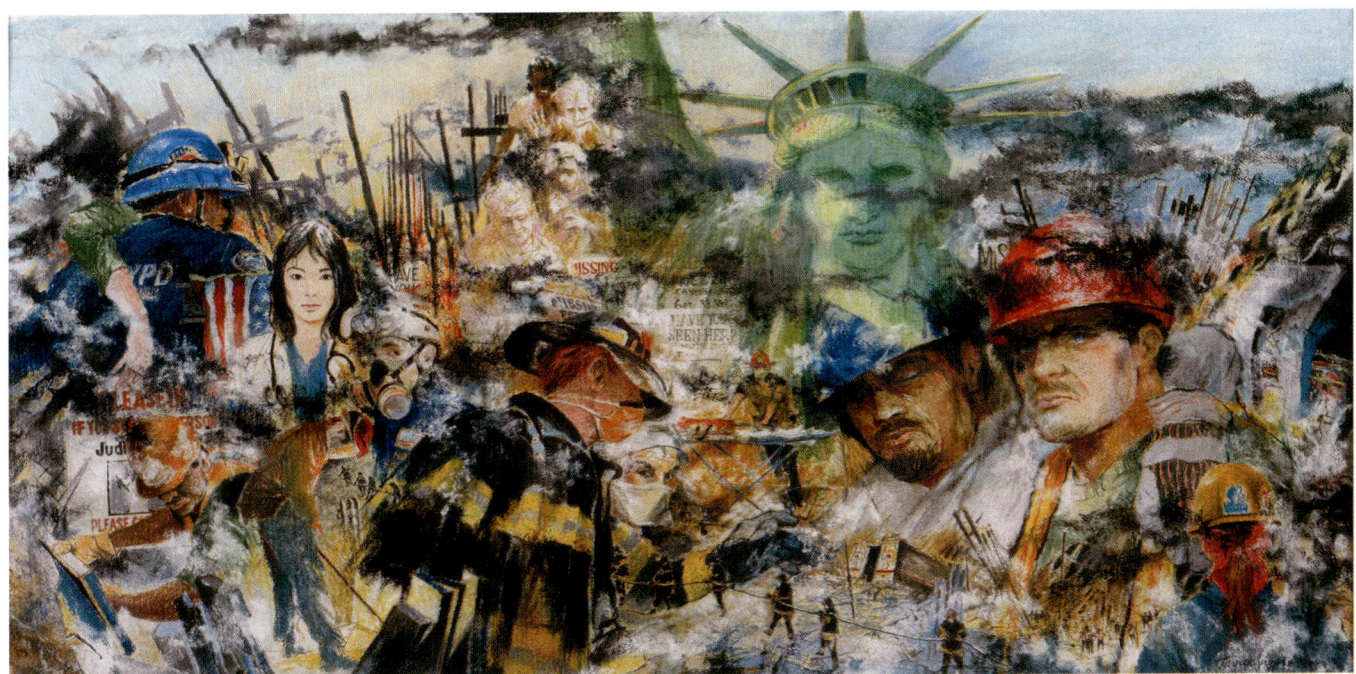

95. *Heroes of 9/11* (Housing Investment Trust mural, Washington, D.C.)

simple and stark and enthralling as firemen struggling up the stairs in a collapsing tower, as a construction worker dragging an injured comrade through the devastation, as a bone-weary policeman who would not be relieved till he found his missing buddy. It was in the valiant hordes of volunteers who came night and day to help claw their way to the fallen. It was the essence of what we believe we are as a people.

When I was asked by Steve Coyle to paint a tribute to these heroes, I was honored to do it. Over a long summer I struggled to find the key that would unlock my painting. When I first perceived an image of the Statue of Liberty's eyes peering down on her children through the poisonous smoke that nearly hid her face, I believed I had a beginning to my painting's journey. It may be the beginning of America's journey as well.

Certainly, it has been a century of stumbles, of sweatshops and colonialism, of exploited children and bigotry, of those individuals with too much and many more with too little, of feudal enmity that reaches through the centuries, and people with no water here on earth even as we reach for the stars. When did we choose to fund prisons rather than schools? Why do two billion people go to bed hungry every night? Enormous, daunting, monumental failures of the human imagination. And yet . . .

I've learned the journey is not yet done. I've learned that the journey need not be done. In my eighth decade on earth I've got pictures I haven't painted yet, but I'm planning to.

I have conclusions I'm still debating about, and I may prove to be right. It's a maybe with possibilities. I delight that, at eighty-seven, my brother bought five new racehorses. When they say "old is," I don't take them seriously. When someone tells me there are better things than a loving wife, I know they're mad. Because artists notice things. It's their business. And if you've been paying any kind of attention sitting in the corner drawing pictures, and I have, then you've learned a few things.

34

The Returning Tide

In the first summer of the new millennium, I returned to Normandy. For more than half a century I had resisted every chance to return to Utah Beach. Like so many veterans, there were simply too many memories to deal with. In my heart, the thought of that beachhead still echoed with sadness. I had seen too much on that stretch of surf and sand. "What's done is done." But, of course, it's never done. And now I had come back.

From the moment we turned off the highway in Saint-Laurent-sur-Mer, I was aware of the silence. Even the gentle murmur of the Channel seemed a long way off. And when we rounded the copse of trees at the entrance, the sudden sight of the dazzling white rows of crosses and Stars of David seemed to blot out even the sounds of the sea. In every direction the severely ruled lines of white stretched endlessly in the silence. What an immaculate and precise parade dress, I thought. No GI or sailor laid this out. This was top brass "doing it properly."

I remembered my ragtaggle boat crews on the days before D-day in Cornwall. "Fall in!" I'd order, hoping to show the locals what a disciplined American amphibious group looked like. And we'd march down the steep, cobbled streets of Fowey to the waiting invasion craft that bobbed at the quay, chanting a motley cadence, "LEFT Left, Left my wife and forty-nine children to die of starvation on nothing but gingerbread. Think I did RIGHT, Right, Right by my country by golly I had a good job and I left, LEFT . . . " They couldn't march worth a damn, but they came alive once we hit the boats.

I stared at the graves, radiating endlessly, in a perfect cadence of silence. These are all kids, I thought, like my crews. We moved off the gravel walks and onto the trimmed lawns, reading names, and states, and outfits of the men buried. Our English friend said, "But there is no indication of their age on the crosses." There's no need, I thought. They're all kids. And they're all dead.

For the past two years, I had been rereading the hundreds of letters I had sent June from England and France during the war. They were full of a young man's passion, curiosity, opinions, prejudices, longing, loneliness, and dreams for the future. In countless letters I talked about "my kids," the crews I was helping to train for D-day. They were a constant challenge to me as their officer. I was only twenty-two myself. Brash, arrogant, funny, brave, foolish, lonely, tender, profane, they were a gangly, often raucous, group to cope with. But often in the silence, the hesitant questions, the needy letters I had to censor, I came to know they were, after all the bluster, just kids.

We walked the cemetery for a long morning, listening to our hearts. All the youthful longing in these graves was once mine. But all the graves were only a heartbreaking part of my youth, part of "my war." For these kids, "my war" was "my life. All of it."

In the afternoon we climbed the dunes of Utah Beach. A breeze shivered the tall grasses, and gulls rode the high wind overhead. The long shallow beachhead was almost empty. A little boy on his bicycle, far out on the wet sand, was all that moved. For six endless months I had worked and lived here, leaving only when Cherbourg and Le Havre were liberated.

I looked in vain for "my war," any trace of the me that once longed to leave this place. All that I found was me, fifty-seven springs, fifty-seven summers, fifty-seven autumns, fifty-seven winters older.

Hand in hand, the child and the man cross the sand, pausing only when the lapping water touches their feet. "Is this where the ocean starts, Daddy?"

The father laughs. "No, son. This is where the ocean ends, and where America begins."

Looking outward. Looking inward. I have despised beaches in wartime. They signified such cruel endings. And I have loved beaches in peacetime. They speak of renewal and continuity. With patience, one can wait there for the next turning of the tide. As the light begins to fade outside my studio, I shake off the weariness of the day by heading for our town beach. I've done it for so long that I sometimes feel it's my beach. Particularly on those days when a chill wind is careening off the water, or a new-fallen snow has piled a white collar at the water's edge. The water beyond the breakwater is inky black, and the heavy gray sky is promising more snow. On those days, the beach is solitary, and only a lonely dog and his huddled-up master might share the stark and beautiful canvas I would never dare to paint. I've walked the beach now for more than fifty years, and nothing really changes except the seasons. The tides keep their somber vigil. The gulls lift and soar and drift down again. The light warms, and the endless children reappear. The same canals get dug to the same fragile sand fortresses that quickly fall to the first timid turning of the tide. And the dads with the beach balls and the moms with the towels and the pink and deep-brown lifeguards start to drift away, emptying the parking lots. The fall's tempestuous skies pile up on the horizon where the last white sails are now racing for home, and pretty soon the beach is my beach again.

After so many years, I can bring those seasons to life in all weather. The shivery, carnal smell of low tide, the murmur, swish, and silence of the water kissing the beach when I

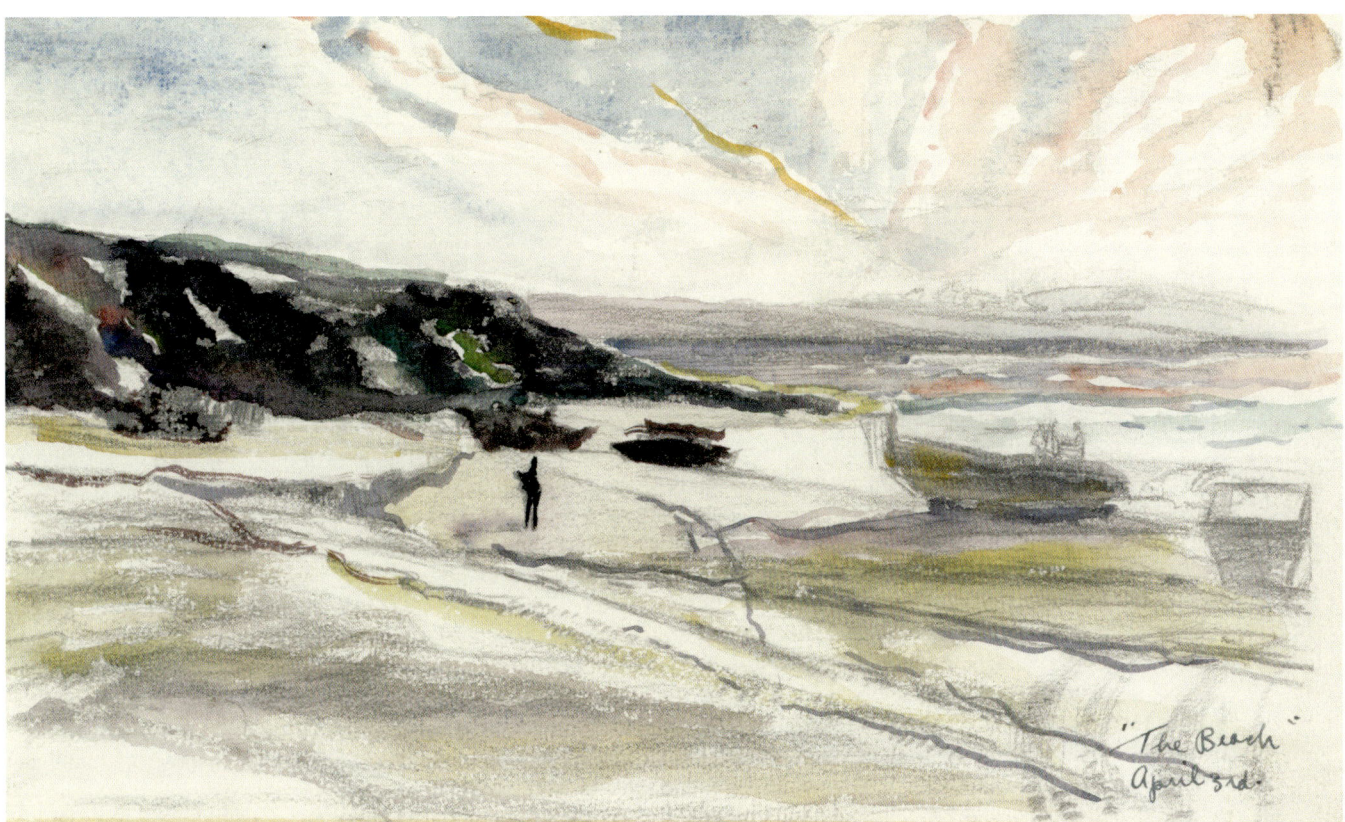

96. *The Beach*

walk at the water's edge all move me. And they all awaken memory. In my mind's eye I can see kids and beach chairs and grandmothers with picnic baskets, and coveys of pretty girls around nonexistent lifeguard chairs even on a November night when the bright stars over the dark sea are the only illumination. And sometimes the dusky beach seems wreathed in smoke, and I can smell cordite in the salt spray. And in the darkening mist I can almost see the hulks of shattered boats. They are bobbing on the outgoing tide, and the only roaring I can hear is the boom-shush of the crashing waves.

Everything is real, and everything goes away, and everything returns. And nothing really changes except the seasons.